Sustainability in the Global-Knowledge Economy

Sustainability in the Global-Knowledge Economy

Editors

Joan Torrent-Sellens
Jorge Sainz-González

MDPI • Basel • Beijing • Wuhan • Barcelona • Belgrade • Manchester • Tokyo • Cluj • Tianjin

Editors
Joan Torrent-Sellens
Universidad Rey Juan Carlos
Spain

Jorge Sainz-González
Institute of Policy Research
University of Bath
UK

Editorial Office
MDPI
St. Alban-Anlage 66
4052 Basel, Switzerland

This is a reprint of articles from the Special Issue published online in the open access journal *Sustainability* (ISSN 2071-1050) (available at: https://www.mdpi.com/journal/sustainability/special_issues/sustainability_global-knowledge_economy).

For citation purposes, cite each article independently as indicated on the article page online and as indicated below:

LastName, A.A.; LastName, B.B.; LastName, C.C. Article Title. *Journal Name* **Year**, *Article Number*, Page Range.

ISBN 978-3-03936-822-8 (Hbk)
ISBN 978-3-03936-823-5 (PDF)

Contents

About the Editors

Joan Torrent-Sellens, Dr., is a Full Professor of Economics at the Faculty of Economics and Business Studies at the Open University of Catalonia (UOC) and group leader of the Information and Communication Technologies Interdisciplinary Research Group (i2TIC: http://i2tic.research.uoc.edu/en/). He holds a degree in Economics and a Master's of Science in Applied Economics from the Autonomous University of Barcelona, and a Ph.D. in Economics (Information and Knowledge Society Doctoral Programme) from the Open University of Catalonia. Dr. Torrent-Sellens specializes in the analysis of the economic, business, labor, health, and wellbeing effects of digitization (http://i2tic.research.uoc.edu/en/people/joan-torrent-sellens/). On this topic, he has published 61 books and book chapters, and 97 articles in high-indexed journals, like the Journal of Business Research, Technological Forecasting and Social Change, and Journal of Travel Research. He has 25 years of teaching and research experience. At the Open University of Catalonia, he has held several teaching management positions, including Dean of the Faculty of Economics and Business Studies, and Founder and Director of the UOC Business School. He has directed 15 competitive and contracted research projects, with funding from entities such as the European Commission, the European Social Fund, the Structural Funds, the Ministry of Science and Innovation in Spain, the Generalitat of Catalonia, the Catalan Employment Service, and the Labour, Economic and Social Council of Catalonia. He has presented 36 communications at international research conferences and directed 12 doctoral theses.

Jorge Sainz (Ph.D. MLL, MBA) is a Professor of Economics at Universidad Rey Juan Carlos. He is currently a Visiting Fellow at the Institute of Policy Research, University of Bath (2018–present), member of the Scientific Board of Iberoamerican Countries Organization (2018–present), and, since 2015, a Fellow of the Royal Spanish Academy of Law and Legislation. He has held several positions in public service including Secretary of Universities in the Ministry of Education, Culture and Sport (2012–2018) and the private sector, for instance, Head of E-Commerce for Yahoo! (2000–2004) and Chief Economist for Intermoney/CIMD (1998–2000). He has also consulted for international organizations, including UNESCO, OECD, and the European Commission, and governments of countries, for example, Australia and Saudi Arabia. He has completed study extension courses and teaching and research stays at Oxford University, London School of Economics, University of Rochester (US), University of Reading, Loyola University (US), etc. He has authored articles in research journals such as the Journal of Business Research, Review of Management, Technological Forecast and Social Change, International Review of Economics and Finance, IZA Journal of Labor Studies, etc.

Preface to "Sustainability in the Global-Knowledge Economy"

The irruption of digital technologies over the last decades has had a profound impact on all economic sectors. The valuation of that impact is still open for discussion, but Corrado, Hulten, and Sichel determined that the share of aggregate intangible capital stock increased three-fold relative to tangible capital during the three decades from 1973 to 2003, reaching a massive 50% of tangible capital, and the figures in developed economies are similar and growing. As the authors note "...knowledge capital should be such an important driver of modern economic growth is hardly surprising, given the evidence from everyday life and the results of basic intertemporal economic theory. What is surprising is that intangibles have been ignored for so long and that they continue to be ignored in financial accounting practice at the firm level."(Corrado, Hulten, and Sichel 2009). Digitization, understood as the phenomenon of intelligent connection between products and activities through the exchange of information thanks to digital technologies, allows the modification of business models impacting both suppliers of such goods and services and consumers. As Porter and Heppelmann highlight, this allows companies to exponentially increase the creation of value for their clients through the modification of their value chains thanks to the appearance of new functionalities, greater security in processes and improvements in efficiency, and the optimization of the possibilities offered to their clients (Porter and Heppelmann 2015).

The optimization of these processes involves the management of massive amounts of data that not only help companies but also public administrations, the education sector, and non-governmental organizations to offer more advanced solutions to their customers that enable them to maximize their value creation. However, not all companies are prepared for the optimization of these processes; the adoption of technologies for massive data analysis is not the only factor to be taken into account, as it also influences the way these technologies are adopted and their use. Decisions on these aspects can change the very essence of the development of the companies' activities, even though the end-user hardly finds any differences, beyond the improvement in service efficiency, product quality, and selection improvement (Ballestar et al. 2019).

Robotization and artificial intelligence are the most pervasive dimensions of technological change of the 4.0 industrial revolution. While the process started before WWII, it was not until the 1970s that the auto industry generalized the replacement of manual workers by robots began seriously. During the following decades, it spread across many industries, beginning in integrated production lines but later grew in all sectors, including the services industry, highlighting the large number of occupations that are at peril of being replaced during the next few years, especially after the impact of the COVID-19 pandemic, which will be labor displacing. Artificial intelligence is also gaining ground in a growing range of activities including security, health, and the most basic operation of integrated domestic appliances at home. But this is likely just the beginning, as it will take over most of a mounting number of decision-making processes that for centuries have been the restricted ground of technically proficient experts and professionals, such as lawyers, economists, doctors, bankers, and engineers (Acemoglu and Restrepo 2019; Autor and Salomons 2018; Faia et al. 2020; Frey and Osborne 2017). This will widely affect employment chances at all levels. It will transform aspects like trade union bargaining power, working conditions of a large number of individuals with low skills, or those that do not possess highly specialized technical skills in the STEM area. It will motivate them to redefine their capabilities and knowledge to void the gloomy perspectives of labor instability, low salaries, and social uncertainty.

Unfortunately, labor is not the only risk to sustainability derived from the growing accumulation of knowledge. As Mahnkopf suggests, electronic texts could save millions of trees, reducing greenhouse gas emissions by millions of tons (Mahnkopf 2019). Though there is an increase in the composition of new materials (fiber, siliceous, plastics, etc.), their production and operation require large amounts of energy for the making. Electricity is needed for ICT infrastructure (the cloud, computer warehouses, and data centers that hold digital content using Big Data, e-commerce, the Internet of Things) which is the backbone of the digital economy. Jones estimates that, by 2030, 21% of the global demand for electricity will come from ICT production and use, showing the relevance of new sectors in the future of the economy and change in consumption patterns (Jones 2018).

However, deep learning also has uses in pattern recognition to define the taxonomy of animal and vegetal species, in estimating biodiversity, and in management and conservation, and the automatization of these tasks due to the vast amount of data that would otherwise be lost. Deep learning is also useful in species distribution models, the analysis of carbon cycles, hazard assessment, and prediction, and forest management thanks to the need for vast amounts of data for classification, modeling, and prediction in forest ecology research. As there is an increase in data recollection and new models adapted to its use, all branches of ecology will take advantage of the new methodologies to gain efficiency, using newly design algorithms to spur knowledge and research on all earth cycle issues (Christin, Hervet, and Lecomte 2019; Liu et al. 2018; Reichstein et al. 2019). But, as Huntingford et al. propose, machine learning models will probably be more useful for the analysis of climate change, as they will be able to deliver "...new insights into the incredibly rich diversity of interconnected Earth System behaviours and their multiple interactions with biochemical cycles... [revealing] ... climate system attributes and enhance forecasting across time scales, it is AI that can then adopt this information to support decisions." (Huntingford et al. 2019).

While former issues are usually downplayed, or just ignored, the latter are somehow exaggerated when speaking about the impact of the knowledge economy on sustainability. The following pages will detail its positive impacts in areas like logistics, agriculture, etc., leaving space for more perspectives on the process, which is arguably one of the most relevant in the history of humankind and should help overcome some of the issues related to environmental decay and climate change.

References

Acemoglu, Daron, and Pascual Restrepo. 2019. "The Wrong Kind of AI? Artificial Intelligence and the Future of Labor Demand." IZA Discussion Paper (12292). Available online: http://www.nber.org/papers/w25682.pdf (accessed on 5 January 2020).

Autor, David, and Anna Salomons. 2018. Brookings Papers on Economic Activity Is Automation Labor-Displacing? Productivity Growth, Employment, and the Labor Share. Available online: https://www.brookings.edu/bpea-articles/is-automation- labor-displacing-productivity-growth-employment-and-the-labor-share/ (accessed on 30 December 2019).

Ballestar, María Teresa, Luis Miguel Doncel, Jorge Sainz, and Arturo Ortigosa-Blanch. 2019. A Novel Machine Learning Approach for Evaluation of Public Policies: An Application in Relation to the Performance of University Researchers. *Technological Forecasting and Social Change* 149.

Christin, Sylvain, Éric Hervet, and Nicolas Lecomte. 2019. Applications for Deep Learning in Ecology. *Methods in Ecology and Evolution* 10: 1632–44. doi:10.1111/2041-210X.13256.

Corrado, Carol, Charles Hulten, and Daniel Sichel. 2009. Intangible Capital and U.S. Economic Growth. *Review of Income and Wealth* 55: 661–85.

Faia, Ester, Sébastien Laffitte, Maximilian Mayer, and Gianmarco Ottaviano. 2020. IZA working papers Automation , Globalization and Vanishing Jobs: A Labor Market Sorting View.

Frey, Carl Benedikt, and Michael A. Osborne. 2017. The Future of Employment: How Susceptible Are Jobs to Computerisation? *Technological Forecasting and Social Change* 114: 254–80.

Huntingford, Chris et al. 2019. Machine Learning and Artificial Intelligence to Aid Climate Change Research and Preparedness. *Environmental Research Letters* 14.

Jones, Nicola. 2018. How to Stop Data Centres from Gobbling up the World's Electricity. *Nature* 561: 163–66.

Liu, Zelin et al. 2018. Application of Machine-Learning Methods in Forest Ecology: Recent Progress and Future Challenges. *Environmental Reviews* 26: 339–50. doi:10.1139/er-2018-0034.

Mahnkopf, Birgit. 2019. EuroMemo Group Discussion Paper No. 01/2019 The '4 Th Wave of Industrial Revolution'—A Promise Blind to Social Consequences, Power and Ecological Impact in the Era of 'Digital Capitalism'.

Porter, Michael E., and James E. Heppelmann. 2015. How Smart, Connected Products Are Transforming Companies. *Harvard Business Review* 2015.

Reichstein, Markus et al. 2019. Deep Learning and Process Understanding for Data-Driven Earth System Science. *Nature* 566: 195–204. doi:10.1038/s41586-019-0912-1.

Joan Torrent-Sellens, Jorge Sainz-González
Editors

sustainability

MDPI

Article

The Impact of Intangible Assets and Sub-Components of Intangible Assets on Sustainable Growth and Firm Value: Evidence from Turkish Listed Firms

Murat Ocak [1,*] and Derya Fındık [2]

1 Department of Business Information Management, T.C. Trakya University, Uzunköprü School of Applied Sciences, Edirne 22000, Turkey

2 Department of Management Information Systems, T.C. Ankara Yıldırım Beyazıt University, Business School, Ankara 06010, Turkey; dfindik@ybu.edu.tr

* Correspondence: muratocak@trakya.edu.tr

Received: 23 August 2019; Accepted: 24 September 2019; Published: 27 September 2019

Abstract: This study explores the effect of intangible assets and sub-components of intangible assets on sustainable growth and firm value in Turkey. The cumulative (i.e., aggregative) value of intangible assets of firms and sub-components of intangible assets were used as test variables in the current study. Further, intangible assets of the firms were divided into three sub-components using the classification of Corrado, Hulten and Sichel, namely computerized information and database, innovative property, and economic competence. Firms listed on Borsa İstanbul were analyzed to test the hypotheses. Two different measures of sustainable growth of firms and unique measure of firm value were used as dependent variables. The final sample includes 1353 observations for nine years between 2005–2013 in Turkey. Ordinary least square (OLS) and Heckman two-stage estimation procedures were employed to test the hypotheses. Estimation results of OLS and Heckman two-stage procedures show that the cumulative value of intangible assets affect the sustainable growth rates of firms and firm value positively. When the cumulative value of intangible assets was classified into three sub-components, both computerized information and database and economic competence impact the sustainable growth rates of firms and firm value.

Keywords: intangible assets; sustainable growth; firm value; computerized information and database; economic competence; innovative property; Turkey; Borsa Istanbul

1. Introduction

In the literature, there are many definitions of intangibles assets. While some of these definitions made by authors refer to one type of specific item among intangible assets (such as brand, trademark, etc.), other authors discuss definitions in a broader context. According to Mooney [1], Siegel and Shim [2], and Andrews and De Serres [3], who discussed intangible assets in a broader context, intangible assets have no physical substance and represent a right granted by the government or by another company. Furthermore, according to Augier and Teece [4], intangible assets are non-current assets and are different from tangible (physical) assets. These differences are that intangible assets are used by one party, their transfer costs are hard to calibrate, their property rights are limited, and the enforcement of property rights is relatively difficult.

There are many types of intangible assets such as patents, copyright, trademarks, design, mineral exploration, brand, software, formula, trade secrets, capitalized research and development, goodwill, databases, domain, human capital, motion pictures, consumer lists, customer loyalty, licenses, market share, and marketing rights [3,5–7]. Even though different countries have enforced local regulations about how to record intangible assets, the International Accounting Standards Board (IASB) determined some criteria to account, record, report, and value intangible assets at the international level. Thus, many countries have adopted the standards of the IASB into local regulations or use a two-book system to prepare their financial statements in accordance with the standards of IASB and their local regulations, as in Turkey. According to International Accounting Standard 38 [7], intangible assets should be identifiable, should be controlled by the firm, and should provide future economic benefits to the firm, and the cost of intangible assets can be measured reliably if firms report these kinds of items as an asset. In Turkey, firms listed on Borsa İstanbul should prepare their financial statements in accordance with the directions of the IASB. Thus, intangible investments made by firms are included in the financial statements of firms as an asset, if firms abide by the IASB's reporting criteria.

There are many studies that explore the effects of intangible assets or the sub-components of intangible assets or some types of specific intangible assets (such as patent, trademark, R&D) on firm performance [8–12], on firm value [13], on firm level and country level productivity [14–16], on stock price [17–19], on economic growth [3,20,21], on analyst coverage, and analyst following [22,23]. Most recently, some scholars have focused on the relationship between firm governance structures and intangible assets and the sub-components of intangible assets (particularly R&D) [12,24–27].

The outcomes of this research show that firms now invest more in intangible assets than in tangible assets because intangible assets play an effective role in sustaining a firm's competitive advantage [9] due to not being easy to imitate [27] and being an important determinant of firm internalization [10]. Intangible assets such as software and R&D are critical investments that sustain a firm's market presence in future years by reducing costs and increasing profits, and intangibles are strategic investments for the long-run growth path of firms [21]. The sustainable growth of a firm can be considered a comprehensive mechanism to evaluate the long-run sustainability of a firm [28]. On the other hand, investing in intangible assets is important for the knowledge economy because intangible assets containing information elements such as R&D, patents, or software rather than tangible assets play an important role in the sustainable growth of firms and firm value. In this regard, intangible assets of firms may affect the sustainable growth of firms and it will be interesting to discuss the association between the intangible assets and sub-components of intangible assets classified by Corrado et al. [29–32] and the sustainable growth rate of firms. Recently, from the narrow perspective of intangible assets, Xu and Wang [33] researched the effect of intellectual capital which is a common form of intangible investment on firms' sustainable growth rate and found that intellectual capital has a positive impact on the sustainable growth of firms in Korea. We take into account the intangible value of a firm in broader context, covering the aggregative value of intangible assets of firms and the sub-components of intangible assets classified by Corrado et al. [29–32]. The first research question is, do these kinds of strategic investments, intangible assets, make firms benefit from sustainable growth? Which kind of sub-components of intangible assets make firms more likely to have sustainable growth? Intangible assets affect firm value positively [13], because much research has empirically documented the positive effect of intangible assets on firm value. However, which kinds of sub-component of intangible assets are more effective to enhance firm value is still unknown. This issue has not been discussed using the classification of Corrado et al. [29–32] regarding intangible assets.

In this study, we used the cumulative value of intangible assets of firms and the sub-components of intangible assets classified by Corrado et al. [29–32] as variables of interest. In this most commonly used classification, the researchers attempt to categorize three main sources of intangible assets [16,29–32]. These are "Computerized Information and Databases," "Innovative Property," and "Economic Competence." While "innovative property" strongly emphasizes the creation of new ideas and includes items such as patents, rights, films, licenses, and R&D, "economic competence" emphasizes the economic impact of intangibles such as agreements and special costs. "Computerized information and databases" includes software and databases [26]. We employed two measures of sustainable growth of firms and unique measure of firm value as dependent variables. Our estimation model also includes firm structure–specific (firm size, firm leverage, firm performance, firm age) and firm governance–specific (board independency, board gender diversity, top management gender diversity,

CEO duality) control variables. Two different econometric approaches are used to estimate the results. One is ordinary least square, the other is the Heckman two-stage estimation procedure. The Heckman selection model was employed because female participation in the top management level of firms affects firms' intangibles [26,27] and thus indirectly affects sustainable growth of firms and firm value. The results of the two estimation procedures document that intangible assets of firms affect firm value and sustainable growth of firms positively. In addition, two sub-components of intangible assets, namely, "computerized information and database" and "economic competence," positively affect firm value and the sustainable growth of firm.

The paper contributes to the existing literature as follows. First, we provide evidence of the relationship between intangible assets, sustainable growth and firm value of firms listed on Borsa İstanbul for the first time. Second, it determines which kind of sub-components of intangible assets affect the sustainable growth rate of firms and firm value. Third, we used Turkish listed firms and thus, the outcomes of this paper shed light on the effect of intangible assets on the sustainable growth of firms and firm value in emerging markets. The literature on the effect of intangible capital on firm value in Turkey focuses more on a single component of intangible capital, intellectual capital and found a positive relationship between intellectual capital and firm value & performance [34–38]. In this paper, we used various sub-components of intangible capital and its effect both on sustainable growth and firm value.

The following subheadings present literature review and hypotheses regarding relationship among intangible assets and sub-components of intangible assets with sustainable growth and firm value. Then, the research design (sample selection, estimation model) is presented. Finally, the results of this paper are explained.

2. Literature Review and Hypothesis Development

2.1. *Intangible Assets and Sustainable Growth*

The term sustainable growth emerged in the 1970s in the field of business. Higgins [39] used the term to address firms' optimal growth from a financial perspective. Accordingly, it indicates a maximum rate that a firm grows at relying on its own resources without using any financial tools outside the company.

As far as the relationship between intangible investment and sustainable growth is considered, firms in general make a large amount of physical investment, which is the main source of production. However, they have difficulty with generating non-physical capital including intellectual capital, R&D activities, and innovative activities, and some studies found that the ownership of a large amount of physical capital accelerates the sustainable growth rate of firms [40]. Another stream of literature, on the other hand, presents contrasting results [33,41–46]. Accordingly, intangible investment in various forms positively affects a firm's sustainable growth. A common form of intangible investment is intellectual capital, which is defined as a set of resources including knowledge, capabilities, networks, operation processes, individual, and organizational relations. Xu and Wang [33] found that intellectual capital has a positive effect on financial performance of Korean manufacturing companies. Furthermore, a similar analysis is also tested for another industry. Xu and Wang [41] concluded that intellectual capital contributes to financial performance in the textile industry. In a similar vein, Mukherjee and Şen [42] revealed that intellectual capital is an influencing factor for corporate sustainable growth as much as other factors, including physical capital, relational capital, innovation capital, and process capital. Moreover, Ying et al. [43] argued that intellectual capital affects sustainable growth of firms indirectly. First, it enhances managers' capabilities to discover strategic resources for the firm, which in turn results in performance improvement. Liang et al. [44] emphasized the role of organizational capabilities such as developing new products and changing organizational structure to experience the performance-enhancing effect of information technology. Some authors use R&D expenditure to proxy intangible assets and found that R&D activities positively affect firm growth [45,46]. Xu and Wang [33] found that advertising stimulates R&D activities through increasing the reputation of the firms' current products and services. Based on these previous studies, we hypothesize that

- H1: Firms with greater intangible assets tend to have better sustainable growth rate;
- H1A: Firms with greater innovative property tend to have better sustainable growth rate;
- H1B: Firms with greater computerized information and databases tend to have better sustainable growth rate;
- H1C: Firms with greater economic competency tend to have better sustainable growth rate.

We expect that the cumulative value of intangible assets and the sub-components of intangible assets (innovative property, computerized information and database, economic competency) have a positive and significant effect on the sustainable growth of firms if the hypotheses (H1, H1A, H1B, H1C) are supported.

2.2. *Intangible Assets and Firm Value*

There is an extant literature on the relationship between intangible assets and firm value, which is commonly measured as Tobin's Q (see Table 1). Some of these studies focus on specific industries such as semiconductors [37,47,48], communications [49], food [50], and pharmaceuticals and chemicals [51].

Megna and Klock [13], one of the first studies analyzing the effect of intangible capital on firm value, used patents and R&D to proxy intangible capital stock of the firms in the semiconductor industry for the period 1972–1990 and found that intangible capital is an important determinant of firm value. When firm-specific effects are taken into account, Tobin's q varies from one firm to another in the same industry even after adjusting for intangible capital. In other words, the effect of intangibles on firm value is not sufficient to explain the variation between firms. Shane and Klock [47] used patent citations as an alternative indicator for intangible capital and detected a contrasting result to the previous evidence. Accordingly, patent citations do not have a significant effect on Tobin's Q. Chin et al. [48], on the contrary, tested a similar hypothesis and the analysis revealed a positive and significant effect of patent citations on firms, which are valuable players within the value chain in the semiconductor industry. As far as the communications industry is concerned, Klock and Megna [49] used four types of intangible capital, namely R&D, radio spectrum licenses, advertising, and customer base, and found that licenses and advertising contribute to the variation in this industry, but the effect of licenses on Tobin's Q is larger than that of advertising. Wu and Bjornson [50] analyzed the effect of advertising activity and found that advertising activity positively affects the firm value regardless of the changing economic and social conditions in the food industry. In the chemicals and pharmaceutical industry, Gleason and Klock [51] found a similar pattern between intangible capital, which was proxied by R&D and advertising activity, and firm value. We observe further evidences examining the effect of intangible assets on firm value in manufacturing sectors [52–55], technology sectors [36,56], and telecommunications [49]. Tseng and James [52] used four types of intangible capital such as human capital, relationship capital, innovation capital, and organizational capital to construct intellectual capital and found that there is a positive relationship between intellectual capital and firm value, which is measured as Tobin's Q, market/book value, and value added intellectual coefficient. Moreover, Salman et al. [53] revealed that the effect of these subcomponents varies. For instance, the effect of human capital on firm value is larger than that of other types of capital. Ehie and Olibe [54] through using another type of intangible capital, found that R&D investment in the manufacturing sector generates a larger positive effect on firm value than in the services sector. Dženopoljac et al. [55], with a specific emphasis on technology sector, found that there are no differences among ICT sectors in terms of financial performance. Among other components of intangible capital, human capital has the highest impact on firm performance for firms operating in ICT sector [36].

Table 1. Main articles on the relationship between intangible assets and firm value.

Author	Publication Year	Title	Data	Methodology	Results
Megna and Klock [13]	1993	The impact of intangible capital on Tobin's q in the semiconductor industry	11 firms operating in semiconductor industry for the years between 1972–1990	Nonlinear least square estimates	Intangible capital explains the variation in Tobin's q to a certain extent. However, there are other factors playing important role in the substantial differences in q within semiconductor industry.
Klock et al. [56]	1996	Tobin's q, intangible capital, and financial policy	100 large manufacturing firms for the years between 1977–1983	OLS	The inclusion of intangible capital strengthens the financial performance of firms.
Wu and Bjornson [50]	1996	Value of advertising by food manufacturers as investment in intangible capital	Compustat PC plus database for large firms in US capital markets	Cross sectional time series regression	Food manufacturing firms' advertising activity is strongly related to intangible capital value.
Haneda and Odagiri [57]	1997	Appropriation of returns from technological assets and the values of patents and R&D in Japanese high-tech firms	40 firms in electrical equipment industry, 41 firms in chemical industry, and 24 firms in drugs industry	Fixed Effects	Tobin's q is positively related to the technological assets, especially in the pharmaceutical industry
Shane and Klock [47]	1997	The relationship between patent citations and Tobin's q in the semiconductor industry	11 firms operating in semiconductor industry for the years between 1977–1990	OLS	Patent citations do not have a significant effect on Tobin's Q
Bosworth and Rogers [58]	1998	Research and development, intangible assets and performance of large Australian companies	IBIS database for the years between 1991–1993	OLS	Intangible assets are important determinants of market value.
Bharadwaj et al. [59]	1999	Information technology effects on firm performance as measured by Tobin's q	631 firms for the years between 1988–1993	Least-squares regression	For the time period investigated, IT investments had a significant positive association with Tobin's q value
Klock and Megna [49]	2000	Measuring and valuing intangible capital in the wireless communications industry	14 firms operating in the communications industry for the years between 1984–1993	OLS	Licenses and advertising explain over 60% of the variation in Tobin's q.
Gleason and Klock [51]	2003	Intangible capital in the pharmaceutical and chemical industry	All firms operating in chemical industry for the years between 1982–2001 (Compustat)	OLS	Intangible capital is a statistically significant determinant of Tobin's q and explains twenty percent of the variation.
Villalonga [9]	2004	Intangible resources, Tobin's q, and sustainability of performance differences	1641 US public operations firms between 1981–1997	Hedonic regression	From a resource-based perspective, intangibles play an effective role in sustaining a firm's competitive advantage.
Hall et al. [60]	2005	Market value and patent citations	NBER 1963–1999		Patent citations have positive effect on Tobin's q.

Table 1. *Cont.*

Author	Publication Year	Title	Data	Methodology	Results
Chin et al. [48]	2006	Patent citation, R&D spillover, and Tobin's Q: Evidence from Taiwan Semiconductor industry	Taiwanese firms between 1990–2002	OLS	The positive effect of patent citation on Tobin's Q is observed as the firm is a crucial player in the value chain.
Lin et al. [61]	2006	Patent portfolio diversity, technology strategy, and firm value	US 1985–1999	OLS	Technology stocks are used as a moderator that explains the relationship between technology diversity and firm performance. Based on the assumptions of the competence-base, firms who do not have high technology stocks should use R&D resources to develop a specific technology field.
Anandarajan et al. [62]	2008	The effect of innovative activity on firm performance: The experience of Taiwan	Semiconductor firms in Taiwanese Stock Exchange between 1990–2002	OLS	Markets tend to give greater emphasis to innovative activities when patents are granted to foreign firms by the U.S. Patent Office.
Parcharidis and Varsakelis [63]	2010	R&D and Tobin's q in an emerging market: the case of the Athens stock exchange	Greek firms for the years between 1996–2004	OLS	The Greek firms' R&D investment effect on the market value of a firm is similar to that of results from US and European studies.
Antonelli and Colombelli [64]	2011	The generation and exploitation of technological change: market value and total factor productivity	Firms in UK, Germany, France, and Italy for the years between 1995–2005	2SLS regression	TFP is a reliable indicator of firms' innovative capabilities. When we control for firm's R&D investments and intangible assets, the effects of TFP on market value remain highly significant.
Rahko [65]	2014	Market value of R&D, patents, and organizational capital: Finnish evidence	56,000 firm*year observations for the years between 1995 and 2008	NLS regression	Organizational capital, R&D, patents, and patent citations have positive and significant effects on market value.
Gamayuni [66]	2015	The effect of intangible asset, financial performance and financial policies on the firm value	Public companies in Indonesia in the years 2007–2009	OLS	Intangible assets have positive and significant effect on financial performance (ROA) and firm value.
Kumar and Sundarraj [67]	2015	Schumpeterian innovation patterns and firm performance of global technology companies	Global 1990–2009	OLS	Creative-accumulation patterns increase firm performance.
Peters and Taylor [68]	2015	Intangible capital and investment-q relation	Compustat firms	OLS	Intangible capital also generates a stronger investment-cash flow relation.

Besides these industry-specific studies, we also observed some evidence analyzing variation in Tobin's Q regarding intangible capital, which address a positive effect of intangible assets in the form of R&D, patents, patent citations, software investments, licenses, and organizational capital on firm value (see Table 1). Based on the previous evidence we determined the following hypotheses:

- H2: Firms with greater intangible assets tend to have better firm value;
- H2A: Firms with greater innovative property tend to have better firm value;
- H2B: Firms with greater computerized information and databases tend to have better firm value;
- H2C: Firms with greater economic competency tend to have better firm value.

We expect that the cumulative value of intangible assets and the sub-components of intangible assets (innovative property, computerized information and database, economic competency) have positive and significant effect on firm value if the hypotheses (H2, H2A, H2B, H2C) are supported.

3. Research Design

3.1. Sample Selection and Data Collection

Although there is no precise information regarding the total number of firms in Turkey, the listed firms in Borsa İstanbul constitute only a small part of the total number. Firms in Turkey are generally small firms and family firms. According to Turkish Statistical Institute and Organisation for Economic Co-operation and Development, as of 2015, the percentage of firms in manufacturing and services in total firms (except agricultural firms) are respectively 12% and 88%. In this research, the manufacturing covers eight main sub-sectors; food, textile, wood, chemistry, metal, machinery and equipment, transport vehicles, and furniture, while the service covers wholesale and retail trade, transport, construction, education, health, tourism, and entertainment [69]. In this paper, we examined Turkish firms listed on Borsa İstanbul to test the hypotheses. The final sample comprises 1353 observations between 2005–2013 and covers four main sectors, namely manufacturing, technology, telecommunication, and trading. The dataset starts from 2005 because, in Turkey, International Financial Reporting Standards (IFRS) have been applied since 2004, and different valuation techniques before IFRS and after IFRS may affect the results of the study. The dataset ends in 2013 because of a data access problem and difficulties with the hand-collection process. Information regarding the sub-components of intangible assets is located in the footnotes of financial statements. We reached the footnotes of financial statements of each firm and collected the information regarding which kind of intangible assets firms invest in, and then we classified these items in three sub-components following the paper by Corrado et al. [29–32]. Financial firms, holdings, firms in the extractive sector (i.e., mining), and tourism firms are excluded because they are subject to different regulations and the structure of their financial statements is slightly different. Besides, some firms did not disclose information regarding their corporate governance structures and the sub-components of intangible assets. Thus, we classified them as missing data. The total number of firms were retrieved from the Capital Market Depository of Turkey (MKK) [70] using their annual statistics. The Capital Market Depository of Turkey provides its members with registration, settlement, and custody services [70]. Besides, The Capital Market Depository of Turkey also provides information regarding the ownership structures, dividend payments, public offerings of listed firms in Borsa İstanbul. Then, we excluded the above-mentioned firms and missing data. Table 2 presents the sample selection procedure and final sample. The dataset is unbalanced.

Table 2. Sample selection procedure and final sample by year.

Panel A: Sample Selection Procedure										
Sector/Year	2005	2006	2007	2008	2009	2010	2011	2012	2013	Tot.
Number of firms	319	335	335	335	335	352	375	418	439	3243
Excluded and missing data	238	229	223	175	168	178	189	233	257	1890
Total obs.	81	106	112	160	167	174	186	185	182	1353
Total obs./ The number of firms	25.39%	31.64%	33.43%	47.76%	49.85%	49.43%	49.6%	44.25%	41.45%	41.72%
Panel B: Final sample by year and sector										
Sector/Year	2005	2006	2007	2008	2009	2010	2011	2012	2013	Tot.
Manufacturing	64	82	87	130	137	142	148	147	144	1081
Technology	8	11	12	13	13	15	16	16	16	120
Telecommunication	3	4	4	5	5	5	5	5	5	41
Trading	6	9	9	12	12	12	17	17	17	111
Total obs.	81	106	112	160	167	174	186	185	182	1353

Information regarding the dependent variables in the current study (sustainable growth and firm value) are obtained from the Financial Information News Network (FINNET) database [71]. FINNET database is one of the common databases which provides detailed information and updates regarding the financial statements items of listed firms in Borsa Istanbul. This database does not provide information regarding the corporate governance structures of firms. We reached data regarding the calculation of sustainable growth rates of firms from FINNET database, and then we measured the sustainable growth rates for each firm. FINNET database presents the final scores for firm value. If they are not available, we accessed the financial statements of firms to measure their sustainable growth rates and firm value. The variables of interest (intangible assets and three sub-components, namely "Computerized Information and Databases," "Innovative Properties," and "Economic Competence") were manually collected from firms' financial reports, and the footnotes of financial statements. First, the financial reports of firms were obtained from the Public Disclosure Platform of Turkey (KAP) for each year [72]. The Public Disclosure Platform of Turkey provides the listed firms' financial statements and their footnotes. Besides this platform presents the detailed information regarding merger and takeover, related party transactions, dividend payment policies of firms, credit rating, and sustainability reports [72]. Then, we reached the footnotes of financial reports regarding the intangible assets of firms. These footnotes show which kind of intangible assets firms hold. Therefore, we classified the intangible assets of firms into three sub-headings as mentioned in the paper by Corrado et al [29–32]. (Please see Section 3.2.3, for more detailed information regarding how intangible assets are classified into three sub-headings.)

Data regarding control variables such as a firm's board structure (Board Gender Diversity, Board Independency, Duality) and top management structure (Gender Diversity in Top Management) were hand-collected because there is no database that discloses the corporate governance structures of firms in Turkey. First, we reached the firms' activity reports or corporate governance compliance reports, then we determined the percentages of females and independent members on the board of directors of firms, and firms with CEO duality for each year. All activity reports and corporate governance compliance reports were retrieved from firms' websites. In the current study, top managers refer to the lists of managers who have a right to manage daily activities of the business. This information, and the percentage of females at the top management level of firms, was manually obtained from the firms' annual reports. Information regarding firm-specific control variables such as leverage, firm size, and financial performance was obtained from the FINNET database [71]. Finally, we manually calculated firm age using corporate webpages or activity reports of firms. The ownership structure (the percentage of institutional owners) of firms were retrieved from the database of the MKK [70].

3.2. Model

Ordinary least squares (OLS) is mainly used to test our hypotheses in this study. The estimation models are as follows:

$$\begin{gathered}\mathrm{SGR}_{i,t} \text{ or } \mathrm{SGR2}_{i,t}.\ (\text{or } \mathrm{FV}_{i,t}) = \beta_0 + \beta_1 \text{ Intangibles}_{i,t} + \beta_2 \text{ Board Female Percent}_{i,t} + \\ \beta_3 \text{ Board Independence}_{i,t} + \beta_4 \text{ Duality}_{i,t} + \beta_5 \text{ Top Female Percent}_{i,t} + \beta_6 \text{ Firm Size}_{i,t} + \\ \beta_7 \text{ Leverage}_{i,t} + \beta_8 \text{ Firm Performance}_{i,t} + \beta_9 \text{ Firm Age}_{i,t} + \beta_{10} \text{ Institutional Owner}_{i,t} + \\ \Sigma\text{Sector Dummies} + \Sigma\text{Year Dummies} + \varepsilon\end{gathered} \tag{1}$$

While the above model (1) is utilized to investigate the effect of the cumulative value of intangible assets of firms on sustainable growth rate (*SGR1* and *SGR2*) and firm value (*FV*), the below model (2) is utilized to estimate the effect of each sub-component (namely, computerized information and databases, innovative property and economic competence) of intangible assets on sustainable growth rate (*SGR1* and *SGR2*) and firm value (*FV*) of firms. The second model shows us which sub-component of intangible assets is more important in improving sustainable growth and firm value. All control variables are included in all models.

$$\begin{gathered}\mathrm{SGR}_{i,t} \text{ or } \mathrm{SGR2}_{i,t}.\ (\text{or } \mathrm{FV}_{i,t}) = \beta_0 + \beta 1 \text{ Computerized Info}_{i,t} + \beta 2 \text{ Innovative Property}_{i,t} \\ + \beta 3 \text{ Economic Competence}_{i,t} + \beta_4 \text{ Board Female Percent}_{i,t} + \beta_5 \text{ Board Independence}_{i,t} \\ + \beta_6 \text{ Duality}_{i,t} + \beta_7 \text{ Top Female Percent}_{i,t} + \beta_8 \text{ Firm Size}_{i,t} + \beta_9 \text{ Leverage}_{i,t} + \beta_{10} \text{ Firm} \\ \text{Performance}_{i,t} + \beta_{11} \text{ Firm Age}_{i,t} + \beta_{12} \text{ Institutional Owner}_{i,t} + \Sigma\text{Sector Dummies} \\ + \Sigma\text{Year Dummies} + \varepsilon\end{gathered} \tag{2}$$

The coefficient of β_1 in model 1 (*Intangibles*) is also expected to be positive, while the coefficients of β_1, β_2, β_3 in the model 2 (*Computerized Info*, *Innovative Property*, *Economic Competence*) are also expected to be positive.

3.2.1. Dependent Variables

Sustainable Growth

Two types of sustainable growth rate measures (*SGR1* and *SGR2*, respectively) are employed as dependent variables in this study due to enhancing the validity of results. The first rate formulated by Higgins [39] and many researchers [33,73–75] were used or modified this formula to calculate firms' sustainable growth rate in their studies. According to this formula (*SGR1*), sustainable growth reflects firm's retention policy, cost containment ability, asset utilization efficiency, and financial strategy [76]. The calculation of the first rate is as follows:

$$\text{SGR1} = \text{Profit Margin} \times \text{Asset Turnover} \times \text{Retention Ratio} \times \text{Financial Leverage} \tag{3}$$

Profit margin is calculated as net income divided by sales. Asset turnover is measured as sales divided by total assets. Financial leverage is calculated as total debts divided by total assets. Retention ratio is calculated as retained earnings divided by net income [33,39,73,77].

The second measure of sustainable growth rate (SGR2) was also used by many researchers [73,77–79]. Some researchers refer to this rate as internal growth rate in their studies [79,80]. This rate is the maximum growth rate that can be achieved without debt or equity external financing [80]. The formulation of the second rate is as follows:

$$\text{SGR2} = \text{ROE} \times \text{Retention Ratio}/1\text{- ROE} \times \text{Retention Ratio} \tag{4}$$

ROE is the return on equity which is calculated as net income divided by shareholders' equity. The calculation of retention ratio is mentioned above.

Firm Value

Firm value (*FV*) is measured as market value of assets divided by book value of assets [81,82].

$$FV = \text{Market value of assets/Book value of assets} \quad (5)$$

Book value of assets refers to the value of firm according to the balance sheet of firm, (i.e. total equity of firm), while market value of assets is calculated as the total number of shares of firms is multiplied by the price of a share. We retrieved this information from FINNET database [71].

3.2.2. Variables of Interest

Intangible assets and sub-components of intangible assets are used as the variables of interest in this study. The cumulative amount of intangible assets and sub-components of intangible assets are employed as the variables of interest. The amount of these variables refers to accumulated intangible assets and sub-components of intangible assets over the years by firms. Cumulative intangible assets (*Intangibles*) are calculated as the total amount of cumulative intangible assets divided by non-current assets. There are many classifications [60,83–88] regarding intangible assets in the earlier literature. For example, Sveiby [85] also divided intangible assets into three sub-components including employee competence and external (e.g., relationship between suppliers and customers, brandnames, trademarks, image) and internal intangibles (e.g., patents, concepts, model, computer). Kaplan and Norton [87] also classified intangible assets into three categories: human capital (skills, talent, knowledge), information capital (databases, information systems, networks), and organization capital (culture, leadership). It is difficult to score such classifications. We follow the most commonly used classification [3,16,20,21,89] made by Corrado et al. [29–32] because testing the effect of each intangible asset item can be difficult. For instance, each firm may not have to invest in or have intangible assets like motion pictures or patents, which are items in the innovative property classification. In this case, using only investments in motion pictures or patents as the variable of interest may not be meaningful due to insufficient number of observations. On the other hand, Corrado et al. [29–32], on the other hand, made this classification based on balance sheet items. Reaching the balance sheet items of firms enables us to make this classification. The disadvantage of this classification compared to the other classifications is that some items such as employee competence, human capital, customer-based capital are not considered in this classification. Thus, following the paper by Corrado et al. [29–32], each item regarding intangible assets are divided into three sub-components in this study. These are "Computerized Information and Databases," "Innovative Property," and "Economic Competence."

These sub-components still contain a number of items as follows. Computerized information and databases (*Computerized Info*), which refers to knowledge embedded in computer programs and computerized databases [30], is composed of the total cumulative amounts of software, information systems, domains, and consumer databases in this study. Innovative property (*Innovative Property*), which refers to knowledge acquired through scientific research and development and non-scientific inventive and creative activities [30], comprises the total cumulative amounts of capitalized research and development, copyrights, designs, licenses, and patents in this study. Economic competence (*Economic Competence*), which refers to knowledge embedded in firm-specific human and structural resources including brand names [30] or which covers investments to retain or gain market share [31], is composed of the total cumulative amounts of trademarks, special costs, agreements, rights, customer lists, and dealer lists in this study. All sub-components are divided by non-current assets.

More detailed information regarding the classification of sub-components of intangible assets is provided in Table 3. Fındık and Ocak [12] were used a similar classification to investigate the effect of intangible assets on firm performance (ROA) in Turkey.

Table 3. Detailed information regarding the classification of sub-components of intangible assets.

Computerized Information and Database	Innovative Property	Economic Competency
Software Computer programs Information systems Data processing Domains Customer databases	Patent Licenses Wholesale licenses Electricity generation licenses Energy generation licenses Technology licenses Mineral exploration licenses GSM and telecommunication Licenses Motion picture Films Development expenses Industrial design Depletable assets Research expenses Preparation and development Expenses Rights Water resources rights Mining rights Concession rights Land lease rights Betting rights Rights for tax exemption Irrevocable rights Slot rights	Advances given Brands Trademarks Bottling agreements Pre-operating expenses Special cost Communication networks with Dealers Customer networks Production concession Agreements Service concession agreements Dealer lists Customer lists Accumulated orders Distribution agreements Non-compete agreements Favorable lease contracts

3.2.3. Control Variables

In this study, some firm governance-specific (Board and Top Management Levels) and firm-specific control variables are employed. Institutional owner percentage is used as a control variable. Firm governance-specific variables are controlled because prior research shows that firms with good governance structure invest more in intangible assets, particularly in research and development [24,26,90–102]. Firms are also aware that good governance leads to sustainable growth and it is gaining recognition as a key factor in driving sustainable growth [103–105] and good governance leads to higher firm value [106,107]. Board independency (*Board Independence*), board female percentage (*Board Female Percent*), CEO duality (*Duality*) and females in the top management level of firms are handled as the components of corporate governance. *Board Independence* is calculated as the number of independent directors on the board of a firm divided by total number of directors. *Board Female Percent* is calculated as the total number of female directors on a firm's board divided by total number of directors. *Top Female Percent* is calculated as the total number of females in s firm's top management team level divided by total numbers of managers at top management level. *Duality* equals 1 if the chairman and CEO are the same person, 0 otherwise.

Firm structure-specific variables are also controlled in this study because recent studies documented that large firms, firms with low leveraging, profitable firms and older firms have more opportunities for sustainable growth [33,73,75,79,108,109] and these structural features of firms can be decisive for investing in intangible assets [11,26], the governance structures of firms [110]. The structural features of firms may have an effect on firm value [111]. Firm size (*Firm Size*) is the natural logarithm of total assets of a firm. Financial leverage (*Leverage*) is calculated as the total debts divided by total assets. Financial performance (*Firm Performance*) is measured as net income divided by total assets. Firm age (*Firm Age*) is the natural logarithm of the number of years since establishment. One of the types of the ownership structures of firms (institutional owners) is controlled in this study because previous studies emphasize that the ownership structures of firm may have an impact on sustainable growth [108] and firm value [112]. Institutional ownership (*Institutional Owner*) is the percentage of total shares of institutional owners. Finally, sector dummies (Sector Dummies) and year dummies (Year Dummies) are included because of their potentially unobservable effects and because, during the period investigated, Turkish firms are exposed to the negative effects of the financial crisis. The global financial crisis in 2008 decreases financial performances [113]. To control for heteroscedasticity, we obtained robust standard errors by clustering firms.

4. Results

This section covers descriptive statistics, correlation matrix and OLS and Heckman two-stage estimation results.

4.1. Descriptive Statistics

This subheading covers basic statistics regarding variables that are used in estimation models. Table 4 presents descriptive statistics regarding variables. The mean value of *SGR1* is 0.0342. The range of values of *SGR1* varied from −0.0370 to 0.7537. The mean value of *SGR2* is 0.0032, and the range values of *SGR2* varied from −0.0574 to 0.1245. The average value of firm value (*FV*) is 2.0484, and the range of values of *FV* varied from 0 to 74.600. The mean value of *SGR1* is slightly higher than the value for sustainable growth rate which was calculated by Xu and Wang [33] and lower than the value of sustainable growth rate calculated by Feng et al. [108]. The mean value of *Intangibles* is 0.0763. The mean values regarding the sub-components of intangible assets indicate that firms have more cumulative innovative property (*Innovative Property*) (0.0547) than the other sub-components of intangible assets, namely computerized information and databases (*Computerized Info*) (0.0064) and economic competence (*Economic Competence*) (0.0163).

Table 4. Descriptive statistics.

Variable	Mean	Std. Dev.	Min	Max
SGR1	0.0342	0.0479	−0.0370	0.7537
SGR2	0.0032	0.0072	−0.0574	0.1245
FV	2.0484	3.7418	0	74.600
Intangibles	0.0763	0.1444	0	0.9859
Computerized Info	0.0064	0.0376	0	0.4620
Innovative Property	0.0547	0.1171	0	0.9857
Economic Competence	0.0163	0.0651	0	0.6580
Board Female Percent	0.1149	0.1468	0	0.8000
Board Independence	0.1075	0.1507	0	0.5000
Duality	0.0901	0.2865	0	1
Top Female Percent	0.1130	0.1460	0	1
Top Female Dummy	0.5173	0.4998	0	1
Firm Size	19.280	1.5238	15.322	23.957
Leverage	0.4943	0.4808	0.0176	8.6743
Firm Performance	0.0301	0.1444	−3.2284	1.0050
Firm Age	3.4712	0.4729	0.6931	4.6249
Institutional Owner	0.3615	0.3000	0	0.9897

Female (*Board Female Percent*) and independent member (*Board Independence*) percentages on boards are respectively 0.1149 and 0.1075. Of the observations, on average, 9.01% have CEO duality (*Duality*). The percentage of females at the top management level of firms is 11.30%. Of observations, 51.73% have a female at the top management level of firms. The average firm size is 19.280 (approximately 215 Million Turkish Lira 40 Million Dollars). The average values of leverage (*Leverage*) and financial performance (*Firm Performance*) are respectively 0.4943 and 0.0301. The mean value of firm age (*Firm Age*) is 3.4712 (Raw form of firm age is 32 years approximately). The mean value of institutional owners' percentage (*Institutional Owner*) is 0.3615.

4.2. Correlation Matrix

The correlation matrix in Table 5 is used to control multicollinearity among the variables. The results regarding correlation coefficients show that there is no multicollinearity problem among the variables. Intangible assets (*Intangibles*) are positively correlated with sustainable growth rates (*SGR1* and *SGR2*) and firm value (*FV*). The values of two sub-components (*Computerized Info* and *Economic Competence*) of cumulative intangible assets are positively correlated with the sustainable growth rates (*SGR1* and *SGR2*) and firm value (*FV*). Innovative property is only positively correlated with one type of sustainable growth rates (*SGR1*). Hence, independent members on the board of firm (*Board Independence*) is positively correlated with intangible assets (*Intangibles*) and two sub-components of intangible assets (*Innovative Property, Economic Competence*). On the other hand, *Duality* is negatively and significantly correlated with all sub-components of intangible assets (*Computerized Info, Innovative Property*, and *Economic Competence*). We separately ran *Intangibles* and the sub-components (*Computerized Info, Innovative Property*, and *Economic Competence*) in different estimation models because the total amounts of the sub-components of intangible assets may substitute for *Intangibles*.

Table 5. Correlation matrix.

Panel A: Correlation Coefficients Among Variable *SGR1* to *Board Independence*								
Variables	**1**	**2**	**3**	**4**	**5**	**6**	**7**	**8**
(1) SGR1	1							
(2) SGR2	0.644 ***	1						
(3) FV	0.052 *	0.0722 **	1					
(4) Intangibles	0.156 ***	0.123 ***	0.123 ***	1				
(5) Computerized Info	0.130 ***	0.087 **	0.114 ***	0.362 ***	1			
(6) Innovative Property	0.049 *	0.014	0.036	0.627 ***	0.106 ***	1		
(7) Economic Competence	0.095 ***	0.067 **	0.066 **	0.509 ***	−0.007	−0.004	1	
(8) Board Independence	−0.006	−0.035	−0.015	0.157 ***	0.037	0.133 ***	0.089 ***	1
(9) Board Female Percent	−0.021	0.026	−0.016	−0.043 *	−0.024	−0.050 *	0.026	−0.075 ***
(10) Duality	0.049 *	0.011	−0.024	−0.038	−0.051 *	0.053 *	−0.077 ***	0.033
(11) Firm Size	0.367 ***	0.194 ***	0.037	0.161***	0.137 ***	0.058 **	0.120 ***	0.110 ***
(12) Leverage	−0.015	−0.116 ***	0.152 ***	0.155***	0.022	0.147 ***	0.055 *	0.114 ***
(13) Firm Age	0.136 ***	0.137 ***	0.019	−0.100***	−0.099 ***	−0.114 ***	0.013	0.040
(14) Firm Performance	0.224 ***	0.175 ***	0.108 ***	0.033	0.039	0.001	−0.038	−0.104 ***
(15) Institutional Owner	0.298 ***	0.151 ***	0.157 ***	0.160 ***	0.155 ***	0.025	0.135 ***	0.045 *
(16) Top Female Percent	0.069 **	0.0161	−0.046	0.070 **	0.100 ***	0.056 **	0.039	0.039
Panel B: Correlation coefficients among variable *Board Female Percent* to *Top Female Percent*								
Variables	**9**	**10**	**11**	**12**	**13**	**14**	**15**	**16**
(9) Board Female Percent	1							
(10) Duality	0.072 **	1						
(11) Firm Size	−0.159 ***	−0.104 ***	1					
(12) Leverage	−0.094 ***	−0.010	0.129***	1				
(13) Firm Age	−0.011	−0.016	0.191***	−0.023	1			
(14) Firm Performance	−0.025	−0.040	0.263***	−0.399 ***	0.058 **	1		
(15) Institutional Owner	−0.090 ***	0.002	0.584***	0.006	0.075 ***	0.222 ***	1	
(16) Top Female Percent	0.145 **	0.056 **	-0.069**	−0.003	−0.003	−0.024	−0.030	1

Notes: * $p < 0.10$, ** $p < 0.05$, *** $p < 0.01$.

4.3. Main Estimation Results

This sub-heading presents the OLS estimation results. Table 6 presents the effects of intangible assets (*Intangibles*) and the sub-components of intangible assets (namely, *Computerized Info*, *Innovative Property*, and *Economic Competence*) on sustainable growth (SGR1 in column 1 and 4 and *SGR2* in column 2 and 5) and firm value (*FV* in column 3 and 6). We obtained robust standard errors by clustering firms to control for heteroscedasticity. Besides, we tested the normality of the data and the results of these assumption show that the data is normally distributed.

Table 6. Main estimation results.

	(1)	(2)	(3)	(4)	(5)	(6)
VARIABLES	SGR1	SGR2	FV	SGR1	SGR2	FV
Intangibles	0.0237 ***	0.168 **	0.310 *			
	(0.00789)	(0.0690)	(0.163)			
Computerized Info				0.101 ***	0.856 ***	1.506 **
				(0.0285)	(0.295)	(0.607)
Innovative Property				−0.00358	0.0320	−0.0732
				(0.00943)	(0.0789)	(0.194)
Economic Competence				0.0272 *	0.259 *	0.579 *
				(0.0162)	(0.136)	(0.330)
Board Independence	−0.00749	−0.142	−0.240	−0.00542	−0.0640	−0.172
	(0.0116)	(0.103)	(0.249)	(0.0116)	(0.102)	(0.249)
Board Female Percent	0.00881	0.236 ***	−0.0550	0.00829	0.217 ***	−0.0524
	(0.00780)	(0.0676)	(0.170)	(0.00782)	(0.0669)	(0.170)
Duality	0.00960 **	0.0362	−0.0629	0.0104 ***	0.0408	−0.0531
	(0.00377)	(0.0331)	(0.0769)	(0.00380)	(0.0330)	(0.0776)
Top Female Percent	0.00898	−0.0388	0.352 **	0.00840	−0.0513	0.324 *
	(0.00762)	(0.0661)	(0.165)	(0.00771)	(0.0656)	(0.167)
Firm Size	0.00707 ***	0.0565 ***	−0.109 ***	0.00698 ***	0.0606 ***	-0.108 ***
	(0.000936)	(0.00808)	(0.0205)	(0.000936)	(0.00969)	(0.0205)
Leverage	−0.00541 **	−0.0611 ***	0.906 ***	−0.00449 *	−0.117 **	0.924 ***
	(0.00238)	(0.0180)	(0.121)	(0.00239)	(0.0502)	(0.123)
Firm Age	0.00750 ***	0.0412 *	0.126 **	0.00821 ***	0.0482 **	0.134 **
	(0.00249)	(0.0216)	(0.0532)	(0.00250)	(0.0213)	(0.0534)
Firm Performance	−0.0240 ***	0.0974 ***	1.543 ***	−0.0226 ***	0.791 ***	1.642 ***
	(0.00830)	(0.0375)	(0.300)	(0.00836)	(0.156)	(0.304)
Institutional Owner	0.0255 ***	0.0715 *	0.635 ***	0.0256 ***	0.0455	0.621 ***
	(0.00444)	(0.0384)	(0.0960)	(0.00444)	(0.0379)	(0.0960)
Constant	−0.135 ***	−1.039 ***	2.587 ***	−0.136 ***	−1.140 ***	2.544 ***
	(0.0183)	(0.157)	(0.390)	(0.0184)	(0.183)	(0.392)
Year Fixed	Yes	Yes	Yes	Yes	Yes	Yes
Sector Fixed	Yes	Yes	Yes	Yes	Yes	Yes
Observations	1353	1353	1353	1353	1353	1353
F Value	15.00 ***	8.17 ***	12.57 ***	14.05 ***	9.38 ***	11.56 ***
R^2	0.200	0.129	0.189	0.206	0.157	0.192
Test of Normality						
Jarque-Bera	4.519	4.743	0.7433	4.416	3.891	2.263
Chi2	0.1044	0.0933	0.6896	0.1099	0.1429	0.3225

Notes: * $p < 0.10$, ** $p < 0.05$, *** $p < 0.01$, Standard errors in parentheses.

Table 6 shows that the intangible assets positively and significantly affect sustainable growth rates of firms (*SGR1* and *SGR2*) (Column 1: 0.0237 and Column 2: 0.168). Moreover, the intangible assets of firms (*Intangibles*) affect firm value (*FV*) positively and significantly (Column 3: 0.310). We accept H1 and H2. The same table shows that computerized information and databases (*Computerized Info*) and economic competence (*Economic Competence*) are positively and significantly related to the rates of sustainable growth (*SGR1* and *SGR2*) (Column 4: 0.101; 0.0272 and Column 5: 0.856; 0.259). Besides, computerized information and databases (*Computerized Info*) and economic competence (*Economic Competence*) are positively and significantly associated with firm value (*FV*) (Column 6: 1.506, 0.579). We accept H1B, H1C, H2B, and H2C. It was found that innovative property (*Innovative Property*) had no effect on sustainable growth rates (*SGR1* and *SGR2*) and firm value (*FV*) (Column 4: −0.00358; Column 5: 0.0320; Column 6: 0.0732). Thus, we do not accept H1A and H2A. The magnitudes of coefficients (0.101 and 0.856 and 1.506 vs 0.0272 and 0.259 and 0.579) show that the computerized information and databases (which includes software, information systems, domains, and consumer databases) is a more important element than economic competence (which includes brand names, trademarks, special costs, agreements, rights, customer lists, dealer lists) to enhance sustainable growth and firm value. On the other hand, the reason for the insignificant association between innovative property (*Innovative Property*) and sustainable growth (*SGR1* and SGR2) and firm value (*FV*) is exposed when the context of the sub-component of innovative property (*Innovative Property*) is investigated (please see the Section 3.2.3). The sub-component of intangible assets *Innovative Property* comprises capitalized research and development, copyrights, designs, licenses, and patents. The research and development item in the innovative property classification is highly risky and the return on this item may spread over years [93]. Many patents in the innovative property classification may provide only limited protection and be created for strategic purposes only distantly related to firm's own innovation efforts [11,73,114]. Thus, innovative property may not affect sustainable growth and firm value for this reason.

The results regarding control variables are as follows. While the percentage of independent members on the boards of firms (*Board Independence*) negatively but insignificantly affected sustainable growth rates (*SGR1* and SGR2) and firm value (*FV*) (−0.00749, −0.142, −0.240, −0.00542, −0.0640, and −0.172, respectively) in all columns, the percentage of females on the boards of firms (*Board Female Percent*) significantly and positively influences sustainable growth rate 2 (SGR2) (Column 2: 0.236; Column 5: 0.217). CEO duality (*Duality*) is positively and significantly associated with sustainable growth rate 1 (*SGR1*) (Column 1: 0.00960; Column 4: 0.0104). The percentage of females in top management positions significantly and positively affects only firm value (*FV*) (Column 3: 0.352; Column 6: 0.324). The results show that the percentage of institutional owners (*Institutional Owner*) (0.0255, 0.0715, 0.635, 0.0256, and 0.621, respectively) and firm age (*Firm Age*) (0.00750, 0.0412, 0.126, 0.00821, 0.0482, and 0.134, respectively) generally have positive and significant effects on sustainable growth rates (*SGR1* and *SGR2*) and firm value (*FV*). While firm leverage (*Leverage*) negatively and significantly affects the sustainable growth rates (*SGR1* and *SGR2*) (−0.0541, −0.0611, −0.00449, and −0.117, respectively), it has a positive and significant effect on firm value (*FV*) (0.906 and 0.924). On the other hand, firm size (*Firm Size*) has a negative and significant effect on firm value (*FV*) (−0.109 and −0.108), and it positively and significantly affects the sustainable growth rates (*SGR1* and *SGR2*) (0.00707, 0.0565, 0.00698, and 0.0606, respectively).

4.4. Heckman Estimation Results

Some recent studies, especially studies in Turkey, indicate that females at the top management level of firms are more likely to invest in intangible assets, particularly in R&D and the innovative property type of intangible assets [26,27]. (In the current study, the correlation table also shows that females at top management level (*Top Female Percent*) positively and significantly correlated with intangible assets and the sub-components of intangible assets.) These studies assert that females are more innovative than males [99] and they may bring more innovative ideas such as intangible assets to a firm [24]. Thus, female participation at the top management level of firms affects firms' intangibles and it indirectly affects sustainable growth of firms and firm value. We adopted a model with some firm-specific characteristics as the determinants of female participation at the top management level of firms. The first stage of the Heckman two-stage estimation model is as follows:

$$\begin{aligned}\text{Top Female Dummy}_{it} = {} & \beta_0 + \beta_1 \text{ Board Female Percent}_{i,t} + \beta_2 \text{ Board Independence}_{i,t} \\ & + \beta_3 \text{ Duality}_{i,t} + \beta_4 \text{ Firm Size}_{i,t} + \beta_5 \text{ Leverage}_{i,t} + \beta_6 \text{ Firm Performance}_{i,t} \\ & + \beta_7 \text{ Firm Age}_{i,t} + \beta_8 \text{ Institutional Owner}_{i,t} + \Sigma\text{Sector Dummies} + \Sigma\text{Year Dummies} + \varepsilon\end{aligned} \quad (6)$$

In the first stage of the Heckman two-stage estimation procedures, we determined which firms are more likely to have females at their top management level. Even though discussions on the appointment of a female to the top levels of firms refers to the board of directors of firms, we argue that these discussions are valid for top management level of firms. Thus, we used some board-specific attributes and firm-specific characteristics in the first stage of selection model. Prior literature stated that female managers and boards with more independent directors are more likely to hire females [115,116]. Besides, CEO who holds the board chairperson may enforce the female participation [117,118]. While large firms may face more pressure to appoint females to the top levels of firms, old firms have more conservative structure and they are less likely to appoint females to top levels of firms [118,119] and higher percentage of institutional owners increases the female presence [118]. We controlled firm performance because presentation of females in top levels of firms increases the performance of firms, thus firms with high performance are more likely to present on top levels of firms [120]. We used sector and year fixed effects because of potential effects. After calculation of the inverse Mills ratio (*IMR*), we re-ran our OLS models with the addition of the *IMR*. *Top Female Dummy* is equal to 1 if there is a female in the top managements of firms, 0 otherwise. Other variables in the first stage of the Heckman two-stage estimation model are explained above. The results of the first stage of Heckman two-stage estimation model shows that high leveraged firms and firms with high board gender diversity are more likely to hire females at the top management levels. However, firms with high board independence are less likely to hire females at the top management level. The second stages of Heckman two-stage estimation models are as follows:

$$\begin{aligned} \text{SGR1}_{i,t} \text{ or } \text{SGR2}_{i,t} \ (\text{or } \text{FV}_{i,t}) &= \beta_0 + \beta_1 \text{ Intangibles}_{i,t} + \beta_2 \text{ Board Female Percent}_{i,t} \\ &+ \beta_3 \text{ Board Independence}_{i,t} + \beta_4 \text{ Duality}_{i,t} + \beta_5 \text{ Top Female Percent}_{i,t} + \beta_6 \text{ Firm Size}_{i,t} \\ &+ \beta_7 \text{ Leverage}_{i,t} + \beta_8 \text{ Firm Performance}_{i,t} + \beta_9 \text{ Firm Age}_{i,t} + \beta_{10} \text{ Institutional Owner}_{i,t} \\ &+ \text{IMR} + \Sigma\text{Sector Dummies} + \Sigma\text{Year Dummies} + \varepsilon \end{aligned} \tag{7}$$

$$\begin{aligned} \text{SGR}_{i,t} \text{ or } \text{SGR22}_{i,t}. \ (\text{or } \text{FV}_{i,t}) &= \beta_0 + \beta_1\text{Computerized Info}_{i,t} + \beta_2\text{Innovative Property}_{i,t} \\ &+ \beta_3\text{Economic Competence}_{i,t} + \beta_4 \text{ Board Female Percent}_{i,t} + \beta_5 \text{ Board Independence}_{i,t} \\ &+\beta_6 \text{ Duality}_{i,t} + \beta_7 \text{ Firm Size}_{i,t} + \beta_8 \text{ Leverage}_{i,t} + \beta_9 \text{ Firm Performance}_{i,t} + \beta_{10} \text{ Firm} \\ &\text{Age}_{i,t} + \beta_{11} \text{ Institutional Owner}_{i,t} + \text{IMR} + \Sigma\text{Sector Dummies} + \Sigma\text{Year Dummies} + \varepsilon \end{aligned} \tag{8}$$

The other columns (2, 3, 4, 5, 6, and 7) in Table 7 present the results regarding the second stage of Heckman two-stage estimation. Intangible assets positively and significantly affect the sustainable growth of firms (*SGR1* and *SGR2*) (Column 2: 0.0250; Column3: 0.357) and firm value (*FV*) (Column4: 0.338). Besides, we found that the sub-components of intangible assets, computerized information and database have a positive and significant impact on sustainable growth rates (*SGR1* and SGR2) and firm value (*FV*) (Column 5: 0.0976; Column 6: 0.823; Column 7: 1.727). On the other hand, economic competence affects only one type of sustainable growth rate (*SGR1*) and firm value (*FV*) (Column 5: 0.0279 and Column 7: 0589). We found no association among innovative property, sustainable growth rates and firm value as in the OLS estimation results. The results of the Heckman two-stage estimation procedure generally confirm the results of the OLS estimation procedure.

Table 7. Heckman estimation results.

	(1)	(2)	(3)	(4)	(5)	(6)	(7)
VARIABLES	Top Female Dummy	SGR1	SGR2	FV	SGR1	SGR2	FV
Intangibles		0.0250 ***	0.357**	0.338**			
		(0.0078)	(0.141)	(0.161)			
Computerized Info					0.0976 ***	0.823 **	1.727 ***
					(0.0307)	(0.327)	(0.639)
Innovative Property					−0.00373	0.0248	0.0443
					(0.00953)	(0.0809)	(0.196)
Economic Competence					0.0279 *	0.208	0.589 *
					(0.0162)	(0.137)	(0.327)
Board Independence	−1.0203 **	−0.0077	−0.0423	−0.239	−0.00549	−0.132	−0.191
	(0.3944)	(0.0116)	(0.2086)	(0.247)	(0.0116)	(0.103)	(0.247)
Board Female Percent	1.2148 ***	0.0072	0.2861 **	−0.0773	0.00785	0.234 ***	−0.0830
	(0.2712)	(0.0077)	(0.1404)	(0.168)	(0.00784)	(0.0680)	(0.169)
Duality	0.0780	0.0090 **	0.0634	−0.0751	0.0102 ***	0.0403	−0.0615
	(0.1264)	(0.0037)	(0.0677)	(0.0763)	(0.00380)	(0.0335)	(0.0770)
Top Female Percent	–	0.0080	0.0424	0.345 **	0.00759	−0.0414	0.316 *
		(0.0076)	(0.1375)	(0.163)	(0.00774)	(0.0671)	(0.166)
Firm Size	−0.0076	0.0033	−0.1267 *	−0.475 ***	0.00340	−0.0129	−0.461 ***
	(0.0288)	(0.0026)	(0.0713)	(0.0975)	(0.00306)	(0.0345)	(0.100)
Leverage	0.2106 **	0.0078	0.3795 *	2.379 ***	0.00879	0.159	2.326 ***
	(0.1029)	(0.0069)	(0.2175)	(0.405)	(0.00792)	(0.105)	(0.413)
Firm Age	0.1101	0.0190 ***	0.5377 ***	1.020 ***	0.0164 ***	0.179 ***	0.991 ***
	(0.0846)	(0.0055)	(0.1416)	(0.217)	(0.00535)	(0.0684)	(0.223)
Firm Performance	−0.4540	−0.0219 ***	0.1693 **	1.987 ***	−0.0211 **	0.127 ***	2.062 ***
	(0.3782)	(0.0083)	(0.0837)	(0.318)	(0.00840)	(0.0391)	(0.322)
Institutional Owner	0.1926	0.0396 ***	0.8493 ***	1.831 ***	0.0398 ***	0.306 **	1.767 ***
	(0.1416)	(0.0080)	(0.2477)	(0.328)	(0.00918)	(0.121)	(0.338)
IMR	–	0.1038 **	4.086 **	8.674 ***	0.106 *	1.764 **	8.289 ***
		(0.0533)	(1.740)	(2.307)	(0.0629)	(0.843)	(2.374)
Year Fixed	Yes	Yes	Yes	Yes	Yes	Yes	Yes
Sector Fixed	Yes	Yes	Yes	Yes	Yes	Yes	Yes
Constant	−0.8829 **	−0.226 ***	−3.996 ***	−3.832 **	−0.219 ***	−2.243 ***	−3.548 **
	(0.3663)	(0.0387)	(1.207)	(1.681)	(0.0410)	(0.585)	(1.723)
Observations	1,353	1,353	1,353	1,353	1,353	1,353	1,353
F Value	73.41 ***	14.42 ***	7.45 ***	13.21 ***	13.44 ***	7.50 ***	12.17 ***
Pseudo R^2 & R^2	0.0401	0.201	0.115	0.205	0.206	0.135	0.208

Notes: * $p < 0.10$, ** $p < 0.05$, *** $p < 0.01$, Standard errors in parentheses.

5. Discussion

This aim of this is to analyze the effects of intangible assets and sub-components of intangible assets, namely computerized information and databases, innovative property, and economic competence, on firm value and the sustainable growth of firms listed on Borsa İstanbul from 2005 to 2013. Two different estimation procedures of the OLS and Heckman two-stage are used to test the hypotheses.

Based on OLS and Heckman estimation results, intangible assets have an impact on sustainable growth and firm value. Also, two sub-components of intangible assets, namely computerized information and databases and economic competence, affect the sustainable growth rates of firms and firm value positively and significantly. We found no association between the other sub-component of intangible assets, innovative property, with the sustainable growth of firms and firm value.

A possible explanation for this is that innovative property comprises R&D items and the return on this item may spread over years [93]. Many patents in innovative property classification may provide only limited protection and be created for strategic purposes only distantly related to firm's own innovation efforts [11,73,114]. Thus, based on our research, innovative property does not have an impact on sustainable growth rates of firms and firm value.

The findings of the research imply that managers of firms should take into account the importance of intangible assets for sustainable growth and firm value and thus, they should know that more investment in these kinds of strategic assets will increase the success of a firm. As far as the relationship between computerized information and databases and performance indicators is concerned, firms through investing in this subcomponent need to improve the skills of the current employees or hire new ones to increase performance improvement effect of the computerized information and databases. Additionally, investing in these assets will necessitate the changes in the organization of the work. For instance, some specific operations that require a long time to complete will be implemented in a shorter time, thus firms will be able to discover new markets.

The study has some limitations. First, a small sample was used compared to a similar study by Xu and Wang [33]. Second, the sample covers only nine years between 2005 and 2013. Most of the data was collected by hand. Data access problems and the hand-collection process caused us to work with this data.

Future research may use a larger sample and could extend the year range or may add alternative corporate governance characteristics, firm-specific characteristics or alternative sustainable growth measures to the research model. The hypotheses of the study may be tested using data from different countries. Therefore, the effects of the amounts of important items in each sub-component of intangible assets such as software, brands, and trademarks on sustainable growth and firm value may be tested. Lagged values for the sub-components of intangible assets, particularly innovative property, may be used as test variables in future research. Alternatively, the effect of different classification made by some authors [60,84–88] on firm value of the sustainable growth of firms may be tested in the future study.

Author Contributions: The data was collected by M.O. The research is designed by M.O. and D.F. The paper is written by M.O. and D.F. Analysis of data was performed by M.O.

Funding: This research received no external funding.

Conflicts of Interest: The authors declare no conflict of interest.

References

1. Mooney, K. *The Essential of Accounting Dictionary*, 1th ed.; Sphinx Publishing: Naperville, IL, USA, 2008.
2. Siegel, J.G.; Shim, J.K. *Dictionary of Accounting Terms*, 1th ed.; Barron's Educational Series; Inc.: New York, NY, USA, 2000.
3. Andrews, D.; de Serres, A. Intangible assets, resource allocation and growth: A framework for analysis. *OECD Econ. Dep. Working Pap.* **2012**. [CrossRef]
4. Augier, M.; Teece, D. An economic perspective on intellectual capital. In *Perspective on Intellectual Capital: Multidisciplinary Insight into Management, Measurement, and Reporting*, 1th Ed.; Marr, B., Ed.; Elsevier Inc.: Oxford, UK, 2005; pp. 3–27.
5. Gardberg, N.A.; Fombrun, C.J. Corporate citizenship: Creating assets across institutional environments. *Acad. Manag. Rev.* **2006**, *31*, 329–346. [CrossRef]
6. Wyatt, A. Accounting recognition of intangible assets: Theory and evidence on economic determinants. *Account. Rev.* **2005**, *80*, 967–1003. [CrossRef]
7. IAS 38 (International Accounting Standard 38), Intangible Assets. Available online: https://www.ifrs.org/issued-standards/list-of-standards/ias-38-intangible-assets/ (accessed on 22 January 2019).
8. St-Pierre, J.; Audet, J. Intangible assets and performance: Analysis on manufacturing SMEs. *J. Intellect. Cap.* **2011**, *12*, 202–223. [CrossRef]
9. Villalonga, B. Intangible Resources, Tobin's q, and sustainability of performance differences. *J. Econ. Behav. Org.* **2004**, *54*, 205–230. [CrossRef]
10. Denicoali, S.; Zucchella, A. Strange, R. Knowledge assets and firm international performance. *Int. Bus. Rev.* **2014**, *23*, 55–62. [CrossRef]
11. Artz, K.W.; Norman, P.M.; Hatfield, D.E.; Cardinal, L.B. A longitudinal study of the impact of R&D, patents, and product innovation on firm performance. *J. Prod. Innov. Manag.* **2010**, *27*, 725–740.
12. Fındık, D.; Ocak, M. Türkiye'de maddi olmayan varlık yatırımlarının işletmelerin finansal performansı üzerine etkisi. *Ege Acad. Rev.* **2016**, *16*, 397–414.
13. Megna, P.; Klock, M. The impact of intangible capital on Tobin's q in the semiconductor industry. *Am. Econ. Rev.* **1993**, *83*, 265–269.

14. Brynjolfsson, E.; Hitt, L.M.; Yang, S. Intangible assets: Computers and organizational capital. *Brook. Pap. Econ. Act.* **2002**, *2002*, 137–181. [CrossRef]
15. Dettori, B.; Marrocu, E.; Paci, R. Total factor productivity, intangible assets and spatial dependence in the European regions. *Reg. Stud.* **2012**, *46*, 1401–1416. [CrossRef]
16. Marrano, M.G.; Haskel, J.; Wallis, G. What happened to the knowledge economy? ICT, intangible investment, and Britain's productivity record revisited. *Rev. Income Wealth* **2009**, *55*, 686–716. [CrossRef]
17. Ely, K.; Waymire, G. Intangible assets and stock prices in the pre-sec era. *J. Account. Res.* **1999**, *37*, 17–44. [CrossRef]
18. Ritter, A.; Wells, P. Identifiable intangible asset disclosures, stock prices and future earnings. *Account. Financ.* **2006**, *46*, 843–863. [CrossRef]
19. Krasnikov, A.; Mishra, S.; Orozco, D. Evaluating the financial impact of branding using trademarks: A framework and empirical evidence. *J. Market.* **2009**, *73*, 154–166. [CrossRef]
20. Fukao, K.; Hamagata, S.; Miyagawa, T.; Tonogi, K. Intangible investment in Japan: Measurement and contribution to economic growth. *Rev. Income Wealth* **2009**, *55*, 717–736. [CrossRef]
21. Van Ark, B.; Hao, J.X.; Corrado, C.; Hulten, C. Measuring intangible capital and its contribution to economic growth in Europe. *EIB Papers* **2009**, *14*, 62–93.
22. Matolcsy, Z.; Wyatt, A. Capitalised intangibles and financial analysts. *Account. Financ.* **2006**, *46*, 457–479. [CrossRef]
23. Bart, M.E.; Kasznik, R.; McNichols, M.F. Analyst coverage and intangible assets. *J. Account. Res.* **2001**, *39*, 1–34. [CrossRef]
24. Midavaine, J.; Dolfsma, W.; Aalbers, R. Board diversity and R&D investment. *Manag. Decis.* **2016**, *54*, 558–569.
25. He, J.; Wang, H.C. Innovative knowledge assets and economic performance: The asymmetric roles of incentives and monitoring. *Acad. Manag. J.* **2009**, *52*, 919–938. [CrossRef]
26. Fındık, D.; Ocak, M. Gender diversity and independency: Threat or opportunity in managing innovative property? In *Handbook of Research on Managerial Thinking in Global Business Economics*, 1th ed.; Dinçer, H., Yüksel, S., Eds.; IGI Global: Hershey, PA, USA, 2019; pp. 298–317.
27. Fındık, D.; Ocak, M. Cinsiyet Farklılığı ve Bağımsızlık: Maddi Olmayan Varlıkların Yönetiminde Fırsat mı Yoksa Tehdit Edici Bir Unsur mu? In Proceedings of the 25th National Management and Organization Congress, Ankara, Turkey, 25–27 May 2017.
28. Mukherjee, T.; Sen, S.S. Sustainable growth rate and its determinants: A study on some selected companies in India. *Glob. Multi.* **2018**, *10*, 100–108. [CrossRef]
29. Corrado, C.; Hulten, C.; Sichel, D. Measuring capital and technology: An expanded framework. Available online: https://www.federalreserve.gov/pubs/feds/2004/200465/200465pap.pdf (accessed on 15 January 2019).
30. Corrado, C.; Hulten, C.; Sichel, D. Measuring capital and technology: An expanded framework. In *Measuring Capital in The New Economy*, 1th ed.; Corrado, C., Haltiwanger, J., Sichel, D., Eds.; University of Chicago Press: Chicago, IL, USA, 2005; pp. 11–46.
31. Corrado, C.; Hulten, C.; Sichel, D. *Intangible capital and economic growth*; FEDS Working Paper No. 2006-24: Washington, DC, USA, 2006.
32. Corrado, C.; Hulten, C.; Sichel, D. Intangible investment and US economic growth. *Rev. Inco. Weal.* **2009**, *55*, 661–685. [CrossRef]
33. Xu, J.; Wang, B. Intellectual capital, financial performance and companies' sustainable growth: Evidence from the Korean manufacturing industry. *Sustainability* **2018**, *10*, 1. [CrossRef]
34. Bozbura, T.F. Measurement and application of intellectual capital in Turkey. *Learn. Organ.* **2004**, *11*, 357–367. [CrossRef]
35. Zerenler, M.; Hasiloglu, S.B.; Sezgin, M. Intellectual capital and innovation performance: Empirical evidence in the Turkish automotive supplier. *J. Tech. Manage. Innov.* **2008**, *3*, 31–40. [CrossRef]
36. Calisir, F.; Altin Gumussoy, C.; Elvan Bayraktaroğlu, A.; Deniz, E. Intellectual capital in the quoted Turkish ITC sector. *J. Intellec. Cap.* **2010**, *11*, 538–554. [CrossRef]
37. Yalama, A. The relationship between intellectual capital and banking performance in Turkey: Evidence from panel data. *Int. J. Learn. Intellec. Cap.* **2013**, *10*, 71–87. [CrossRef]

38. Ozkan, N.; Cakan, S.; Kayacan, M. Intellectual capital and financial performance: A study of the Turkish Banking Sector. *Borsa Istanb. Rev.* **2017**, *17*, 190–198. [CrossRef]
39. Higgins, R.C. How much growth can a firm afford? *Financ. Manag.* **1977**, *6*, 7–16. [CrossRef]
40. Yu, F.; Zhang, L. Does intellectual capital really create value? In Proceedings of the IEEE 4th International Conference on Wireless Communications, Networking and Mobile Computing, Sydney, Australia, 29–30 June 2018.
41. Xu, J.; Wang, B. Intellectual Capital Performance of the Textile Industry in Emerging Markets: A Comparison with China and South Korea. *Sustainability* **2019**, *11*, 2354. [CrossRef]
42. Mukherjee, T.; Sen, S.S. Intellectual Capital and Corporate Sustainable Growth: The Indian Evidence. *J. Bus. Econ. Environ. Stud.* **2019**, *9*, 5–15. [CrossRef]
43. Ying, Q.; Hassan, H.; Ahmad, H. The role of a manager's intangible capabilities in resource acquisition and sustainable competitive performance. *Sustainability* **2019**, *11*, 527. [CrossRef]
44. Liang, T.P.; You, J.J.; Liu, C.C. A resource-based perspective on information technology and firm performance: A meta analysis. *Ind. Manag. Data Syst.* **2010**, *110*, 1138–1158. [CrossRef]
45. Mudambi, R.; Swift, T. Proactive R&D management and firm growth: A punctuated equilibrium model. *Res. Policy* **2011**, *40*, 429–440.
46. Demir, K.A.; Tolga, İ.B. A sustainable growth rate metric based on R&D experience for government R&D organizations. *J. Glob. Strateg. Manag.* **2014**, *8*, 27–37.
47. Shane, H.; Klock, M. The relation between patent citations and Tobin's Q in the semiconductor industry. *Rev. Quant. Financ. Account.* **1997**, *9*, 131–146. [CrossRef]
48. Chin, C.L.; Lee, P.; Chi, H.Y.; Anandarajan, A. Patent citation, R&D spillover, and Tobin's Q: Evidence from Taiwan semiconductor industry. *Rev. Quant. Financ. Account.* **2006**, *26*, 67–84.
49. Klock, M.; Megna, P. Measuring and valuing intangible capital in the wireless communications industry. *Quart. Rev. Econ. Financ.* **2000**, *40*, 519–532. [CrossRef]
50. Wu, Q.; Bjornson, B. Value of advertising by food manufacturers as investment in intangible capital. *Agribusiness* **1996**, *12*, 147–156. [CrossRef]
51. Gleason, K.I.; Klock, M. Intangible capital in the pharmaceutical & chemical industry. Available online: https://scholarworks.uno.edu/cgi/viewcontent.cgi?article=1009&context=econ_wp (accessed on 10 August 2019).
52. Tseng, C.Y.; James Goo, Y.J. Intellectual capital and corporate value in an emerging economy: Empirical study of Taiwanese manufacturers. *RD Manag.* **2005**, *35*, 187–201. [CrossRef]
53. Salman, R.T.; Mansor, M.; Babatunde, A.D.; Tayib, M. Impact of intellectual capital on return on asset in Nigerian manufacturing companies. *Interdiscipl. J. Res. Bus.* **2012**, *2*, 21–30.
54. Ehie, I.C.; Olibe, K. The effect of R&D investment on firm value: An examination of US manufacturing and service industries. *Int. J. Prod. Econ.* **2010**, *128*, 127–135.
55. Dženopoljac, V.; Janoševic, S.; Bontis, N. Intellectual capital and financial performance in the Serbian ICT industry. *J. Intellec. Cap.* **2016**, *17*, 373–396. [CrossRef]
56. Klock, M.; Baum, C.F.; Thies, C.F. Tobin's Q, intangible capital, and financial policy. *J. Econ. Bus.* **1996**, *48*, 387–400. [CrossRef]
57. Haneda, S.; Odagiri, H. Appropriation of returns from technological assets and the values of patents and R&D in Japanese high-tech firms. *Econ. Innov. New Tech.* **1998**, *7*, 303–321.
58. Bosworth, D.; Rogers, M. *Research and Development, Intangible Assets and the Performance of Large Australian Companies*; Melbourne Institute of Applied Economic and Social Research: Melbourne, Australia, 1998.
59. Bharadwaj, A.S.; Bharadwaj, S.G.; Konsynski, B.R. Information technology effects on firm performance as measured by Tobin's q. *Manag. Sci.* **1999**, *45*, 1008–1024. [CrossRef]
60. Hall, B.H.; Jaffe, A.; Trajtenberg, M. Market value and patent citations. *RAND J. Econ.* **2005**, *36*, 16–38.
61. Lin, B.W.; Chen, C.J.; Wu, H.L. Patent portfolio diversity, technology strategy, and firm value. *IEEE Trans. Eng. Manag.* **2006**, *53*, 17–26.
62. Anandarajan, A.; Chin, C.L.; Chi, H.Y.; Lee, P. The effect of innovative activity on firm performance: The experience of Taiwan. *Adv. Account.* **2007**, *23*, 1–30. [CrossRef]
63. Parcharidis, E.G.; Varsakelis, N.C. R&D and Tobin's q in an emerging financial market: The case of the Athens Stock Exchange. *Manag. Dec. Econ.* **2010**, *31*, 353–361.
64. Antonelli, C.; Colombelli, A. The generation and exploitation of technological change: Market value and total factor productivity. *J. Tech. Transfer.* **2011**, *36*, 353–382. [CrossRef]

65. Rahko, J. Market value of R&D, patents, and organizational capital: Finnish evidence. *Econ. Innov. New Tech.* **2004**, *23*, 353–377.
66. Gamayuni, R.R. The effect of intangible asset, financial performance and financial policies on the firm value. *Int. J. Sci. Tech. Res.* **2015**, *4*, 202–212.
67. Kumar, V.; Sundarraj, R.P. Schumpeterian innovation patterns and firm-performance of global technology companies. *Eur. J. Innov. Manag.* **2016**, *19*, 276–296. [CrossRef]
68. Peters, R.H.; Taylor, L.A. Intangible capital and the investment-q relation. *J. Financ. Econ.* **2017**, *123*, 251–272. [CrossRef]
69. Koru, A.T.; Dinçer, N.N. Türkiye'de sanayi ve hizmet sektörleri. *İkt. Ve Top.* **2018**, *88*, 5–11.
70. MKK (Merkezi Kayıt Kuruluşu- Central Securities Depository of Turkey). Available online: https://www.mkk.com.tr (accessed on 15 October 2017).
71. FINNET (Financial Information News Network). Available online: https://www.finnet.com.tr/FinnetStore/tr/ (accessed on 15 October 2017).
72. KAP (Kamuyu Aydınlatma Platformu- Public Disclosure Platform). Available online: https://www.kap.org.tr/en/ (accessed on 16 October 2017).
73. Arora, L.; Kumar, S.; Verma, P. The anatomy of sustainable growth rate of Indian manufacturing firms. *Glob. Bus. Rev.* **2018**, *19*, 1050–1071. [CrossRef]
74. Vasiu, D.E.; Illie, L. Sustainable growth rate. An analysis regarding the most traded companies on the Bucharest stock exchange. In *Emerging Issues in the Global Economy*, 1th ed.; Mărginean, S.C., Ogrean, C., Orăştean, R., Eds.; Springer: Berlin, Germany, 2018; pp. 381–394.
75. Fonseka, M.M.; Ramos, C.G.; Tian, G.-L. The most appropriate sustainable growth rate model for managers and researchers. *J. Appl. Bus. Res.* **2012**, *28*, 481–500. [CrossRef]
76. Lockwood, L.; Prombutr, W. Sustainable growth and stock returns. *J. Financ. Res.* **2010**, *33*, 519–538. [CrossRef]
77. Firer, C. Investment basics: XXXI. sustainable growth models. *Invest. Anal. J.* **1995**, *24*, 57–58. [CrossRef]
78. Demirgüç-Kunt, A.; Maksimovic, V. Law, finance, and firm growth. *J. Financ.* **1998**, *53*, 2107–2137. [CrossRef]
79. Amouzesh, N.; Moeinfar, Z.; Mousavi, Z. Sustainable growth and firm performance: Evidence from Iran stock exchange. *Int. J. Bus. Soc. Sci.* **2011**, *2*, 249–255.
80. Brick, I.E.; Chen, H.-Y.; Hsieh, C.-H.; Lee, C.-F. A comparison of alternative models for estimating firm's growth rate. *Rev. Quant. Financ. Account.* **2016**, *47*, 369–393. [CrossRef]
81. Lee, K.; Lee, H. How Does CSR activity affect sustainable growth and value of corporations? Evidence from Korea. *Sustainability* **2019**, *11*, 508. [CrossRef]
82. Chen, M.-C.; Cheng, S.-J.; Hwang, Y. An empirical investigation of the relationship between intellectual capital and firms' market value and financial performance. *J. Intellect. Cap.* **2005**, *6*, 159–176. [CrossRef]
83. Hall, R. The strategic analysis of intangible resources. *Strateg. Manag. J.* **1992**, *13*, 135–144. [CrossRef]
84. Hendriksen, E.S.; van Breda, M.F. *Accounting Theory*, 3th ed.; Wiley & Sons: Hoboken, NJ, USA, 1992.
85. Sveiby, K. The intangible assets monitor. *J. Hum. Res. Cost. Account.* **1997**, *2*, 73–97. [CrossRef]
86. Hammerer, G. Intangible Investments in Austria. *OECD Workshop New ST Indic. Knowl. Based Econ.* Working Paper, **1996**.
87. Kaplan, R.S.; Notron, D.P. Measuring the strategic readiness of intangible assets. *Harv. Bus. Rev.* **2004**, *82*, 52–63.
88. Cohen, J.A. *Intangible Assets: Valuation and Economic Benefit*, 1th ed.; John Wiley & Sons, Inc.: Hoboken, NJ, USA, 2005.
89. Borgo, M.D.; Goodridge, P.; Haskel, J.; Pesole, A. Productivity and growth in UK industries: An intangible investment approach. *Oxf. Bull. Econ. Stat.* **2013**, *75*, 806–834. [CrossRef]
90. Chen, H.-L.; Hsu, W.-T. Family ownership, board independence, and R&D investment. *Fam. Bus. Rev.* **2009**, *22*, 347–362.
91. Guldiken, O.; Darendeli, I.S. Too much of a good thing: Board monitoring and R&D investments. *J. Bus. Res.* **2016**, *69*, 2931–2938.
92. Rossi, F.; Cebula, R.J. Does the board of directors affect the extent of corporate R&D? Empirical evidence from public corporations in Italy. *Econ. Bull.* **2015**, *35*, 2567–2580.
93. Baysinger, B.D.; Kosnik, R.D.; Turk, T.A. Effects of board and ownership structure on corporate R&D strategy. *Acad. Manag. J.* **1991**, *34*, 205–214.

94. Dong, J.; Gou, Y.-N. Corporate governance structure, managerial discretion, and the R&D investment in China. *Int. Rev. Econ. Financ.* **2010**, *19*, 180–188.
95. Shapiro, D.; Tang, Y.; Wang, M.; Zhang, W. The effects of corporate governance and ownership on the innovation performance of Chinese SMEs. *J. Chinese Econ. Bus. Stud.* **2015**, *13*, 311–335. [CrossRef]
96. Rapp, M.S.; Udoieva, I.A. Corporate governance and its impact on R&D investment in emerging markets. *Emerg. Mar. Financ. Trad.* **2017**, *53*, 2159–2178.
97. Faccio, M.; Marchica, M.-T.; Mura, R. CEO gender, corporate risk-taking, and the efficiency of capital allocation. *J. Corp. Financ.* **2016**, *39*, 193–209. [CrossRef]
98. Honoré, F.; Munari, F.; La Potterie, B. Corporate governance practices and companies' R&D intensity: Evidence from European countries. *Res. Policy* **2015**, *44*, 533–543.
99. Mahadeo, J.D.; Soobaroyen, T.; Hanuman, V.O. Board composition and financial performance: Uncovering the effects of diversity in an emerging economy. *J. Bus. Ethics* **2012**, *105*, 375–388. [CrossRef]
100. Block, J.; Miller, D.; Jaskiewicz, P.; Spiegel, F. Economic and technological importance of innovations in large family and founder firms: An analysis of patent data. *Fam. Bus. Rev.* **2013**, *26*, 180–199. [CrossRef]
101. Zahra, S.A.; Neubaum, D.O.; Huse, M. Entrepreneurship in medium-size companies: Exploring the effects of ownership and governance systems. *J. Manag.* **2000**, *26*, 947–976. [CrossRef]
102. Miller, T.; Triana, M. Demographic diversity in the boardroom: Mediators of the board diversity-firm performance relationship. *J. Manag. Stud.* **2009**, *46*, 754–786. [CrossRef]
103. Kyereboah-Coleman, A.; Biekpe, N. The relationship between board size, board composition, CEO duality and firm performance: Experience from Ghana. *Corp. Owner. Cont.* **2007**, *4*, 114–122. [CrossRef]
104. Li, X.; Liu, Z.; Ren, F. Study on relationship between board characteristics and sustainable growth of family listed companies. *Sci. J. Bus. Manag.* **2015**, *3*, 11–16. [CrossRef]
105. GCGF (Global Corporate Governance Forum), Corporate Governance Better Companies Better Societies. Available online: http://documents.worldbank.org/curated/pt/261621468330946276/pdf/628830NEWS0Glo00Box0361495B0PUBLIC0.pdf (accessed on 3 July 2019).
106. Ammann, M.; Oesch, D.; Schmid, M.M. Corporate governance and firm value: International evidence. *J. Emp. Financ.* **2011**, *18*, 36–55. [CrossRef]
107. Black, B.S.; Kim, W.; Jang, H.; Park, K.-S. How corporate governance affects firm value: Evidence on channels from Korea. Available online: http://ssrn.com/abstract=844744 (accessed on 3 July 2018).
108. Feng, Y.; Chen, H.H.; Tang, J. The impact of social responsibility and ownership structure on sustainable financial development of China's energy industry. *Sustainability* **2018**, *10*, 301. [CrossRef]
109. Hemalin, A. Influence of family ownership on small business growth. Evidence from French SMEs. *Small Bus. Econ.* **2013**, *41*, 563–579. [CrossRef]
110. Linck, J.S.; Netter, J.M.; Yang, T. The determinants of board structure. *J. Financ. Econ.* **2008**, *87*, 308–328. [CrossRef]
111. Klein, P.; Shapiro, D.; Young, J. Corporate governance, family ownership and firm value: The Canadian evidence. *Corp. Gov. Int. Rev.* **2005**, *13*, 769–784. [CrossRef]
112. McConnell, J.J.; Servaes, H. Additional evidence on equity ownership and corporate value. *J. Financ. Econ.* **1990**, *27*, 595–612. [CrossRef]
113. Ocak, M.; Güçlü, F.C. Finansal kriz, finansal performance ve yönetim kurulundaki bağımsız üyeler: 2008 küresel finans krizinde BİST imalat sektörüne yönelik bir araştırma. *Muh. Bil. Dün. Derg.* **2014**, *16*, 75–96.
114. Griliches, Z. The Search for R&D Spillovers. *Nat. Bur. Econ. Res. Working Paper No. 3768* **1991**.
115. Bossler, M.; Mosthaf, A.; Schank, T. Are female managers more likely to hire more female managers? Evidence from Germany. *ILR Rev.* **2019**. [CrossRef]
116. Thams, Y.; Bendell, B.L.; Terjesen, S. Explaining women's presence on corporate boards: The institutionalization of progressive gender-related policies. *J. Bus. Res.* **2018**, *86*, 130–140. [CrossRef]
117. Ozdemir, O.; Upneja, A. Board structure and CEO compensation: Evidence from U.S. lodging industry. *Int. J. Hos. Manag.* **2012**, *31*, 856–863. [CrossRef]
118. Schrand, L.; Ascherl, C.; Schaefers, W. Gender diversity and financial performance: Evidence from US REITS. *J. Prop. Res.* **2018**, *35*, 296–320. [CrossRef]

119. Darmadi, S. Do women in top management affect firm performance? Evidence from Indonesia. *Corp. Gov.* **2013**, *13*, 288–304. [CrossRef]
120. Dezsö, C.L.; Ross, D.G. Does female representation in top management improve firm performance? A panel data investigation. *Strateg. Manag. J.* **2012**, *33*, 1072–1089.

sustainability

MDPI

Article

Knowledge Management and the Sustainable Development of Social Work

Simon Colnar [1,*], Vlado Dimovski [1] and David Bogataj [1,2]

[1] School of Economics and Business, University of Ljubljana, 1000 Ljubljana, Slovenia; vlado.dimovski@ef.uni-lj.si (V.D.); david.bogataj@ef.uni-lj.si or david.bogataj@gmail.com (D.B.)

[2] Department of Management and Engineering, University of Padua, 35122 Padua, Italy

* Correspondence: simon.colnar@ef.uni-lj.si; Tel.: +386-31-787-710

Received: 14 October 2019; Accepted: 9 November 2019; Published: 13 November 2019

Abstract: The growing shortage of skilled social workers, accompanied by an ageing population and the increasing number of fragile, elderly individuals that require social services, poses a serious challenge for our society. The magnitude of this problem is seen in the various predictions hypothesizing that, globally, there is likely to be a shortfall of millions of social workers for the successful provision of social services. To make matters worse, there are not enough social work students to fill that void, whereas the existing employee turnover is another serious concern for the social work field. Policy makers in many countries do not yet understand the pattern of growing needs and have no tool to forecast the future increase in educational requirements for creating a pool of adequately skilled social workers. In addition to this, understanding the patterns of workforce entrance and exit for social workers and the dynamics of transition becomes important for national policy and decision makers. In our paper, we build on current research about knowledge management in social work settings to demonstrate that knowledge management can have a positive impact in helping to fulfil the important role of social work in any ageing society. With our research, we contribute to the underdeveloped literature about knowledge management in the public sector and especially in social work settings and to the knowledge-based view of the organization. We present a multiple decrement model of social workers' entrance and transition from social work student and social worker trainee to fully productive social worker, to their exit, whether by changed profession, retirement or death. We argue that the availability of social workers in a national economy depends on the development and operationalization of appropriate policies, where knowledge management can be influential. Our model allows measuring the quality of the national policy system related to the social work profession, something which has not been achieved yet, and shows how knowledge management solutions can positively influence the whole field of social work. We apply an objective measuring tool, grounded in an already developed actuarial–mathematical method. Our case relies on the collection and analysis of relevant data found in publicly available statistical reports for Slovenia. Existing data enables us to provide assumptions on how to better forecast the transition of social workers.

Keywords: knowledge management; social work; sustainable development of social work; social work centers; multiple decrement model

1. Introduction

Social sustainability can be defined as a process for creating sustainable, successful environments that promote wellbeing, by understanding what people need from the places where they live and work [1]. Moreover, social sustainability combines design of the physical realm with design of the social world, namely infrastructure to support social and cultural life, social amenities, systems for citizen engagement and space for people and places to evolve [2]. The social dimension of sustainability has gained rather inadequate attention and recognition in previous studies, considering that this aspect is typically difficult to define and operationalize [3,4]. Consequently, most of the previous initiatives have primarily focused on the economic and environmental aspects of sustainable development, while overlooking the social dimension of sustainability [5,6]. Social sustainability, however, is integral to the quality of a human system, as it fosters lasting conditions for human wellbeing, particularly for the most vulnerable individuals or groups [3,7], including the elderly. Mutual development of knowledge management and social sustainability could potentially enhance the overall performance levels of social work organizations. Moreover, if knowledge management initiatives are properly implemented, they may positively influence the sustainability of the entire social system in any ageing society. Additionally, we argue that the sustainability of any social system is not only a problem of public finances but that it is also about ensuring an adequate number of skilled social workers. Currently, we are dealing with a decrease in the availability of social workers, while at the same time, the requirement of social services for the elderly is constantly growing. Therefore, we must determine whether we have enough social workers available for the sustainable provision of wellbeing for service users in social work. Such initiatives may also positively influence the sustainability of public finances, following possible efficiency improvements [8].

Knowledge and the way it is managed has been with humankind since the beginning of time [9]. Nowadays, in the knowledge economy, an organization's ability to manage knowledge effectively is increasingly more crucial [10]. Similarly, authors [11] believe that knowledge management can equip employees with real time information so that they can react appropriately and make decisions that will allow them to successfully fulfil organizational goals. Previous research already established four basic knowledge management process stages, namely creating knowledge, storing and retrieving knowledge, transferring knowledge and implementing knowledge [12]. Knowledge creation typically involves tapping the tacit and, in most cases, highly subjective, insights, informal skills and practice (or know-how) of individual employees in ways that an organization can act on [13]. For organizations, it is also important to appropriately arrange and store their knowledge, as it enables them quicker and easier access and distribution of knowledge within the organization [14]. Furthermore, knowledge transfer is another integral part of knowledge management, as it enables organizations to absorb and appropriately use knowledge of paramount importance for their functioning and follows the key goal of turning knowledge into organizational assets and resources [15]. Among the resources examined, an organization's knowledge or intellectual assets are generally considered the most critical for its long-term successful functioning [16]. Knowledge implementation is the final stage of the knowledge management process that creates real value for the organization by making knowledge active and relevant [17]. In addition, management support can be perceived as the degree to which management understands the importance of knowledge management and the extent to which it participates in its implementation and activities [18]. Additionally, the support and active participation of managers could significantly influence the positive outcomes of knowledge management in organizations [19]. From the perspective of organizations, it is particularly important to determine the effectiveness of knowledge management and its overall contribution to organizational performance. As knowledge is an intangible strategic asset of an organization, its measurement possesses a serious challenge [20]. However, [21] argues that it is possible to measure the effectiveness of knowledge management with changes in soft measures such as enhanced communication, enhanced collaboration, enhanced learning and enhanced performance. Moreover, improvements in the aforementioned aspects could result also in improved service quality.

Knowledge management has captured the attention of researchers in the knowledge-based economy [22], with interest in this academic and practice-oriented discipline witnessing a significant rise in recent years [23–25]. There is also a need nowadays to gain additional insight into how knowledge management is evolving within the context of public sector organizations [26], including social work organizations. Researchers have argued that the adaptation and implementation of knowledge management practices can be beneficial [27] in any type of organization, whether private or public [28], and can play an important role [29] in improving the wellbeing of services users and the quality of services and programs offered to them [30,31]. However, few studies focus on knowledge management initiatives in the public sector, especially in comparison to the private sector [32,33]. The scattered and limited understanding of knowledge management in the context of the public sector [32,34] is a major challenge for organizations, as knowledge becomes more and more a critical resource for their functioning [35]. However, it is also important to acknowledge that dominant discussions related to knowledge management in general are not adapted to fit the context of the public sector and social work [36]. Therefore, we must consider that public sector organizations function in a unique context that differs significantly from the private sector. Simply implementing private sector knowledge management tools and models that worked well in that environment might prove to be counterproductive in the context of the public sector [26], and more so in social work. Another specific related to social work is that in general employees are more reluctant to embrace "quantocentric" cultures and approaches [37]. Moreover, there is growing discontent among social work professionals as the levels of formalization of social work practice increase [38]. Consequently, what is needed for the successful implementation of knowledge management in the public sector is the development of a research area that has been largely unexplored [27]. Public sector organizations and their employees must also acknowledge these challenges when discussing knowledge management initiatives, as the need and significance of knowledge management for the public sector are now overwhelming [39]. Moreover, researchers [39] believe that the only question that remains for public organizations is not if but how can they benefit the most from knowledge management initiatives.

Social work is considered as particularly important because it closely follows its mission to enhance human wellbeing and help meet the basic needs of all people, with particular attention to the needs and empowerment of people who are vulnerable, oppressed, and living in poverty [40]. Its commitment to support and help people makes social work different from many other professions [41], and authors [40] believe that it has an important role to play in any ageing society. In our research, we opted to focus on Slovenian social work centers that are and have been the basic institutions, which through measures and services for social security, cover the predominant part of social protection on the national level. Their founder is the state, and the central role as the coordinators of social protection and welfare services devolves upon them [42]. Currently, there are approximately 1250 employees in Slovenian social work centers [43]. Slovenia is similar to other countries experiencing a shortage of skilled social workers [44]. Due to the existing shortage, guaranteeing the supply of an adequate workforce that is engaged in practice and for educating future social workers is one of the core challenges for all societies. Such shortages should also raise an important concern for national policy and decision makers. We argue that similar to the case of nursing staff shortages [45], specific models for workforce forecasting with regard to social workers will be gaining in importance and recognition. Effective forecasting models help managers and policy and decision makers to predict possible shortages or excesses of workforce and its consequences for organizational activities such as planning of activities and annual budgets [45]. Actual data from 2015 show that the European Union had the second highest old-age dependency ratio (29.2%) after Japan (42.7%). The old-age dependency ratio is expected to rise in the European Union by 25 percentage points by 2070, reaching 54.2% [46]. As such, this ratio is going to have a significant impact on the future functioning of our ageing society. Population ageing accompanied by the decrease in births and increasing life expectancy over the last century has already had a strong influence on the changes in the global age structure [47]. The number of people over 60 will grow from 901 million in 2015 to 1.4 billion in 2030 [48]. In addition to this, for example in Slovenia, there will be 31.5% of persons aged 65 years or more in 2060, in comparison to the 20.4% in 2020 [49]. As the population ages and lives longer, the need for social services increases. Long-term care will become even more important and will require an additional number of skilled social workers [50].

Therefore, we believe it is of crucial importance to develop a better understanding of knowledge management in general in the particular context of the public sector, including social work organizations.

Moreover, appropriately implementing knowledge management in practice through the more systematic and effective capture, dissemination, transfer and implementation of knowledge in the context of the public sector, including social work services, is perceived as important due to its impact on influencing public policies [51], improving the wellbeing of social services users and the quality of services and programs [30,31], as well as ensuring an adequate number of skilled social workers. Knowledge management in the context of social work is intended to add value to services by increasing wellbeing, societal effectiveness and general welfare [52,53], and is not solely focused on generating profit and competitive advantages, as is typically the case in the private sector [34]. Moreover, due to various objective barriers such as time and energy, many of the social work knowledge nowadays remains hidden in organizations [54]. While discussing knowledge management in the context of social work can be very important, it can also be explained with the fact that often the ability of such organizations to achieve their goals is in close correlation to the experience and skills of their employee [55]. Moreover, reference [56] argues that access to knowledge, and the skills of employees to use knowledge effectively, importantly influences realizing the benefits to individuals and their lives, which is something that social organizations primarily aim to achieve. Therefore, a knowledgeable, highly skilled and competent workforce is the integral component when discussing transformation of outcomes for services users. Especially the role of knowledge, which empowers employees with resources, skills and the ability to seek and share knowledge, as well as implement it in practice as an integral part of their everyday tasks and learning activities. Nowadays, social work organizations can already be labelled as knowledge intensive organizations, as they are reliant on the knowledge of their employees so that they can provide services, rather than relying on their physical capital [57]. Therefore, in our paper, we consider knowledge management as the ability of social workers to be able to better utilize their existing resources for achieving the wellbeing of service users. Knowledge management can additionally positively influence the job satisfaction of individual employees [58], which raises motivation levels of individuals [59] and mitigates their turnover intentions [60]. As such, we argue that it can foster the sustainable development of the social dimension of sustainability and social work, which is of paramount importance in ageing societies. However, it is also important to acknowledge the existing conditions of social work such as high staff turnover, lack of training and education, and lack of preparation for additional tasks as they can all hamper the successful functioning of social work organizations and proper implementation of knowledge management [61].

Despite knowledge management being of paramount importance, though, the academic research of knowledge management in the public sector is still in its nascent stage [39]. Knowledge and understanding about knowledge management in social work in particular is scarce [62,63]. Furthermore, authors [26] argue that the public sector research on knowledge management is clearly fragmented, typically being dominated by unrelated research in the education and research sectors. This highlights an important challenge related to knowledge management research in the public sector, as it provokes researchers to tackle the topic also in other public sector fields and organizations such as social work centers in our research. Additionally, authors [26] posit, that researchers have so far neglected fields that would possibly have the largest impact on the society as a whole, including the sustainable development of social work.

In addition to this, we believe that examining the relationship between knowledge management and the availability of social workers is important, given that this aspect has been neglected in previous studies. In our paper, we present a multiple decrement model of social workers' entrance and transition from social work student and social worker trainee to fully productive social worker, to their exit, whether by changed profession, retirement or death. We are also following the proposition advanced by [26], of continuing the evolution of public sector knowledge management and tackling existing research needs to provide insight to other practitioners, academics and national policy and decision makers. We conduct our initial quantitative analysis about existing knowledge management practices on data of 98 employees in Slovenian social work centers, obtained through online questionnaires and in-person contact. We include social work centers as according to [43], a modern, professional and effective system of social care is needed in order to appropriately address the increasingly demanding and complex needs of services users. Moreover, as indicated by [64] the successful resolution of the needs of services users nowadays requires broader knowledge from different fields and [65] argues that the role of knowledge and knowledge management in the whole process can be particularly important. In addition, authors [55] believe that knowledge management is continuously spreading beyond its original private sector focus and is creating links to other disciplines such as social work that were hard to imagine at the beginning of knowledge management. Moreover, as indicated by [66] in the context of Slovenia public sector managers and employees lack sufficient skills and knowledge in (knowledge) management topics. As social work is an important part of the public sector, this gap in knowledge is also present social work. We therefore argue that the potential of knowledge management in social work is high as it is a field that is nowadays underdeveloped and underutilized in practice in social work. We first estimate the extent and effectiveness of existing knowledge management practices using descriptive statistics in the SPSS software (version 24.0). To test the reliability of our measurement instruments, we analyze the Cronbach's α of all nine constructs. Later, the impact of knowledge management on the sustainable development of social work is analyzed using a multiple decrement model. In determining special cases of a multistate transition model, we follow the examples of [67–69].

The primary goal of our study is to contribute to the underdeveloped literature about knowledge management in the public sector [26] and especially in social work settings [62,63]. The intent of our paper is to partially fill this gap with a theoretical analysis followed by an empirical examination that links knowledge management and social work by considering the positive effects of knowledge management on the availability of skilled social workers. In this way, we would respond to certain shortfalls in the existing research and contribute to the theoretical advancement of the field [39]. In addition to this, our paper also continues with the tradition of [70], who started exploring how professional caregivers can organize in more effective ways, in particular how can they share (or transfer) and implement knowledge in order to deliver high-quality services and ensure wellbeing for their users. This new focus on knowledge management in social work setting is extremely promising as an area of exploration in the context of the broader public sector [71]. By particularly focusing on social work organizations, our paper extends previous studies on knowledge management in the public sector as they were typically exploring the education and research sectors [26]. Additionally, in line with the knowledge-based view of the organization [72–74], our study recognizes the important role of knowledge in social work centers as potentially the primary source influencing their functioning. A paradigm shift towards a knowledge-based view of the organization is also suggested by some social work researchers [75,76]. We also aim to contribute the previously neglected aspect of sustainable development, the social dimension of sustainability [5,6]. Empirically, our research will provide support to social work centers in their evaluation of existing knowledge management practice and will potentially emphasize the importance of implementing such initiatives in the future. Moreover, the results of our study are intended to promote the necessity of sustainable development of social work among policy and decision makers who matter, at the national level. Our quantitative approach provides a methodological foundation, as the majority of previous works exploring managerial topics in social work organizations have relied on qualitative approaches, being mainly case studies and interviews [17]. As such, our quantitative paper follows the example of [77] in promoting methodological diversity in the social work field, considering that the scope of social work research is indeed broad and multidisciplinary.

2. Materials and Methods

Primary data from respondents were collected from May 2018 to January 2019. We opted for an adapted online and in-person questionnaire, which was filled out by social work managers and social work employees in Slovenian social work centers with approximately 1250 employees [43]. Our sample frame consists of e-mail contacts of employed individuals available to the Social Chamber of Slovenia and the subsequent personal contacts developed with individual respondents.

We established numerous personal relationships with managers and employees in social work centers and sent several reminders to respondents to fill out our questionnaire in order to tackle the issue of non-response bias. Researchers [78,79] define that common method bias could potentially result from artefactual covariance between independent and dependent variables, where one respondent answers all measures, similar to single source data collected through questionnaires, as is also the case in our study. To counteract the negative aspects of common method bias, we enabled the respondents to remain anonymous at all times and encouraged them to provide answers as honestly as possible. 98 respondents completed the whole questionnaire. We edited and analyzed the data in the SPSS software (version 24.0). The response rate in our study is 7.9%. The largest proportion of respondents work in an organization with 26 to 50 employees (33.3%) and in an organization with 50 or more employees (33.3%). More than two thirds of respondents (71.3%) are aged from 30 to 49 years. 80.2% are women, which is consistent with the observation of authors [80], that social work is predominantly a female profession. 64.5% of respondents have successfully acquired level 7 of education as explained in the Decree on the introduction and use of the classification system of education and training in Slovenia. 78.7% have been employed in their present organizations for at least 6 years.

For individual constructs, which measured the extent and effectiveness of knowledge management in social work centers, we select measurement instruments that are in the scientific environment: (1) well established: developed and/or used by some of the key authors of the examined topics; (2) frequently used: scientific papers that consider the development of measurement instruments are often cited; (3) up to date: the relevant measurement instruments are also used in the latest research. We measure management responsibility with 7 items. Statements intended to measure the opinion of respondents regarding management responsibility and were focused on whether an organization has a specific manager dedicated to knowledge management, the level of management support for knowledge management and the existing incentive structure. We measure knowledge creation with 2 items that were exploring the creation of new ideas in a social work center and its subsequent critical evaluation. Similarly, we measure knowledge storage and retrieval with 2 items. We examine how knowledge is stored and retrieved with a particular focus on whether social work centers have standard procedures and databases. 5 items were used to measure knowledge transfer in organizations with emphasis on whether they have readily available knowledge for transfer and gaining insight about individual employees that possess specific knowledge. To measure knowledge implementation, we used 6 items in order to analyze how knowledge implementation impacts organizational performance and to gain an understanding whether the newly gained knowledge is actually used in their daily practice. We measure enhanced collaboration through 3 items. The items were intended to focus on improved collaboration and improved team work. We utilize 2 items to measure enhanced communication. The items were designed to gain insight into the existing communication structure. Similarly, we measure enhanced learning with 7 items. We examine how this influences the ability to improve innovativeness, learning, competences and experience. To measure enhanced performance, we used 4 items in order to analyze how it impacts improved processes, enables better decision making and contributes towards an overall better functioning organization in a very general manner.

The application of life table techniques to the study of labor force status and mobility was first suggested by [81]. Such a life table can be constructed for a fixed group of people who share a membership-defining event (the cohort) [82], such as members of a defined profession, in our case social workers. Similarly, multistate work-life expectancy models have been used in studies by several authors [82–87], especially focusing on occupational health or pension models. Authors [82] argue that work-life and related expectancies are conceptually the same as health expectancies, both being an expected occupation time, with the difference being that the former occur in the context of labor force activity rather than in health statistics. Therefore, as our focus is on examining the availability of social workers and their entrance into and exit from the profession, we rely on using multiple decrement models, as explained below.

Multiple decrement models that represent a special case of multistate transition models were already developed by [67–69]. For successful forecasting of employment productivity states into which social workers can be organized, we will further develop the model for forecasting the entrance and exit to and from the social work profession. The basic model allows us to forecast the number of social workers entering and exiting the profession in each age cohort and derives the probabilities of transition at various ages on the national level, based on a demographic multiple decrement model [88,89]. The model will enable long term projections of available social workers in different states of productivity. The model will also enable an understanding of the patterns of social workers that enter and exit the workforce and how different policies can influence the dynamics of the existing workforce of social workers at different age cohorts. The increase in number of social workers due to novel policy tools and potential effects of knowledge management has not been included in the model yet. Social workers can move among various states such as social work student, social worker trainee, fully productive social worker, to exit by changing profession, by retirement or in the event of death (see Figure 1). Multiple decrement models are currently being used in disability insurance [88]. In our research, they will be extended as a tool for human resource management and for forecasting the entrance and exit of social workers. In multiple decrement models that have m different states for social workers, there are m + 1 states for transition from one state to another.

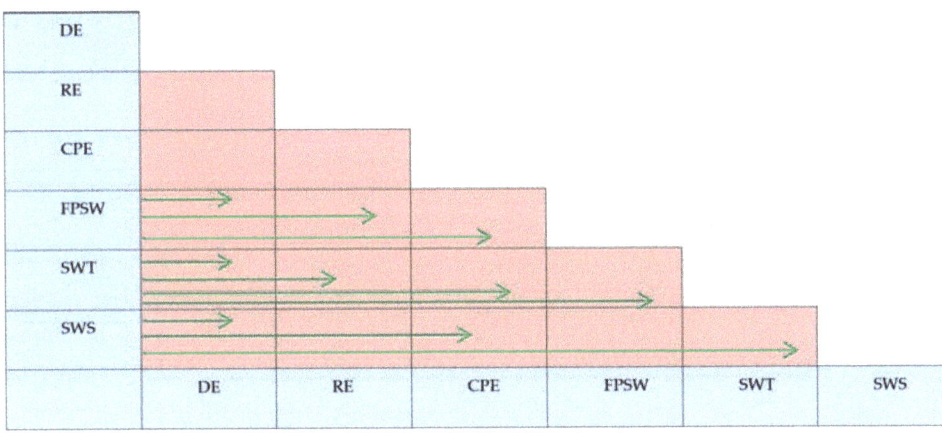

Figure 1. Transitions to and from employment for social workers. Legend: SWS—social work student; SWT—social worker trainee; FPSW—fully productive social worker; CPE—changed profession exit; RE—retirement exit; DE—death exit; significant transitions for policy and decision makers are marked with green arrows.

We denote the initial state where the individual is a social work student as state 0 and transition, which models social workers in state of type j, by the line of the graph from this child node to the state (node) j, j = 1, 2, ... , m. The model should describe the probabilities of transition from state 0 to state j ∈ SW (where SW is a set of different types of social workers) or, in general, from the child node to node j at various time points. All paths to j determine the dynamics of human resource management (state of type j) or different types of social worker exit (by changed profession, retirement or death). In a multiple decrement setup, transition between any two states, from i to j, i > j = 1, 2, ... , m is not possible (directed graph). Let us consider a social worker aged x denoted by (x). We denote the future work period of the social work that they will do in a current state (type of employment) i ∈ SW by $T_i(x)$. Therefore, x + Ti(x) will be the age when the social worker exits the current state i and enters a new state, j ∈ SW. The future work period in the category of type i, $T_i(x)$, is a random variable with probability distribution function.

$$Gi\ (t) = Pr\ (Ti \leq t),\ t \geq 0 \tag{1}$$

The function $G_i(t)$ represents the probability that the social worker will exit the profession due to different reasons, such as death, retirement or a change in profession (state type of j) within t years, for any fixed t. We assume that $G_i(t)$, the probability distribution of T_i is known. We also assume that $G_i(t)$ is continuous and has probability density $g_i(t) = G_i'(t)$. Data for $G_i(t)$ should be available from the national statistics office. As such, we describe:

$$gi\ (t)\ dt = \Pr\ (t < T_i < t + dt,\ i \in SW) \tag{2}$$

where Equation (2) describes the probability that the social worker will transfer from state of type I in the infinitesimal time interval from t to t + dt. Therefore, the probability that a social worker x years old in state of employment i will transfer into a state of employment j within t years is denoted by the t q_x (i,j). Consequently, we have a known relationship:

$$t\ q_x\ (i,j) = G(i,j{:}t) \tag{3}$$

$$t\ p_x\ (i) = 1 - G(i,j{:}t) \tag{4}$$

which denotes the probability that a x years old social worker will remain in his or her current state at least for t years.

The graph starts at the initial state i = SWS (social work student). We can observe all possible paths from SWS through some of the identified child nodes j∈SW, which enable different exits from states. Namely such exits from the social workers' workforce include the possibility of employment in other professions, retirement or death.

Forecasting future distribution of social workers S according to the type of state based on current distribution of social workers among different types of states and matrix of transitions among different types of states for social workers x years old in multiple decrement model (i→j; i ∈ SW, j ∈ SW) will be described by transition equations:

$$\begin{aligned} S_{x+1,\,\tau+1} &= S_{x,\,\tau} P_{x,\tau} = \\ [S_x^{(0)} S_x^{(1)} S_x^{(2)} S_x^{(3)} S_x^{(4)} S_x^{(5)}]_t &\begin{bmatrix} p_x^{(0)} & q_x^{(0,1)} & q_x^{(0,2)} & q_x^{(0,3)} & q_x^{(0,4)} & q_x^{(0,5)} \\ 0 & p_x^{(1)} & q_x^{(1,2)} & q_x^{(1,3)} & q_x^{(1,4)} & q_x^{(1,5)} \\ 0 & 0 & p_x^{(2)} & q_x^{(2,3)} & q_x^{(2,4)} & q_x^{(2,5)} \\ 0 & 0 & 0 & p_x^{(3)} & q_x^{(3,4)} & q_x^{(3,5)} \\ 0 & 0 & 0 & 0 & p_x^{(4)} & q_x^{(4,5)} \end{bmatrix}_t \\ &= [S_{x+1}^{(0)} S_{x+1}^{(1)} S_{x+1}^{(2)} S_{x+1}^{(3)} S_{x+1}^{(4)} S_{x+1}^{(5)}]_{t+1} \end{aligned} \tag{5}$$

Appropriately implementing knowledge management activities can influence the quality of human resource management and thus also the intensity of transitions. The details of the transitions will be modelled as a directed graph. By observing all possible paths from the initial state through transition types of states in different states (transition nodes in the graph), based on national demographic statistics, one can calculate the projected labor supply of different categories. Knowledge management solutions will be needed for such transitions that also remain subjects of further research. Our model will be further developed in the future, based on the theoretical foundations of [68].

3. Empirical Results

3.1. Extent and Effectiveness of Knowledge Management in Social Work Centers

Table 1 presents descriptive statistics for all nine constructs analyzed in our paper that are related to the extent and effectiveness of knowledge management in social work centers.

From the results in Table 1, we can see a moderate mean value for the construct of knowledge transfer (3.51). The mean values for the other four constructs that measure the extent of knowledge management in social work centers show low or at best moderate values. The mean values are: management responsibility (2.77), knowledge implementation (2.81), knowledge creation (2.87), knowledge storage and retrieval (2.94). Our part of the research that focused on the effectiveness of knowledge management in social work centers had a necessary condition. Respondents had to declare that their respective organization formally or informally engages in knowledge management activities. Consequently, this might influence the potential favorable opinions towards the effectiveness of their existing knowledge management efforts. Nevertheless, we found only moderate mean values for all four measured constructs that measure the effectiveness of knowledge management in social work centers. The mean values are as follows: enhanced communication (3.43), enhanced performance (3.50), enhanced collaboration (3.60), improved learning (3.63). The mean values indicate that the activity levels of knowledge management in the practice of social work centers are at best moderate. Similarly, the mean values also suggest that knowledge management is in practice only moderately effective.

Table 1. Mean values, standard deviation and Cronbach's α for all measured constructs.

Variable	Mean	SD	Cronbach's α
1. Management responsibility	2.77	0.97	0.90
2. Knowledge creation	2.87	1.10	0.84
3. Knowledge storage and retrieval	2.94	1.15	0.87
4. Knowledge transfer	3.51	0.86	0.82
5. Knowledge implementation	2.81	0.96	0.91
6. Enhanced collaboration	3.63	0.55	0.90
7. Enhanced communication	3.59	0.47	0.62
8. Enhanced learning	3.58	0.61	0.86
9. Enhanced performance	3.42	0.45	0.42

3.2. Case Study of Slovenian Female Social Workers

As mentioned in previous paragraphs, appropriately implementing knowledge management can influence the intensity of transitions between different states. Moreover, it can positively impact the perceived job satisfaction among individuals [58], that consequently improves the motivation of individuals [59] and reduces their turnover intentions [60]. Therefore, we present the hypothesized impact of knowledge management on the transitions using a sample of Slovenian social workers. As the population of social workers employed in social work centers is too small, we additionally focus on the whole sector of social work. Our assumption is that the transitions will be similar in the social work sector as a whole and in individual social work centers. The number of employees in social work in Slovenia in 2017 was 19,373 [90], of which 1250 are employed in social work centers [43]. We present the age structure in 5-year age cohorts in Table 2:

Table 2. Employees in social work 2017.

Ages	Total	15–19	20–24	25–29	30–34	35–39	40–44	45–49	50–54	55–59	60–64	65+
Social workers	19,373	107	937	1596	2157	2443	2826	3050	3447	2298	492	20

Data source: [90].

The transition matrix could be written based on demographic data and employment tables for different occupation groups for the year 2017, which were collected at the state level by [90]. As social work is predominantly a female dominated profession [80], we focused on female social workers aged 45 years old. The structure of female social workers aged 45 years old who are distinguished due to their different category is represented by the vector S_x, being the sum of net transitions of cohort:

$$S_{45}^{2017} = \left[S_{45}^{(0)} S_{45}^{(1)} S_{45}^{(2)} S_{45}^{(3)} S_{45}^{(4)} S_{45}^{(5)} \right]_{2017} = [0\ 0\ 546\ 0\ 0] \tag{6}$$

$$P_{45}^{2017} = \begin{bmatrix} p_{45}^{(0)} & q_{x45}^{(0,1)} & q_{45}^{(0,2)} & q_{45}^{(0,3)} & q_{45}^{(0,4)} & q_{45}^{(0,5)} \\ 0 & p_{45}^{(1)} & q_{x45}^{(1,2)} & q_{45}^{(1,3)} & q_{45}^{(1,4)} & q_{45}^{(1,5)} \\ 0 & 0 & p_{45}^{(2)} & q_{45}^{(2,3)} & q_{45}^{(2,4)} & q_{45}^{(2,5)} \\ 0 & 0 & 0 & p_{45}^{(3)} & q_{45}^{(3,4)} & q_{45}^{(3,5)} \\ 0 & 0 & 0 & 0 & p_{45}^{(4)} & q_{45}^{(4,5)} \end{bmatrix}_{2017} \quad (7)$$

$$= \begin{bmatrix} 0 & 0.98 & 0 & 0.10 & 0 & 0.01 \\ 0 & 0 & 0.97 & 0.02 & 0 & 0.01 \\ 0 & 0 & 0.92 & 0.05 & 0.02 & 0.01 \\ 0 & 0 & 0 & 0.97 & 0.02 & 0.01 \\ 0 & 0 & 0 & 0 & 0.99 & 0.01 \end{bmatrix} \quad (8)$$

Given the allocation of female social workers by category and the studied cohort in the following year (when they are x + 1 years old), we can calculate:

$$S_{46}^{2018} = S_{45}^{2017} P_{45}^{2017} = [S_{46}^{(0)} S_{46}^{(1)} S_{46}^{(2)} S_{46}^{(3)} S_{46}^{(4)} S_{46}^{(5)}]_{2018} \quad (9)$$

In Table 3, we present the forecast of the availability of female social workers aged 45 in 2017 up to the studied year 2032, when they will be 60 years old. Additionally, in Table 3, we include the hypothesized improvements due to knowledge management activities implemented in social work organizations. The forecast is based on a multiple decrement model.

Table 3. Female Social Workers aged 45 in 2017 to aged 60 in 2032.

		Original						**Improved**					
Year	**Age**	**SWS**	**SWT**	**FPSW**	**CPE**	**RE**	**DE**	**SWS**	**SWT**	**FPSW**	**CPE**	**RE**	**DE**
2017	45	0	0	546.00	0	0	0	0	0	546.00	0	0	0
2018	46	0	0	502.32	27.30	10.92	5.46	0	0	524.16	10.92	5.46	5.46
2019	47	0	0	462.13	51.60	21.40	10.86	0	0	503.19	21.08	10.87	10.86
2020	48	0	0	425.16	73.16	31.46	16.22	0	0	483.07	30.51	16.21	16.22
2021	49	0	0	391.15	92.22	41.12	21.51	0	0	463.74	39.25	21.48	21.51
2022	50	0	0	359.86	109.01	50.37	26.76	0	0	445.19	47.35	26.69	26.76
2023	51	0	0	331.07	123.73	59.25	31.95	0	0	427.39	54.83	31.83	31.95
2024	52	0	0	304.58	136.57	67.75	37.09	0	0	410.29	61.74	36.88	37.09
2025	53	0	0	280.22	147.71	75.89	42.18	0	0	393.88	68.09	41.85	42.18
2026	54	0	0	257.80	157.29	83.69	47.22	0	0	378.12	73.93	46.73	47.22
2027	45	0	0	546.00	0	0	0	0	0	363.00	79.27	51.52	52.20
2028	46	0	0	502.32	27.30	10.92	5.46	0	0	348.48	84.15	56.22	57.15
2029	47	0	0	462.13	51.60	21.40	10.86	0	0	334.54	88.60	60.83	62.03
2030	48	0	0	425.16	73.16	31.46	16.22	0	0	321.16	92.63	65.34	66.87
2031	49	0	0	391.15	92.22	41.12	21.51	0	0	308.31	96.27	69.75	71.66
2032	50	0	0	359.86	109.01	50.37	26.76	0	0	295.97	99.55	74.06	76.41

Data source: [90], own calculations.

Table 4 provides a summary of the important hypothesized improvements due to knowledge management activities implemented in social work organizations.

Table 4. Difference in female Social Workers aged 45 in 2017 to aged 60 in 2032.

		Difference		
Year	**Age**	**FPSW**	**CPE**	**RE**
2017	45	0	0	0
2018	46	21.84	−16.38	−5.46
2019	47	41.06	−30.52	−10.53
2020	48	57.91	−42.65	−15.25

Table 4. *Cont.*

Difference				
Year	Age	FPSW	CPE	RE
2021	49	72.59	−52.97	−19.64
2022	50	85.33	−61.66	−23.68
2023	51	96.32	−68.90	−27.42
2024	52	105.71	−74.83	−30.87
2025	53	113.66	−79.62	−34.04
2026	54	120.32	−83.36	−36.96
2027	45	125.82	−86.19	−39.64
2028	46	130.28	−88.20	−42.08
2029	47	133.79	−89.50	−44.30
2030	48	136.47	−90.16	−46.31
2031	49	138.40	−90.27	−48.14
2032	50	139.65	−89.89	−49.78

Data source: [90], own calculations.

4. Discussion

Nowadays, there is an imperative to seek sustainable development in all dimensions, including the social dimension [91]. Moreover, as [92] emphasizes, in a socially sustainable society individuals do not have to tackle any structural obstacles related to many aspects of their functioning, including health and social services. In addition to this, social workers already recognize social sustainability, as it deals with individual health and wellbeing, nutrition, shelter, education and cultural needs [93]. Sustainability themes also have multiple implications for social work in general, such as social resilience to future economic and ecological shocks [94]. The extent and effectiveness of knowledge management in general indicate that knowledge management practices are less developed in social work centers in comparison to other fields and organizations, especially in the context of the private sector.

4.1. Theoretical Implications

The concept of knowledge management is novel and remains largely unexplored and underutilized in the public sector [27]. Furthermore, knowledge management is especially neglected as a research topic in the field of social work [17,62,63]. Similarly, the aspect of social sustainability has gained inadequate attention and recognition in previous studies [3,4]. In this paper we make four important theoretical contributions to this area.

Our first theoretical contribution to the literature of knowledge management research is applying and testing components of knowledge management to the public sector. In our study, we present a theoretical explanation and empirical validation of how knowledge management can positively influence the availability of skilled social workers. Previous studies suggested that knowledge management initiatives could help organizations to impact public policies through the more systematic and effective capture, dissemination, transfer and implementation of knowledge [51], and in this manner improve the quality of existing services and programs [31]. However, those studies did not explore the relationship between knowledge management and the availability of skilled social workers that we focus on in our research. Thus, our study presents a relevant contribution to the literature as we show how knowledge management can have the potential to influence the availability of skilled social workers and how this could potentially influence the ability of organizations to achieve their goals.

Our second theoretical contribution to the literature involves the knowledge-based view of the organization [72–74]. With our study we aim to draw attention to the importance of knowledge management in social work by establishing the primary components that underlie its functioning. Our research orientation is supported by social work researchers that propose a shift towards the knowledge-based view of social work organizations [75,76]. We aimed to conceptualize and empirically validate how knowledge and knowledge management can help social work organizations to deliver higher quality services. In line with the recommendations of [26], we go beyond the typical framework of knowledge management research in the public sector.

With our third theoretical contribution we devote attention to the previously neglected aspect of sustainable development, the social dimension of sustainability [5,6]. With our fourth theoretical contribution we respond to the need to include more methodological diversity in the scope of social work research [77]. By applying quantitative research methods to a sample of Slovenian social work organizations we add to previous research. The usage of such methods is also important to enhance the ability of social work organizations to understand and effectively respond to their existing challenges [95]. In our study, we focus on a sample of managers and employees working in Slovenian social work centers and measure their individual perceptions of different topics related to knowledge management.

4.2. Practical Implications

We used the results of our research to propose a number of relevant practical recommendations especially for managers and also for employees in social work organizations. Although their primary goal is not to create profit, we do believe they could still benefit from our suggestions. Social work organizations indeed have the responsibility to deliver high-quality services to their users and contribute to the wellbeing of society as a whole [55]. Individuals employed in such organizations have become increasingly more aware that like other organizations functioning in the context of the public sector they must respond to the growing complex demands of their users, while being exposed to a diminishing amount of resources available. Consequently, they are considering making internal improvements in order to maximize their available resources [96]. We believe, that our model provides clear reasoning for how improvements related to knowledge management activities could benefit the social work field.

We argue that there is a potential of knowledge management in influencing public policies [30] by advancing informed debate and decision making [97]. Moreover, it can impact the sustainable development of social work by enhancing the wellbeing of service users by improving the quality of services and programs [30,31]. Typically, bureaucratic organizations can exploit knowledge management advantages by empowering employees that are able to create knowledge networks and more efficiently organize their work in teams [98]. People employed in social work tend to have both communication competencies and team work skills that are both helpful in successful knowledge management initiatives. In addition, knowledge management could help ensure the appropriate number of skilled social workers in social work organizations by motivating social workers [59], enhancing their job satisfaction levels [58] and reducing their turnover intention [60].

Moreover, based on the results of our study, which indicate that knowledge management is underdeveloped in social work centers, we propose improvements in at least four areas that were examined to determine the current levels of knowledge management. Managers who are directly responsible for knowledge management in an organization can enhance the possibility of achieving the desired goals of improved wellbeing of service users, through knowledge management [99]. Therefore, social work centers could reconsider the possibility of a manager that is at least part-time responsible for all knowledge management related activities in an organization as in the majority of cases such a manager is nowadays absent. Management support is fundamental to the success of knowledge management initiatives [100]. We particularly advise managers to actively support and engage in creating and maintaining a supportive workplace environment where employees are motivated to apply and implement knowledge in their work [101]. A clearly defined incentive structure [62,102] typically encourages employees to participate in knowledge management activities. Therefore, social work centers could change their human resource management practices towards more knowledge-based compensation. Such a practice would encourage employees to engage in knowledge-intensive activities through incentive systems that recognize their involvement in knowledge processes. Organizations could potentially function better if they base their incentive system on such knowledge activities [103]. Moreover, such an incentive system could make the profession more desirable for potential students.

As our population is ageing, it is also extremely important to engage more young people to choose the social work profession and enter the educational process. Similarly, important to the success of knowledge management is clear and active communication of expectations and benefits related to knowledge management [62]. Therefore, we would encourage delivering strong messages from management [104]. The mere existence of ideas and knowledge is not enough to improve the functioning of social work centers. Consequently, social work centers should strive to continuously critically evaluate new ideas [105,106], apply new knowledge in practice [107,108] and be aware that the sole existence of knowledge is not enough [12,109]. Information communication technologies directly support knowledge management practices [110]. It would be beneficial for Slovenian social work centers to solve the ongoing challenges regarding information communication technologies [103,111] that are changing their existing working patterns.

Furthermore, we propose improvements in all four topics wherein we aimed to gain insight about the existing effectiveness of knowledge management. As mentioned, informed [97] and improved [112,113] decision making is a prerequisite of influencing public policies. Social work managers should provide guidelines for their subordinates on how to question existing knowledge patterns, how to creatively think about innovative solutions and analyze their applicability and how to utilize this new knowledge in organizational decision-making processes. Also mentioned above, organizing work in teams could prove to be more efficient in practice [98]. Therefore, we encourage social work centers to promote the importance and positive effect of team work to their employees [114]. On the basis of existing literature, we argue that readily available knowledge makes employees more aware of who knows what in their organization [115–117]. We encourage organizations to enhance their efforts in making knowledge readily available to every single employee. Utilizing new knowledge, additional skills and experience can positively influence the functioning of social work centers [118,119]. Therefore, it would be beneficial for organizations to encourage managers and employees to continuously acquire new knowledge, additional skills and experience and focus on constantly improving learning at the individual, group and organizational level [120]. The end goal of knowledge management activities should be to help social work centers achieve excellence in their daily routines [17,121]. We argue that they should engage and provide support for any activity or initiative that can potentially improve the quality of their overall performance [92,112], measured by the wellbeing of social services users. To conclude, we believe it is the responsibility of managers to consider which aspects of knowledge management are most effective in practice, and what role these practices might have on stimulating higher levels of organizational performance.

Considering that the case study of Slovenian female social workers actually shows that the existing patterns of entrance and exit of social workers will decrease the availability of social workers despite the increasing need for staffing, it is of paramount importance to endorse efforts that acknowledge the importance of understanding workforce entrance and exit in the social work profession on a national level in order to provide the required number of well-trained social workers who will provide wellbeing for a growing number of service users in an ageing society. Efforts to maintain or improve the availability of social workers should focus also on the quality of knowledge management activities, as this can contribute towards maintaining fully productive social workers and mitigate any intention among them to change their profession or retire early. Knowledge management measures are typically related to the four already established knowledge management process stages, namely knowledge creation, knowledge storage and retrieval, knowledge transfer and knowledge implementation [11,12] and management support. They would result in improvements in use of the societal resources available to social workers through the so-called soft measures such as enhanced collaboration, enhanced communication, enhanced learning, and indirectly in enhanced performance [21]. As is evident from Table 4, we argue that in the event of successful knowledge management implementation, more female social workers would remain fully productive for a longer period, and they would be less motivated to change their profession due to various reasons, while also staying longer as active participants on the labor market.

4.3. Limitations and Future Research Directions

Despite newly gained insight into knowledge management in the context of social work organizations, our paper is not without limitations. The first limitation is related to our sample frame. Due to the implementation of the GDPR act, our scope for respondents was limited. The second limitation relates to generalizability. We cannot confirm our findings across the whole field of social work, as we included only a proportion of managers and employees employed in social work centers. Third, the transition matrix is only hypothesized based on moderate estimates of how knowledge management would potentially influence the patterns of entrance and exit from the workforce of social workers.

Future research should aim to include more social work organizations, with the aim to draw final conclusions related to the field. It would also be extremely beneficial to compare our results to other European countries. Moreover, our results show that public data regarding workforce entrance and exit in general, and specifically for social workers, should be maintained and regularly published, to afford researchers better access to data regarding workforce availability. As the whole topic of knowledge management is novel and unexplored in social work, it offers several potential opportunities for future exploration for both researchers and practitioners in social work. We would especially urge follow-up studies face-to-face open-ended interviews to gain additional understanding about specific topics that are related to the extent and effectiveness of knowledge management in social work. Such methods would enable researchers to overcome issues related to interpreting the results of questionnaires that only use Likert scale ranges.

5. Conclusions

Our results are highly relevant and discuss the important potential impact of knowledge management on the social work profession due to the fact that: (1) there is an imperative to focus on the social dimension of sustainability as it is integral to the quality of a human system, (2) the existing supply of social workers is not sufficient to provide wellbeing for the growing elderly population, (3) at the moment, involvement in knowledge management activities in social work is not extensive enough to positively influence the functioning of social work organizations that are and will be responsible for taking care of our ageing population. Along with the sustainable development of social work, this represents the possible future path towards satisfying the ever-growing demand for social services. (4) The model we have developed allows better understanding of patterns in the social work profession regarding workforce entrance and exit and can be utilized by: (1) social work organizations that employ social workers, to increase their understanding regarding the social workers' demographics and the potential impact of knowledge management on policies and other improvements; (2) social workers' unions, i.e., with regard to negotiating processes that deal with the existing shortage of social workers; as well as (3) policy and decision makers, when discussing and developing future policies covering this important topic of our ageing society. In the long term, the results of our study regarding knowledge management can make an important contribution in providing support to ensure appropriate social services to our ageing society. Therefore, our contribution is also indirectly towards the sustainability of our society as a whole. To conclude, we believe that while addressing the challenge of ensuring the wellbeing of service users it is also important to acknowledge the institutional framework, as it can potentially act as a major constraint. A thorough reflection on the existing legislation and the way services are currently being provided is necessary. We believe that knowledge management could contribute to improving the existing state of affairs to some degree, however, it cannot yet move social work beyond the challenges related to its institutional framework.

Author Contributions: The contributions of authors are as follows: conceptualization: S.C., V.D. and D.B., abstract: S.C., V.D. and D.B., introduction: S.C., V.D. and D.B., materials and methods: S.C., V.D. and D.B., results: S.C., V.D. and D.B., discussion: S.C., V.D. and D.B., conclusions: S.C., V.D. and D.B. and references: S.C.

Funding: The authors acknowledge that the paper Knowledge Management and the Sustainable Development of Social Work, was financially supported by the Slovenian Research Agency, Program P5-0364—The Impact of

Corporate Governance, Organizational Learning, and Knowledge Management on Modern Organization and by the Slovenian Research Agency, Program J6-9396—Development of Social Infrastructure and Services for Community Based Long-Term Care.

Acknowledgments: We would like to express our deep gratitude to the Social Chamber of Slovenia and its secretary general Vilko Kolbl for their help in acquiring data from our respondents. Additionally, we would also like to thank all of our respondents that filled out our questionnaire related to the topic of knowledge management in Slovenian social work centers and for their consent to participate in this research.

Conflicts of Interest: The authors declare no conflict of interest.

References

1. Social Life: Social Sustainability Definition. Available online: http://www.social-life.co/ (accessed on 23 September 2019).
2. Woodcraft, S.; Bacon, N.; Caistor-Arendar, L.; Hackett, T. *Design for Social Sustainability: A Framework for Creating Thriving New Communities*; Social Life: London, UK, 2012.
3. Ajmal, M.M.; Khan, M.; Hussain, M.; Helo, P. Conceptualizing and incorporating social sustainability in the business world. *Int. J. Sustain. Dev. World Ecol.* **2018**, *25*, 327–339. [CrossRef]
4. Staniškiene, E.; Stankevičiute, Ž. Social sustainability measurement framework: The case of employee perspective in CSR-committed organization. *J. Clean. Prod.* **2018**, *188*, 708–719. [CrossRef]
5. Cuthill, M. Strengthening the "social" in sustainable development: Developing a conceptual framework for social sustainability in a rapid urban growth region in Australia. *Sustain. Dev.* **2010**, *18*, 362–373. [CrossRef]
6. Vavik, T.; Keitsch, M.M. Exploring relationships between universal design and social sustainable development: Some methodological aspects of the debate on the sciences of sustainability. *Sustain. Dev.* **2010**, *18*, 295–305. [CrossRef]
7. Bostrom, M. A missing pillar? Challenges in theorizing and practicing social sustainability: Introduction to the special issue. *Sustain. Sci. Pract. Pol.* **2012**, *8*, 3–14. [CrossRef]
8. De Vries, M.; Nemec, J. Public Sector Reform: An Overview of Recent Literature and Research on NPM and Alternative Paths. *Int. J. Public Sect. Manag.* **2013**, *26*, 4–16. [CrossRef]
9. Jashapara, A. *Knowledge Management: An Integrated Approach*; Pearson Education: London, UK, 2011.
10. Dalkir, K. *Knowledge Management in Theory and Practice*; Elsevier Butterworth-Heinemann: Burlington, NJ, USA, 2005.
11. Hicks, R.; Dattero, R.; Galup, S. The five-tier knowledge management hierarchy. *J. Knowl. Manag.* **2006**, *10*, 19–31. [CrossRef]
12. Alavi, M.; Leidner, D.E. Review: Knowledge management and knowledge management systems: Conceptual foundations and research issues. *MIS Q.* **2001**, *25*, 107–136. [CrossRef]
13. Ward, V.; Smith, S.; Keen, J.; West, R.; House, A. Creating and implementing local health and wellbeing policy: Networks, interactions and collective knowledge creation amongst public sector managers. *Evid. Policy* **2018**, *14*, 477–498. [CrossRef]
14. Heisig, P. Harmonisation of knowledge management—Comparing 160 KM frameworks around the globe. *J. Knowl. Manag.* **2009**, *13*, 4–31. [CrossRef]
15. Dawson, R. Knowledge capabilities as the focus of organizational development and strategy. *J. Knowl. Manag.* **2001**, *4*, 320–327. [CrossRef]
16. Kogut, B.; Zander, U. What firms do? Coordination, identity and learning. *Organ. Sci.* **1996**, *7*, 502–518. [CrossRef]
17. Downes, T.V. An Evaluation of Knowledge Management Practices in Nonprofit Community Services Organizations in Australia. Ph.D. Thesis, Southern Cross University, Lismore, Australia, 2014.
18. Lin, H.F. Antecedents of the stage-based knowledge management evolution. *J. Knowl. Manag.* **2011**, *15*, 136–155. [CrossRef]
19. Azmee, N.N.; Kassim, N.A.; Abdullah, C.Z.H. Dimensions of Knowledge Management Maturity: Top Management Support and Leadership, People, and Information Technology. *J. Inf. Knowl. Manag.* **2017**, *7*, 1–7.
20. Bharadway, S.S.; Chauhan, S.; Raman, A. Impact of Knowledge Management Capabilities on Knowledge Management Effectiveness in Indian Organizations. *J. Decis. Mak.* **2015**, *40*, 421–434. [CrossRef]

21. Anantatmula, V.S. Linking KM effectiveness attributes to organizational performance. *VINE* **2007**, *37*, 133–149. [CrossRef]
22. Kim, Y.W.; Ko, J. HR practices and knowledge sharing behavior: Focusing on the moderating effect of trust in supervisor. *Public Pers. Manag.* **2014**, *43*, 586–607. [CrossRef]
23. Mariano, S.; Awazu, Y. Artifacts in knowledge management research: A systematic literature review and future research directions. *J. Knowl. Manag.* **2016**, *20*, 1333–1352. [CrossRef]
24. Centobelli, P.; Cerchione, R.; Esposito, E. How to deal with knowledge management misalignment: A taxonomy based on a 3D fuzzy methodology. *J. Knowl. Manag.* **2018**, *22*, 538–566. [CrossRef]
25. Centobelli, P.; Cerchione, R.; Esposito, E. Efficiency and effectiveness of knowledge management systems in SMEs. *Prod. Plan. Control* **2019**, *30*, 779–791. [CrossRef]
26. Massaro, M.; Dumay, J.; Garlatti, A. Public sector knowledge management: A structured literature review. *J. Knowl. Manag.* **2015**, *19*, 530–558. [CrossRef]
27. Špaček, D. Knowledge management in public administration—What can be found in research outputs in the Czech Republic—Preliminary findings. In Proceedings of the 20th International Conference on Current Trends in Public Sector Research, Brno, Czech Republic, 21–22 January 2016.
28. Arora, E. Knowledge Management in Public Sector. *J. Arts Sci. Commer.* **2011**, *2*, 165–171.
29. Wiig, K. Knowledge management in public administration. *J. Knowl. Manag.* **2002**, *6*, 224–239. [CrossRef]
30. Hardina, D. Ten characteristics of empowerment-oriented social service organizations. *Adm. Soc. Work* **2005**, *29*, 23–42. [CrossRef]
31. Ukil, M.I. The impact of Employee Empowerment on Employee Satisfaction and Service Quality: Empirical Evidence from Financial Enteprizes in Bangladesh. *Business* **2016**, *17*, 178–189. [CrossRef]
32. Oluikpe, P. Developing a corporate knowledge management strategy. *J. Knowl. Manag.* **2012**, *16*, 862–878. [CrossRef]
33. Ringel-Bickelmaier, C.; Ringel, M. Knowledge management in international organisations. *J. Knowl. Manag.* **2010**, *14*, 524–539. [CrossRef]
34. Cong, X.; Pandya, K.V. Issues of knowledge management in the public sector. *Electron. J. Knowl. Manag.* **2003**, *1*, 25–33.
35. Willem, A.; Buelens, M. Knowledge sharing in public sector organizations: The effect of organizational characteristics on interdepartmental knowledge sharing. *J. Public Adm. Res. Theory* **2007**, *17*, 581–606. [CrossRef]
36. Leung, Z.C.S. Knowledge Management in Social Work: Towards a Conceptual Framework. *J. Technol. Hum. Serv.* **2007**, *25*, 181–198. [CrossRef]
37. McCoyd, J.L.M.; Johnson, Y.M.; Munch, S.; LaSala, M. Quantocentric culture: Ramifications for social work education. *Soc. Work Educ.* **2009**, *28*, 811–827. [CrossRef]
38. Broadhurst, K.; Hall, C.; White, S.; Pithouse, A. Risk, instrumentalism and the humane project in social work: Identifying the informal logics of risk management in children's statutory services. *Br. J. Soc. Work* **2010**, *40*, 352–370. [CrossRef]
39. Al Ahbabi, S.; Singh, S.K.; Balasubramian, S.; Singh Gaur, S. Employee perception of impact of knowledge management processes on public sector performance. *J. Knowl. Manag.* **2019**, *23*, 351–373. [CrossRef]
40. Hartnett, H.P.; Tabone, J.K.; Orlsene, L. Aging at Work: The Importance of Understanding Accommodation in Social Work Practice. *J. Sociol. Soc. Work* **2019**, *7*, 36–43. [CrossRef]
41. Hall, N. Social work through an indigenous lens: Reflections on the state of our profession. In *Social Work: Making a World of Difference: Social Work Around the World IV in the Year of IFSW's 50th Jubilee*; IFSW: Berne, Switzerland; FAFO: Oslo, Norway, 2006.
42. Kuzmanič Korva, D.; Perkovič, M.; Kovač, J.; Rapošta-Tajnšek, P.; Flaker, V. *Preoblikovanje Organiziranosti Centrov za Socialno Delo v Republiki Sloveniji*; Skupnost CSD Slovenije: Ljubljana, Slovenia, 2004.
43. Ministry of Labour, Family, Social Affairs and Equal Opportunities. Available online: http://www.mddsz.gov.si/197/delovna_podrocja/sociala/reorganizacija_centrov_za_socialno_delo/ (accessed on 5 April 2019).
44. Harlow, E. Why don't women want to be social workers anymore? New managerialism, postfeminism and the shortage of social workers in social services departments in England and Wales. *Eur. J. Soc. Work* **2004**, *7*, 167–179. [CrossRef]
45. Squires, A.; Jylha, V.; Jun, J.; Ensio, A.; Kinnune, J. A scoping review of nursing workforce planning and forecasting research. *J. Nurs. Manag.* **2017**, *25*, 587–596. [CrossRef]

46. European Commission. *The 2018 Ageing Report*; European Commission: Luxemburg, 2017.
47. Dimovski, V.; Grah, B.; Colnar, S. Modelling the industrial workforce dynamics and exit in the ageing society. In Proceedings of the 9th IFAC Conference on Manufacturing Modelling, Management and Control, Berlin, Germany, 28–30 August 2019.
48. United Nations, World Population Prospects: The 2015 Revision. Available online: http://esa.un.org/unpd/wpp/ (accessed on 5 July 2019).
49. Eurostat, Eurostat Database: Demographic Balances and Selected Indicators, EUROPOP 2018, Slovenia. Available online: https://www.stat.si/StatWeb/en/news/Index/8316 (accessed on 8 September 2019).
50. Marc, M.; Bartosiewicz, A.; Burzynska, J.; Chmiel, Z.; Januszewicz, P. A nursing shortage-a prospect of global and local policies. *Int. Counc. Nurs.* **2019**, *66*, 9–16. [CrossRef]
51. Riege, A.; Lindsay, N. Knowledge management in the public sector: Stakeholder partnership in the public policy development. *J. Knowl. Manag.* **2006**, *10*, 24–39. [CrossRef]
52. Ortenblad, A. Who is the learning organization for? A stakeholder contingency approach to contextualizing managerial panaceas. In *Handbook of Research on Knowledge Management: Adaptation and Context*; Ortenblad, A., Ed.; Edward Elgar: Cheltenham, UK; Northampton, MA, USA, 2014.
53. Ortenblad, A.; Koris, R. Is the learning organization idea relevant to higher educational institutions? A literature review and a multi-stakeholder contingency approach. *Int. J. Educ. Manag.* **2014**, *28*, 173–214. [CrossRef]
54. Beddoe, L. Investing in the future: Social workers talk about research. *Br. J. Soc. Work* **2011**, *41*, 557–575. [CrossRef]
55. Bloice, L.; Burnett, S. Barriers to knowledge sharing in third sector social care: A case study. *J. Knowl. Manag.* **2016**, *20*, 125–145. [CrossRef]
56. Institute for Research and Innovation in Social Services. Available online: https://lx.iriss.org.uk/sites/default/files/resources/sharing_knowledge_improving_practice_changing_lives.pdf (accessed on 29 October 2019).
57. Lettieri, E.; Borga, F.; Savoldelli, A. Knowledge management in non-profit organizations. *J. Knowl. Manag.* **2004**, *8*, 16–30. [CrossRef]
58. Kianto, A.; Vanhala, M.; Hielmann, P. The impact of knowledge management on job satisfaction. *J. Knowl. Manag.* **2016**, *20*, 621–636. [CrossRef]
59. North, K.; Hornung, T. The Benefits of Knowledge Management—Results of the German Award "Knowledge Manager 2002". *J. Univers. Comput. Sci.* **2002**, *9*, 361–389.
60. Muchinsky, P.M.; Tuttle, M.L. Employee turnover: An empirical and methodological assessment. *J. Vocat. Behav.* **1979**, *14*, 43–77. [CrossRef]
61. Alexanderson, K. Vilja, Kunna, Förstå: Om Implementering av Systematisk Dokumentation för Verksamhetsutveckling i Socialtjänsten [Willingness, Comprehension, Capability: About Implementation of Systematic Documentation for Developing Social Work in the Public Social Work Services]. Ph.D. Thesis, Orebro University Library, Orebro, Sweden, 2006.
62. Austin, M.J.; Ciaassen, J.; Vu, C.M.; Mizrahi, P. Knowledge Management: Implications for Human Service Organizations. *J. Evid. Based Soc. Work* **2008**, *5*, 361–389. [CrossRef]
63. Leung, Z.C.S. Knowledge management in social work—The interplay of knowledge sharing platforms. *Int. Soc. Work* **2014**, *57*, 143–155. [CrossRef]
64. Social Protection Institute of the Republic of Slovenia. Available online: https://www.irssv.si/upload2/Socialni%20polozaj%20v%20Sloveniji%202015_2016_dopolnjeno%20koncno%20porocilo_2.pdf (accessed on 28 October 2019).
65. Bjorkenheim, J. Knowledge and social work in health care: The case of Finland. *Soc. Work Health Care* **2007**, *44*, 261–278. [CrossRef]
66. Ministry of Public Administration. Available online: http://www.mju.gov.si/si/delovna_podrocja/razvoj_projektov_kakovost_javne_uprave_in_kohezijska_politika/strategija_razvoja_javne_uprave/ (accessed on 29 October 2019).
67. Bogataj, D.; McDonnell, D.R.; Bogataj, M. Management, financing and taxation of housing stock in the shrinking cities of aging societies. *Int. J. Prod. Econ.* **2016**, *181*, 2–13. [CrossRef]
68. Bogataj, D.; McDonnell, D.; Bogataj, M. Reverse mortgage schemes financing urban dynamics using the multiple decrement approach. *Springer Proc. Math. Stat.* **2015**, *135*, 27–47. [CrossRef]

69. Rogelj, V.; Bogataj, D. Planning and financing the home and facility-based care using the multiple decrement approach. *J. Decis. Syst.* **2018**, *27*, 132–143. [CrossRef]
70. Kahn, W.A. Caring for the caregivers: Patterns of organizational caregiving. *Adm. Sci. Q.* **1993**, *38*, 539–563. [CrossRef]
71. Henttonen, K.; Kianto, A.; Ritala, P. Knowledge sharing and individual work performance: An empirical study of a public sector organization. *J. Knowl. Manag.* **2016**, *20*, 749–768. [CrossRef]
72. Grant, R. Towards a Knowledge Based Theory of the Firm. *Strateg. Manag. J.* **1996**, *17*, 109–122. [CrossRef]
73. Hislop, D.; Bosua, R.; Helms, R. *Knowledge Management in Organizations—A Critical Introduction*, 4th ed.; Oxford University Press: Oxford, MS, USA, 2018.
74. Kogut, B.; Zander, U. Knowledge of the firm and the evolutionary theory of the multinational corporation. *J. Int. Bus. Stud.* **2003**, *34*, 516–529. [CrossRef]
75. Edge, K. Powerful public sector knowledge management: A school district example. *J. Knowl. Manag.* **2005**, *9*, 42–52. [CrossRef]
76. Fitch, D. Examination of the child protective services decision-making context with implications for decision support system design. *J. Soc. Serv. Res.* **2006**, *32*, 117–134. [CrossRef]
77. Soydan, H. Producing Knowledge for Evidence-Based Practice and the Future of Social Work Research. In *Evidence Based and Knowledge Based Social Work: Research Methods and Approaches in Social Work Research*; Aarhus University Press: Aarhus, Denmark, 2008.
78. Podsakoff, P.M.; MacKenzie, S.B.; Lee, J.Y.; Podsakoff, N.P. Common method biases in behavioral research: A critical review of the literature and recommended remedies. *J. Appl. Psychol.* **2003**, *88*, 879–903. [CrossRef]
79. Podsakoff, P.M.; MacKenzie, S.B.; Podsakoff, N.P. Sources of method bias in social science research and recommendations on how to control it. *Annu. Rev. Psychol.* **2012**, *63*, 539–569. [CrossRef]
80. McPhail, B.A. Setting the Record Straight: Social Work is Not a Female-Dominated Profession. *Soc. Work* **2004**, *49*, 323–326. [CrossRef]
81. Hoem, J.M. Point estimation of forces of transition in demographic models. *J. R. Stat. Soc.* **1970**, *33*, 275–289. [CrossRef]
82. Nurminen, M.; Nurminen, T. Multistate worklife expectancies. *Scand. J. Work Environ. Health* **2005**, *31*, 169–178. [CrossRef] [PubMed]
83. Dudel, C.; Lopez Gomez, M.A.; Benavides, F.G.; Myrskylä, M. The length of working life in Spain: Levels, recent trends, and the impact of the financial crisis. *Eur. J. Popul.* **2018**, *34*, 769–791. [CrossRef] [PubMed]
84. Dudel, C.; Myrskylä, M. Working Life Expectancy at Age 50 in the United States and the Impact of the Great Recession. *Demography* **2017**, *54*, 2101–2123. [CrossRef] [PubMed]
85. Pedersen, J.; Bjorner, J.B. Worklife expectancy in a cohort of Danish employees aged 55–65 years—Comparing a multi-state Cox proportional hazard approach with conventional multi-state life tables. *BMC Public Health* **2017**, *17*, 879. [CrossRef] [PubMed]
86. Schoen, R. Multistate Transfer Rate Estimation from Adjacent Populations. *Popul. Res. Policy Rev.* **2016**, *35*, 217–240. [CrossRef]
87. Nurminen, M. Worklife expectancies of fixed-term Finnish employees in 1997–2006. *Scand. J. Work Environ. Health* **2008**, *34*, 83–95. [CrossRef]
88. Deshmukh, S. *Multiple Decrement Models in Insurance: An Introduction Using R*; Springer: New Delhi, India, 2012.
89. Promislow, S.D. *Fundamentals of Actuarial Mathematics*, 3rd ed.; John Wiley & Sons: Chichester, UK, 2015.
90. Slovenian Statistical Office. Delovno Aktivno Prebivalstvo Po Spol, Skd Dejavnost, Leto, Starostni Razred. Available online: https://pxweb.stat.si/pxweb/Dialog/SaveShow.asp (accessed on 15 July 2019).
91. Belchior Rocha, H. Social Work Practices and the Ecological Sustainability of Socially Vulnerable Communities. *Sustainability* **2018**, *10*, 1312. [CrossRef]
92. Missimer, M.; Robert, K.H.; Broman, G. A strategic approach to social sustainability—Part 2: A principle-based definition. *J. Clean. Prod.* **2017**, *140*, 42–52. [CrossRef]
93. Brennan, E. Definitions for social sustainability and social work paper. In *White Paper Distributed for CSWE Conference*; Portland State University: Portland, OR, USA, 2010.
94. Blake, J. Sustainable communities and social work practice learning: Reflections on emergent, learning partnerships. *J. Pract. Teach. Learn.* **2009**, *9*, 93–114. [CrossRef]

95. Teater, B.; Devaney, J.; Forrester, D.; Scourfield, J.; Carpenter, J. *Quantitative Research Methods for Social Work: Making Social Work Count*, 1st ed.; Palgrave: London, UK, 2016.
96. Dimovski, V.; Penger, S.; Peterlin, J.; Grah, B.; Černe, M.; Klepec, M. *Advanced Management and Leadership Practice*; Pearson Education Limited: Essex, UK, 2017.
97. Myers, P.S. A Normative Model of Knowledge Management Effectiveness. In *Handbook of Research on Knowledge Management: Adaptation and Context*; Ortenblad, A., Ed.; Edward Elgar Publishing: Cheltenham, UK; Northampton, MA, USA, 2014; pp. 28–52.
98. Nishikawa, M. (Re)defining care workers as knowledge workers. *Gend. Work Organ.* **2011**, *18*, 113–135. [CrossRef]
99. Dehgani, R.; Ramsin, R. Methodologies for developing knowledge management systems: An evaluation framework. *J. Knowl. Manag.* **2015**, *19*, 682–710. [CrossRef]
100. Garrido-Moreno, A.; Lockett, N.; Garcia-Morales, V. Paving the way for CRM success: The mediating role of knowledge management and organizational commitment. *Inf. Manag.* **2014**, *51*, 1031–1042. [CrossRef]
101. Akbari, N.; Ghaffari, A. Verifying relationship of knowledge management initiatives and the empowerment of human resources. *J. Knowl. Manag.* **2017**, *21*, 1120–1141. [CrossRef]
102. Bosilj Vukšić, V.; Pejić Bach, M.; Garrido-Moreno, A.; Lockett, N.; Garcia-Morales, V. Exploring the role of knowledge management practices in fostering customer relationship management as a catalyst of marketing innovation. *Balt. J. Manag.* **2015**, *10*, 393–412. [CrossRef]
103. Tapio Inkinen, H.; Kianto, A.; Vanhala, M. Knowledge management practice and innovation performance in Finland. *Balt. J. Manag.* **2015**, *10*, 432–435. [CrossRef]
104. Cabrera, A.; Collins, W.C.; Salgado, J.F. Determinants of individual engagement in knowledge sharing. *Int. J. Hum. Resour. Manag.* **2006**, *17*, 245–264. [CrossRef]
105. Bontis, N. *Information Bombardment: Rising Above the Digital Onslaught*; Institute for Intellectual Capital Research: Hamilton, ON, Canada, 2011.
106. Karamitri, I.; Talias, M.A.; Bellali, T. Knowledge Management practices in healthcare settings: A systematic review. *Int. J. Health Plan. Manag.* **2015**, *32*, 4–18. [CrossRef]
107. Bierly, P.E.; Damanpour, F.; Santoro, M.D. The application of external knowledge: Organizational conditions for exploration and exploitation. *J. Manag. Stud.* **2009**, *46*, 481–509. [CrossRef]
108. Choi, S.Y.; Lee, H.; Yoo, Y. The impact of information technology and transactive memory systems on knowledge sharing, application and team performance. *MIS Q.* **2010**, *34*, 855–870. [CrossRef]
109. Penrose, E.T. *The Theory of the Growth of the Firm*, 4th ed.; Oxford University Press: Oxford, MS, USA, 2009.
110. Andreeva, T.; Kianto, A. Does knowledge management really matter? Linking knowledge management practices, competitiveness and economic performance. *J. Knowl. Manag.* **2012**, 617–636. [CrossRef]
111. Ouriques, R.A.B.; Wnuk, K.; Gorschek, T.; Berntsson Svensson, R. Knowledge Management Strategies and Processes in Agile Software Development: A Systematic Literature Review. *Int. J. Softw. Eng. Knowl. Eng.* **2018**, *29*, 345–380. [CrossRef]
112. King, W.R. *Knowledge Management and Organizational Learning*; Springer: Boston, MA, USA, 2009.
113. Carneiro, A. How does knowledge management influence innovation and competitiveness? *J. Knowl. Manag.* **2000**, *4*, 87–98. [CrossRef]
114. Eppler, M.; Sukowski, O. Managing Team Knowledge: Core Processes, Tools and Enabling Factors. *Eur. Manag. J.* **2000**, *18*, 334–341. [CrossRef]
115. Rodrigues, A.; Azevedo, C.; Calvo, V. Internal communication in organizations: Practical instruments to help the shift change. *J. Educ. Technol. Health* **2016**, *2*, 1–10. [CrossRef]
116. Alavi, M.; Leidner, D. Knowledge Management Systems: Issues, Challenges, and Benefits. *Commun. Assoc. Inf. Syst.* **1999**, *1*, 1–27. [CrossRef]
117. Argote, L. Organizational learning research: Past, present and future. *Manag. Learn.* **2011**, *42*, 439–446. [CrossRef]
118. Senge, P.M. *The Fifth Discipline: The Art & Practice of a Learning Organization*; Doubleday: New York, NY, USA, 1990.
119. Resatsch, F.; Faisst, U. Measuring the performance of knowledge management initiatives. In Proceedings of the Fifth European Conference on Organizational knowledge, learning and Capabilities, Innsbruck, Austria, 2–3 April 2004.

120. Westerlund, M.; Rajala, R. Learning and innovation in inter-organizational network collaboration. *J. Bus. Ind. Mark.* **2010**, *25*, 435–442. [CrossRef]
121. Anantatmula, V.S.; Stankosky, M. KM criteria for different types of organisations. *Int. J. Knowl. Learn.* **2008**, *4*, 18–35. [CrossRef]

sustainability

MDPI

Article

Sustainability through the Digitalization of Industrial Machines: Complementary Factors of Fuel Consumption and Productivity for Forklifts with Sensors

Natallia Pashkevich [1], Darek Haftor [2,*], Mikael Karlsson [3] and Soumitra Chowdhury [4]

1 School of Social Sciences, Södertörn University, 141 89 Huddinge, Sweden; natallia@athaydes.com
2 Department of Informatics and Media, Uppsala University, 751 20 Uppsala, Sweden
3 Research Manager, Bestwood AB, 172 75 Sundbyberg, Sweden; mikael.karlsson@bestwood.se
4 Department of Informatics, Linnaeus University, 351 95 Växjö, Sweden; soumitra.chowdhury@lnu.se
* Correspondence: darek.haftor@im.uu.se

Received: 23 October 2019; Accepted: 23 November 2019; Published: 27 November 2019

Abstract: Increasing the fuel efficiency of industrial machines through digitalization can enable the transport and logistics sector to overcome challenges such as low productivity growth and increasing CO_2 emissions. Modern digitalized machines with embedded sensors that collect and transmit operational data have opened up new avenues for the identification of more efficient machine use. While existing studies of industrial machines have mostly focused on one or a few conditioning factors at a time, this study took a complementary approach, using a large set of known factors that simultaneously conditioned both the fuel consumption and productivity of medium-range forklifts (n = 285) that operated in a natural industrial setting for one full year. The results confirm the importance of a set of factors, including aspects related to the vehicles' travels, drivers, operations, workload spectra, and contextual factors, such as industry and country. As a novel contribution, this study shows that the key conditioning factors interact with each other in a non-linear and non-additive manner. This means that addressing one factor at a time might not provide optimal fuel consumption, and instead all factors need to be addressed simultaneously as a system.

Keywords: digitalization; complementarities; sustainability; fuel consumption; heavy-duty equipment; productivity; sensor data

1. Introduction

In line with the ongoing focus on environmental sustainability in the global economy, the transport and logistics sector is also concerned with the negative environmental impact of using heavy-duty industrial equipment. The depletion of the ozone layer has been a worldwide concern for the last few decades [1], and hazardous materials that affect the ozone layer are emitted through the fuel consumption of various equipment in different industrial sectors. Most heavy-duty industrial equipment, such as forklifts, terminal tractors, cranes, straddle carriers, and reach stackers, are diesel-fueled and have been shown to be a key source for hydrocarbon, NOx, and particulate matter emissions that contribute significantly to the formation of haze/smog [2,3]. Although the number of electric vehicles is increasing [4], reducing fuel consumption from diesel-fueled industrial machines remains one of the key challenges for environmental sustainability [5].

The development of more advanced vehicles has contributed to humans' enhanced capabilities to perform difficult industrial tasks, but this has in turn led to an even stronger response from the environment [6,7]. The growing fuel consumption and carbon emissions from such heavy-duty equipment add to the already existing emissions in the transport and logistics sector [2,8]. For example, without the intervention of governments and clear energy efficiency measures it is predicted that in the European Union greenhouse gas emissions produced by trucks will be around 35% higher in 2030 than the 1990 levels [9]. In comparison to other vehicles, diesel vehicles consume the most fuel [2,10]. At the same time, heavy-duty vehicles are being overloaded in order to reduce operating costs, and this has had significant negative environmental impacts [3]. Thus, because fuel efficiency is directly linked to CO_2 emission [9], vehicle fuel consumption and vehicle productivity [1] should be explicitly considered together in order to reduce these vehicles' environmental impact.

Digitalization and the Internet of Things (IoT) enable us to measure fuel consumption in heavy-duty industrial equipment and to identify factors that influence fuel consumption in a manner that has not previously been possible. The very low transaction costs for operational data collection enabled by digitalization make it possible to collect continuous detailed operational data from a large set of vehicles operating in their actual work contexts. However, in general, the transport and logistics sector is lagging in digitalization, particularly in the European Union [11,12]. Recent concerns include how to transform the massive amounts of data collected from vehicles into useful knowledge [13], and answering this requires more empirical knowledge from longitudinal studies of vehicle use in real-life situations. Given all this, the aim of this study is to identify factors that condition fuel consumption in relation to the productivity of medium-range forklifts that use sensor data.

Studies on road freight transportation and logistics that have analyzed the effect of sensor data on fuel consumption show the importance of factors related to (i) vehicles, (ii) their environments, (iii) their travels, (iii) their drivers, and (iv) their operations [13–16]. However, these studies have focused their attention on only one or a few conditioning factors at a time, while ignoring the complementarity perspective. Previous studies that have summarized fuel consumption factors [17,18] have not demonstrated how these factors interact with each other in an empirical setting, so as to condition the fuel consumption and productivity of forklifts, and this is the first knowledge gap targeted here. While recent studies have focused on truck freight transportation in general, there is a limited number of studies [19–23] that have investigated the factors that condition the fuel consumption and productivity of forklifts, which have different operations from ground transportation, with more starts and stops and shorter travel distances [24]. This is the second knowledge gap addressed in this work. Finally, most studies have focused either on fuel consumption factors or on productivity factors separately, while the present study addresses this knowledge gap by targeting both simultaneously. The work in the present study used empirical data from the actual use of a large set of medium-range forklifts equipped with data sensors and operating in a natural setting over the course of one full year, and this contrasts with other studies looking at small samples of a few machines operating in artificial settings. In order to handle the interactions of the large number of factors (independent variables) studied here, the partial least square regression method was employed for the first time in this context.

Our results demonstrate the importance of a number of conditioning factors, including travel, driver, and operations-related factors related to fuel consumption, such as distance, average speed, and time-related parameters such as production hours, engine hours, hydraulic hours, driving hours, and idling hours. This study shows that operating in certain workload spectra significantly increases fuel consumption. The results also demonstrate the importance of contextual factors and show that specific customer segments and countries realize more efficient fuel consumption than others. One important practical implication of the results provided here is that there is an opportunity to change the behavior of vehicle drivers in order to reduce fuel consumption, which will both increase economic productivity and reduce CO_2 emissions, and thus reduce the negative environmental impact of such vehicles. The results can further be used to monitor driver behavior and to formulate feedback mechanisms and training packages, and can be used to further develop fuel and productivity-related factors. With regards to theory, unlike the partiality of previous studies, this study demonstrates that several factors must be addressed simultaneously and in a complementary manner in order to reduce fuel consumption and thereby increase the productivity and reduce the CO_2 emissions of medium-range forklifts.

The remainder of this paper is organized as follows. The next section presents work related to key drivers affecting fuel consumption. We then present the research methodology, which is followed by a description of the results. Following that, a discussion and conclusion are presented.

2. Related Work

Digitalization has profoundly affected modern nations, organizations, and individuals [12]. The Industrial IoT and new digital environments, such as big data, mobile and service platforms, cloud computing, and social media, enable new combinations of resources, communication channels, products, services, and digital business models [8,25–28]. Numerous sensors, camera images, and barcode scans produce a vast amount of data, and this creates a great opportunity to uncover hidden patterns that might affect fuel consumption and thus CO_2 emissions without reducing equipment productivity in unexpected ways [14,20]. However, making sense of these services and data is a challenge for both manufacturers and customers [11,12], and these advancements in technology, smart services, and large, complex datasets raise many questions regarding the use of digital technologies for environmental sustainability. One such question is how to use and analyze large sets of sensor data in order to reduce the fuel consumption of heavy equipment without reducing productivity.

Over the past few years there has been an increasing number of studies on the factors affecting fuel consumption and CO_2 emissions in the field of road freight transportation and logistics. For example, it was previously found that engine load conditions [29], vehicle speed [30,31], payload [32,33], fleet size and mix [33], driver behavior [34–36], and surface roughness [37] are key factors that affect vehicle fuel consumption. All of these factors were later summarized in the following five key groups of factors (Table 1) that significantly affect the fuel consumption of road freight transport [17,18]: (i) vehicle-related (vehicle weight, shape, engine and transmission models, and fuel and oil type); (ii) environment-related (surface and temperature conditions); (iii) travel-related (speed and acceleration/deceleration); (iv) driver-related (driver behavior, gear selection, and idling); and (v) operations-related (fleet size, mix, payload, and empty kilometers).

Factors affecting fuel consumption have been widely studied in the road freight transportation and logistics fields, but factors affecting the fuel consumption of forklifts have received little attention. Forklift operations differ from ground transportation in that in the former there is a need for more starting and stopping and the distances traveled are much shorter [24]. Most of the studies that have addressed forklift efficiency and fuel consumption have focused on operational features and have developed a number of models that indirectly affect the fuel consumption of forklifts through order sequencing, storage allocation, and path minimization [19–23]. However, these models are criticized for having low flexibility, restricted applicability to the particular operating conditions, and difficulty being adapted to different warehouse layouts. Thus, these models are difficult to apply in more complex real-life settings. Moreover, while driver behavior has a direct influence on fuel consumption and efficiency, it is often neglected in these models. For example, in a recent study [24], it was observed that drivers with similar tasks had different driving behaviors and that average speed was the most significant variable affecting the fuel consumption of forklifts.

A number of studies have also investigated the impact of information and communication technologies (ICT) on fuel consumption and thus on CO_2 emissions. For ICT-based scheduling systems with telematics applications for data communication, it has been shown that positioning and navigation have a rate of return of 40–75% due to savings in fuel consumption [38,39], and the introduction of semi-automated computerized route optimization and scheduling systems and onboard monitoring computers has positively affected fuel efficiency [40]. ICT use at different levels—including vehicle, company, supply chain, and network levels—has also been shown to have a positive effect on reducing mileage, fuel consumption, and CO_2 emissions [41]. Internet-based freight applications that match the consignor's demand and the carrier's supply provide an efficient way to find the right truck and to organize the delivery process in a way that decreases empty travel distances, and thus improves average vehicle load and fuel efficiency while reducing CO_2 emissions [18].

Table 1. Factors affecting fuel consumption.

Categories	Factors
Vehicle-related	Vehicle curb weight Vehicle shape Engine size/type Engine temperature Transmission Fuel type/composition Oil viscosity Other characteristics (maintenance, age, accessories, etc.)
Environment-related	Roadway gradient Wind conditions Ambient temperature Altitude Pavement type Other characteristics (humidity, surfaceconditions, etc.)
Travel-related	Speed Acceleration/deceleration Congestion
Driver-related	Driver aggressiveness Gear selection Idling time
Operations-related	Fleet size and mix Payload Empty kilometers Number of stops

Source: [17,18].

With the advancement of ICT and the proliferation of sensors, companies are now able to capture multivariate time series datasets related to vehicle use. Over the last decade, a number of studies have analyzed large amounts of road freight transportation data in order to identify key parameters and their effects on fuel consumption. For example, data from a global positioning system have been shown to be effective in predicting the driving and idling fuel consumption rates of heavy vehicle fleets [13,15,42]. Among the key parameters collected from the sensor data of heavy-duty vehicles, the most important for fuel consumption are vehicle configuration, speed, payload factors, traffic congestion, and regenerative braking [43]. Differences in the operating environment of long-haul trucks and customer usage also play an important role in fuel efficiency [44], and the analysis of logging data revealed real-world driving behaviors that have a major influence on fuel economy [16]. In addition, big data analysis obtained from digital tachographs demonstrated the importance of driving patterns such as acceleration/deceleration, speed, and revolutions per minute [14] on fuel efficiency. Overall, these studies confirmed previously established factors for efficient fuel consumption.

While recent studies, including sensor-based studies, have already discovered a number of factors that affect vehicle fuel consumption, the majority of them have studied these factors separately, and thus only provide a partial understanding of existing fuel consumption factors. To overcome this, a specific theory of complementarities has been advanced to show that changing only one factor might not come close to achieving the benefits that are available using a system of specific complementarities that are addressed in a purposeful and synchronized manner [45]. In the present study, we apply a methodology that can potentially demonstrate which complementary factors can be studied together in order to improve fuel efficiency. We also focus on fuel consumption as a dependent variable but do not disregard the relationship between fuel consumption and the productivity of a vehicle. Moreover, in the present study we focus on one specific and homogeneous type of heavy-duty vehicle—medium-range forklifts—and thus present a unique and detailed analysis of factors that affect fuel consumption.

3. Method

This study's empirical basis was a particular company that is a leading global provider of heavy industrial vehicles with lifting capabilities, such as forklifts, reach stackers, and terminal tractors. The company's key customer segments include industrial ports, saw mills, and steel mills. The choice of company can be explained by the crucial importance of the transport and logistics sector for economic growth and employment [11,46,47], and current studies demonstrate that this industry has undergone significant development in terms of activities and employment [48]. The demand for road freight transport and logistics services is continuously growing [49], and thus the productivity of this industry has a significant impact on environmental sustainability with regard to CO_2 emission reductions [41]. Although the road freight transport industry is important for the social and economic development of a country, this industry is characterized by environmental, social, and competitive pressures, as well as by demanding customers [50]. Under these conditions, digital technologies are seen as the main enabling tool for effective and efficient operations [18,41], and transport and logistics companies increasingly depend on their ability to use these technologies in analyzing fuel consumption in order to move freight on time with reduced damage to the environment.

The study of the company's vehicles was motivated by several factors. Connectivity of vehicles is a part of the company's strategy, and the number of connected vehicles is constantly increasing. The company is in the transition process with the introduction of sensor data technologies and has a large enough set of vehicles with data sensors sending daily operational data from various countries and customer segments. The sensors on the vehicles send a vast amount of data to the company cloud regarding the usage and performance of the vehicles, e.g., accumulated distance, forward and reverse directions, speed, time, load, temperature, and fuel. The data indicate that diesel fuel consumption varies quite significantly between different customers, and this was the impetus for this study to attempt to identify key determinants of fuel consumption in relation to productivity. Below, the data collection procedures and analytical method are presented in detail.

3.1. Sample and Data Collection

For the purpose of analyzing what factors affect fuel consumption, a homogeneous group of vehicles, i.e., medium-range (9–18 tons) forklifts, which are primarily designed to lift and move materials over short distances, were chosen, and the data were collected daily from 1 January 2017 to 31 December 2017. The main concern from the company under investigation was that the available data indicate that diesel fuel consumption varies quite significantly between different industry segments. The final data sample was represented by 285 forklifts constructed during 2012–2017, including 13 forklift models, 5 engine models, and 3 transmission models. The forklifts operated in 16 countries, primarily in the US (16.5%), Great Britain (13.9%), and Germany (12.5%), and in 15 industry segments (Figure 1), including sawmills (34%), material handling and logistics (26%), brick and concrete industry (9%), and steel mills (6%).

Descriptive statistics are presented in Table A1 (Appendix A). The independent (explanatory) variables used in this study were chosen based on previous studies that identified them as significant for fuel consumption. Among these variables are vehicle distance, speed, number of idles, shock and overload occurrences, engine, driving and idle time, and time spent in different driving modes, time spent and number of lifts in different workload spectra, and variables related to ambient, engine coolant, hydraulic, and transmission oil temperature. For the 285 forklifts, the average forklift drove 29.8 km per day with an average speed of 6.6 km per hour, carrying a total weight of 661 ton and lifting 176 loads. The average time per day that the engine was running while the vehicle was moving or using load handling function was 9.5 h, and the average number of hours a vehicle was idling was 4.1 h. The average time during which a vehicle carried a very heavy load was 0.2 h. On average, the majority of forklifts spent their working time in different workload spectra, but most of them did not spend significant time in heavy load spectra. The average ambient temperature was 16 °C, and the engine coolant temperature, hydraulic fluid temperature, and transmission oil temperature did not exceed their limits. The dependent (output) variables were provided by the company and included average fuel consumption per day, engine hour, load, ton, and ton-meter. On average, one forklift consumed 65 L of diesel fuel per day, 7 L per hour, 1.6 L per load, 0.7 L per ton, and 0.02 L per ton-meter.

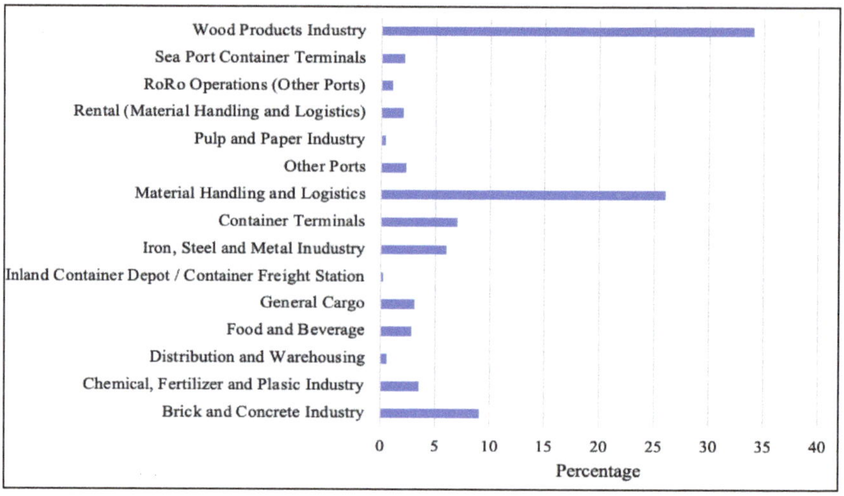

Figure 1. Distribution of vehicles among industry segments.

3.2. Data Preparation and Analysis

The aim of this study was to explore fuel consumption factors using a number of underlying explanatory variables. Partial least-squares regression (PLSR) is a regression method that allows for the identification of latent variables (linear combinations of explanatory variables) and their effects on response variables [51]. Over the last decade, this method has become widely used in various fields of business research, including the Information Systems discipline, marketing, and strategic and operations management [52]. In addition, this method has become popular in the analysis of factors affecting fuel consumption [53,54]. MATLAB software was used for the PLSR analysis.

PLSR is a method that is used for modeling linear regressions between multiple, possibly correlated, explanatory variables and multiple dependent variables. This method combines the basic functions of canonical correlation analysis, principal component analysis, and multiple regressions [55]. The least-squares solution for multiple linear regression [56]:

$$Y = XB + \varepsilon, \tag{1}$$

is given by:

$$B = (X^T X)^{-1} X^T Y. \tag{2}$$

The problem is that $X^T X$ is singular, either because the number of columns (variables) in X exceeds the number of rows (objects) or because of collinearity. PLSR circumvents this by decomposing X to orthogonal scores T and loadings P:

$$X = T P. \tag{3}$$

Furthermore, PLSR regresses Y on the first column of the scores, and its aim is to incorporate information on both X and Y in the definition of the loadings and scores. The loadings and scores are chosen in such a way as to describe, as much as possible, the covariate between X and Y.

PLSR overcomes two key challenges of classical regression methods, namely a large number of correlated explanatory variables and a small sample size with a large number of predictors [57]. Another important advantage of PLSR is that it does not have many specific assumptions for the analyzed data. The data only need to be relatively normally distributed (Figure A1, Appendix B) and cleansed of influential outliers prior to analysis [58]. Correlation coefficients between explanatory variables were strong and significant in most cases, demonstrating potential multicollinearity. Therefore, PLSR was an appropriate method for analyzing the available data.

4. Results

The PLSR technique was used to analyze the effect of the explanatory variables on fuel-related dependent variables. First, the prediction ability of key PLSR models with dependent variables, such as liters per day, liters per hour, liters per load, liters per ton, liter per ton-meter, was established by the percentage of variation accounted for by the principal components. Second, key drivers of fuel consumption in relation to productivity were extracted by analyzing the normal probability plots and bar loads of the most important regression variables.

4.1. Prediction Ability

The choice of PLS factors was made by exploring the percentage of the variance explained in the response variables (Figure A2, Appendix C) and the root mean of the dependent variables. Table 2 provides the percentage variation accounted for by the PLS factors.

The first nine PLS factors included all of the variance information for X and Y. First, by using 39.063% of the information in potential influencing factors, the first nine PLS factors explained 95.984% of the variance in fuel consumption per day. Second, for 40.722% of the information in potential influencing factors for liters per hour, the first nine PLS factors explained 59.729% of the variance. The percentage of variations accounted for by PLS factors demonstrates that fuel per time unit (day and hour) are promising dependent variables to explain fuel consumption reductions based on the available explanatory variables. Third, for 40.451% of the information in potential influencing factors, the first nine PLS factors explained 38.719% of the variance in liters per load. Fourth, for 40.259% of the information in potential influencing factors, the first nine PLS factors explained 32.045% of the variance in liters per ton. Fifth, for 41.377% of the information in potential influencing factors, the first nine PLS factors explained 28.251% of the variance in liters per ton-meter. The percentage of variation accounted for by PLS factors demonstrates that the models do not have strong predictive ability from the explanatory variables in relation to the constructed variables of fuel consumption per load, per ton, and per ton-meters. Thus, more explanatory variables can improve the predictive ability in relation to fuel consumption per load, per ton, and per ton-meters. These dependent variables can also be subject to further examination of whether they account for relevant activities and measures in the physical world in order to find ways to reduce fuel consumption.

4.2. Key Determinants of Fuel Consumption and Productivity

Normal probability plots and bar loads were used to demonstrate the most important regression variables. Normal probability plots helped us to find cut-off limits in order to select important variables for fuel consumption (Figure A1, Appendix B). We began our analysis by focusing on fuel consumption per day and per hour (Figure 2) and further analyzed what factors affect fuel consumption per load, per ton, and per ton-meter (Figure 3). On the left-hand side of each figure, bar loads demonstrate the weight of the most influential factors of fuel consumption decrease and the right-hand side shows the weight of the most important factors that affect fuel consumption increase.

Table 2. Variation accounted for by partial least-squares factors.

Latent Factor	Percentage of Explained Variance for X	Cumulative Percentage of Explained Variance for X	Percentage of Explained Variance for Y	Cumulative Percentage of Explained Variance for Y	Root Mean Squared Error of Prediction
		Liters per day			
1	16.372	16.372	90.645	90.645	12.604
2	5.428	21.800	2.803	93.448	10.548
3	3.245	25.045	1.424	94.872	9.331
4	2.691	27.736	0.542	95.414	8.824
5	2.064	29.800	0.258	95.672	8.573
6	2.168	31.968	0.130	95.802	8.443
7	2.069	34.037	0.091	95.893	8.351
8	2.658	36.695	0.051	95.944	8.299
9	2.368	39.063	0.040	95.984	8.258
		Liters per hour			
1	15.079	15.079	24.089	24.089	1.485
2	7.374	22.453	21.527	45.616	1.257
3	4.218	26.671	5.083	50.699	1.197
4	3.687	30.358	3.530	54.229	1.153
5	2.481	32.839	2.325	56.554	1.124
6	1.930	34.769	1.598	58.152	1.103
7	1.530	36.299	1.086	59.238	1.088
8	2.706	39.005	0.258	59.496	1.085
9	1.717	40.722	0.233	59.729	1.082
		Liters per load			
1	14.698	14.698	18.262	18.262	1.126
2	8.888	23.586	13.841	32.103	1.026
3	3.801	27.387	2.870	34.973	1.004
4	1.924	29.311	1.789	36.762	0.990
5	2.312	31.623	0.832	37.594	0.984
6	2.810	34.433	0.419	38.013	0.980
7	2.278	36.711	0.343	38.356	0.978
8	2.167	38.878	0.222	38.578	0.976
9	1.573	40.451	0.141	38.719	0.975
		Liters per ton			
1	15.628	15.628	14.153	14.153	0.528
2	7.723	23.351	12.18	26.333	0.489
3	3.795	27.146	2.602	28.935	0.481
4	2.159	29.305	1.621	30.556	0.465
5	2.574	31.879	0.654	31.210	0.473
6	2.701	34.580	0.326	31.536	0.472
7	2.179	36.759	0.260	31.796	0.471
8	1.871	38.630	0.151	31.947	0.470
9	1.629	40.259	0.098	32.045	0.470
		Liters per ton-meter			
1	11.463	11.463	13.663	13.663	0.017
2	11.89	23.353	7.814	21.477	0.016
3	3.963	27.316	2.839	24.316	0.106
4	2.466	29.782	1.888	26.204	0.015
5	3.012	32.794	0.795	26.999	0.015
6	2.520	35.314	0.508	27.507	0.015
7	2.187	37.501	0.386	27.893	0.015
8	2.018	39.519	0.221	28.114	0.015
9	1.858	41.377	0.137	28.251	0.015

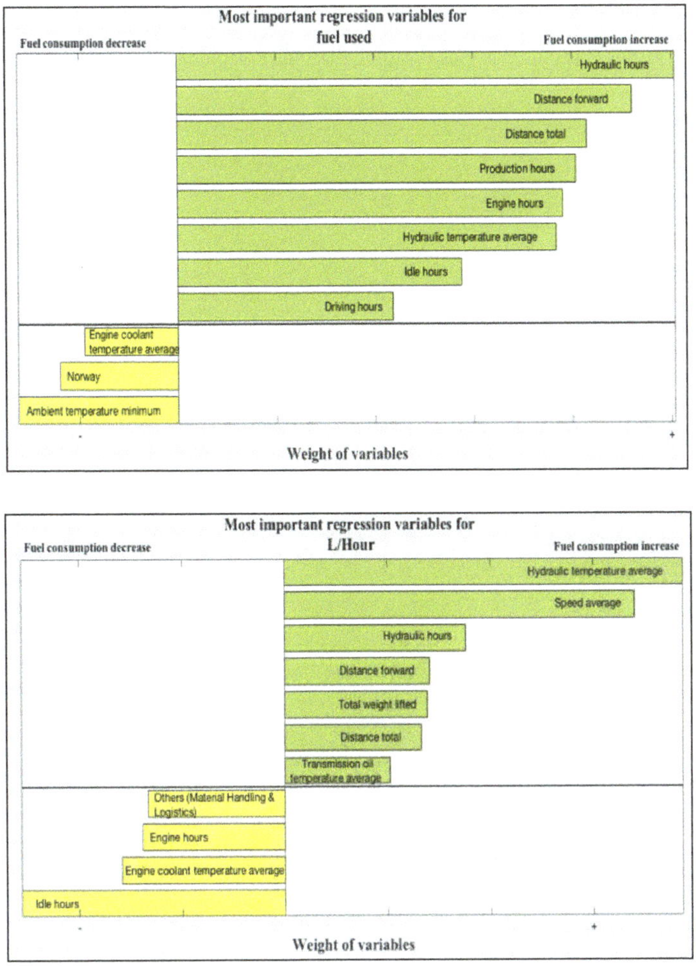

Figure 2. Bar loads of the most relevant variables for fuel consumption per time (liter/day, liter/hour).

The results demonstrated that high fuel consumption per day was mainly caused by distance driven and time-related parameters, such as production, engine, hydraulic driving, and idling hours. Low fuel consumption per day was strongly associated with minimum ambient temperature, and among the different countries, Norway demonstrated the most efficient fuel usage. High fuel consumption per hour depended strongly on distance driven, average speed, and weight lifted. In comparison to other customer segments, the material handling and logistics segment was shown to be the most fuel efficient. Overall, the results demonstrate the importance of travel-related, operations-related, and driver-related factors on fuel consumption per unit of time. Interestingly, the results demonstrated that leaving machines idling for a shorter time period might lead to fuel savings per hour, but in the long run this led to high fuel consumption per day. The results also demonstrated that high hydraulic fluid temperatures can waste fuel, and thus this has to be addressed through maintenance in order to maintain a stable hydraulic system.

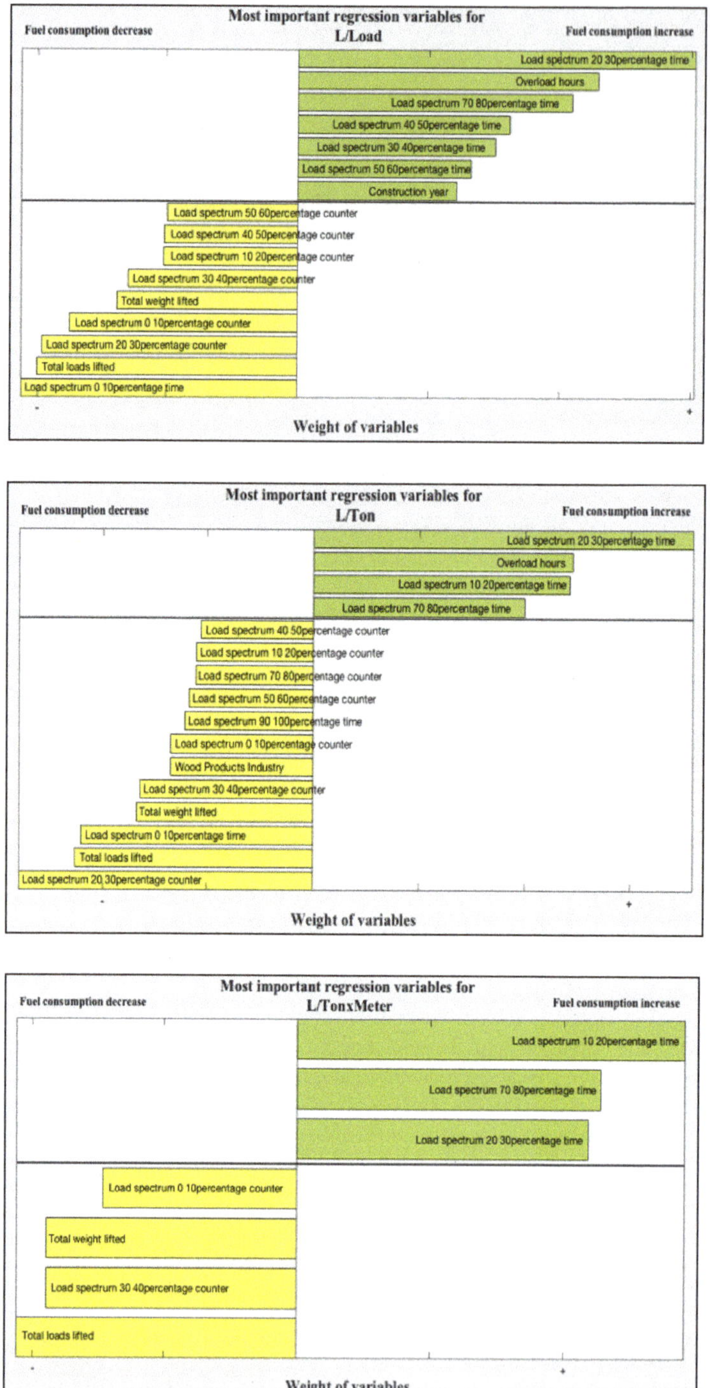

Figure 3. Bar loads of the most relevant variables for fuel consumption and productivity (liter/load, liter/ton, liter/ton-meter).

The results further demonstrated that high fuel consumption per load, per ton, and per ton-meter was associated with time spent in a specific load spectrum. For example, time spent in the load spectrum of 20–30 tons was associated with high fuel consumption per load, per ton, and per ton-meter. Interestingly, a number of lifts in specific load spectra and time spent in these lead spectra in some cases have different effects on fuel consumption. While these factors and their effect as such are interesting, the present study's aim was not to consider one or two factors and their effect on fuel consumption but the whole system of factors together. Overload hours were also associated with high fuel consumption per load and ton. For other segments, the wood products industry was shown to be efficient in terms of fuel consumption and productivity. Although somewhat counterintuitive, total loads lifted and total weight were associated with fuel-saving per load, per ton, and per ton-meter. On the one hand, this can be explained by short distances driven by forklifts, on the other hand, while the less loaded a forklift the less efficient it is, a heavier loaded forklift is more efficient until a certain level and a non-linear behaviour occurs because of the scale effects. This can also be explained by all three dependent variables not having a fixed ratio of driving/lifting/weight for vehicles, and thus to establish how fuel consumption can decrease without losing productivity these variables must be reconsidered.

5. Discussion

While fuel costs are increasing and governments are taking actions towards reducing greenhouse gas emissions, manufacturers and users of heavy-duty equipment are struggling to reduce fuel consumption while improving the productivity of vehicles. Although factors related to fuel consumption are a heavily researched area in road freight transportation and logistics field, the current state of knowledge demonstrates a gap with respect to complementary factors and their interactions, which can reduce fuel consumption and improve the productivity of heavy-duty equipment [1] and, therefore, align with both ecological sustainability and economic productivity. Moreover, making sense of newly collected data via sensors over an extended time period presents another challenge in relation to fuel consumption and productivity. This study attempted to respond to the need for companies to move towards cleaner productivity by finding patterns in a large dataset that are indicative of fuel efficiency and cleaner productivity of heavy-duty equipment, which, in our case, was medium-range forklifts. The present study advances the current literature in the following important ways.

First, our results contribute to the literature that investigates factors of fuel consumption and productivity in the field of road freight transportation and logistics [13,14,16]. In contrast to previous studies, which approached fuel consumption factors in a monolithic manner, studying one or a few factors per study, the present study shows that when several factors are considered at the same time and for a larger set of forklifts that operate in natural settings for a longer time, a more complex situation emerges regarding the factors that affect fuel consumption and thus CO_2 emission. For the first time, this study shows that various factors that have been established as drivers of fuel consumption, when considered jointly, may manifest conflicting contradictors and non-linear behaviour.

Second, our results also contribute to the limited literature that focuses on models that indirectly affect fuel consumption of forklifts through order sequencing, storage allocation, and path minimization [19–23]. These studies are mostly criticized for restricted applicability to the particular operating conditions and difficult application in complex real-life settings. In the present study, we collected and analyzed longitudinal data of forklifts in real-life use. The results from this study reveal that mostly travel-, driver-, and operations-related factors complement each other to increase fuel consumption per unit time, including distance, average speed, and time-related parameters, such as production, engine, hydraulic, driving, and idle hours. The results also demonstrate the importance of the environment- and vehicle-related variables. Additionally, particular industry segments and countries are shown to be more effective in terms of fuel consumption.

Third, besides complementary fuel consumption drivers, the present study supports currently limited evidence on the importance of driver behaviour of forklifts [24]. In contrast to current studies that focus on driver behaviour in freight transportation and logistics in general, there is a limited number of studies that investigate driver behaviour of forklifts in relation to fuel consumption and productivity. The results of the present study demonstrate that driver behavior such as compliance to speed limits and idling can significantly affect the fuel consumption per time unit of a forklift. The impact on fuel efficiency and productivity by this behavior is often highlighted as a promising research direction to identify fuel-saving practices, and the results from this study confirm the importance of driver behaviour as a complementary factor.

The results of the present paper are important for practitioners who focus on drivers of fuel consumption and productivity. In general, the present study demonstrates that several factors available through sensors, of various kinds, should be elaborated in a deliberately synchronized manner in order to improve the fuel consumption and productivity of a vehicle. This study guides practitioners by informing that when considered jointly, various factors that have been established as drivers of fuel consumption may manifest conflicting contradictors.

This study has the following limitations. First, we used only one homogeneous group of vehicles—medium-range forklifts. The analysis can further be applied to a different range of forklifts and adjusted to different types of heavy-duty vehicles, such as reach stackers and tractors. Second, the daily dataset was analyzed for one year and is expandable to include more vehicles and to uncover new patterns in fuel consumption over a longer time. The data from the sensors were sent every second; thus, a more detailed analysis of fine-grained data might also bring new insights into patterns of fuel consumption. Third, the analysis was done on the vehicle level and might further be extended by focusing on the individual driver level. Therefore, future studies over a longer time span and on a larger scale might help to discover new patterns that can be used to adjust fuel consumption and productivity. Finally, while we applied the systems approach of the complementarity theory [59], future experimental studies can explore the nature of the interactions of the various factors identified.

6. Conclusions

In the present paper, an analysis of sensor data aimed at discovering drivers of fuel consumption and productivity was carried out. Most previous studies have focused only on one or a few factors that affect fuel consumption in terms of liters of fuel consumed, and little attention has been paid to complementary relationships among them and their effect on fuel consumption and productivity, which was the target in the present study. An evaluation of the effect of several explanatory variables on fuel consumption revealed the considerable effect of distance, average speed, and time-related variables on overall fuel consumption per unit time. The analysis also demonstrated the importance of activities in different workload spectra and overload hours in relation to fuel consumption per load, per ton, and per ton-meter. In addition, for activity-based parameters, particular industry segments and countries were shown to be more efficient in terms of fuel consumption. In contrast to previous studies, this study demonstrated which combinations of fuel consumption factors can be used to further establish complementary relationships between factors. The results of the study can further be used to conduct controllable experiments to explore the nature of the interactions among particular factors, among which complementary relationships emerge. The results of the study can also be used in a more detailed analysis of forklift activities in different workload spectra and for different dependent variables. The results can also be used to further explore practices in fuel consumption in different countries and industry segments to formulate a list of the best practices. Thus, further analysis can bring new insights into how to reduce fuel consumption and become more cost effective without losing vehicle productivity.

Author Contributions: The individual responsibilities and contributions of the authors are listed as follows: N.P., D.H. and S.C. designed the research; N.P. collected the literature and the data; D.H. guided the research process and revised and edited the manuscript; N.P. and M.K. analyzed the data; N.P., D.H. and M.K. interpreted the results; N.P. wrote the original version of the manuscript; S.C. revised and edited the manuscript.

Funding: This research received no external funding.

Conflicts of Interest: The authors declare no conflict of interest.

Appendix A

Table A1. Descriptive statistics of variables used in the analysis.

Variables	Unit of Measurement	Description	Mean	Standard Deviation
		Counters		
Distance forward	km	Total distance forward covered by a vehicle during a specific time period	24.463	20.707
Distance in reverse	km	Total distance in reverse covered by a vehicle during a specific time period	5.333	6.412
Total distance	km	Total distance covered by a vehicle during a specific time period	29.796	24.230
Idle occurrences	number	Number of times when a vehicle has been idling without performing/producing	8.310	8.867
Shock occurrences	number	Number of shocks (hard braking, crashing into the bumper, crossing a railway, and any other jarring events) experienced by a vehicle	58.240	102.521
Number of overloads	number	Number of times a vehicle lifted more than its rated capacity	15.250	49.380
Total weight	ton	Total number of tons being lifted by a vehicle during a specific time period	660.731	727.788
Total loads lifted	number	Number of loads lifted by a vehicle during a specific time period	175.850	172.781
Speed average	km/h	The average speed a vehicle achieves during a given time period	6.623	3.161
Speed maximum	km/h	The maximum speed of a vehicle within a set time period	20.320	6.763
Diesel level maximum	%	The filling levels of diesel fuel	84.910	22.906
Battery voltage	V	The voltage of the battery	17.188	12.718
		Time		
Driving time	hour	Total number of hours a vehicle is driven (speed greater than 0)	5.273	3.778
Hydraulic time	hour	Total hours of hydraulic function use	2.540	2.004
Idling time	hour	Time the engine is running but the vehicle is not moving or using load handling functions	4.102	3.519
Engine time	hour	Time the engine is running when vehicle is moving or using load handling functions	9.509	6.660
Time in ECO mode	hour	Time the vehicle has been driving in Eco driving mode	0.919	0.925
Time in Normal mode	hour	Time the vehicle has been driving in Normal driving mode	1.814	1.298
Time in Power mode	hour	Time the vehicle has been driving in Power driving mode	2.239	1.560
Production time	hour	Engine time minus idle time	5.408	3.936

Table A1. *Cont.*

Variables	Unit of Measurement	Description	Mean	Standard Deviation
Time in overload	hour	Time during which a vehicle carried a very heavy load	0.187	0.750
		Load spectra (time)		
Load spectrum 0–10percentage time	hour	Time during which a vehicle operated in load spectrum 0–10	2.517	2.418
Load spectrum 11–20percentage time	hour	Time during which a vehicle operated in load spectrum 11–20	0.488	0.582
Load spectrum 21–30percentage time	hour	Time during which a vehicle operated in load spectrum 21–30	0.571	0.814
Load spectrum 31–40percentage time	hour	Time during which a vehicle operated in load spectrum 31–40	0.444	0.687
Load spectrum 41–50percentage time	hour	Time during which a vehicle operated in load spectrum 41–50	0.288	0.383
Load spectrum 51–60percentage time	hour	Time during which a vehicle operated in load spectrum 51–60	0.238	0.369
Load spectrum 71–80percentage time	hour	Time during which a vehicle operated in load spectrum 71–80	0.132	0.264
Load spectrum 81–90percetage time	hour	Time during which a vehicle operated in load spectrum 81–90	0.094	0.271
Load spectrum 91–100percentage time	hour	Time during which a vehicle operated in load spectrum 91–100	0.063	0.193
Load spectrum above 101percentage time	hour	Time during which a vehicle operated in load spectrum above 100	0.255	0.524
		Load Spectra (Number of Lifts)		
Load spectrum 0–10percentage counter	number	Number of lifts in load spectrum 0–10	36.670	48.323
Load spectrum 11–20 percentage counter	number	Number of lifts in load spectrum 11–20	31.755	41.679
Load spectrum 21–30percentage counter	number	Number of lifts in load spectrum 21–30	27.693	37.146
Load spectrum 31–40percentage counter	number	Number of lifts in load spectrum 31–40	18.240	25.740

Table A1. *Cont.*

Variables	Unit of Measurement	Description	Mean	Standard Deviation
Load spectrum 41–50percentage counter	number	Number of lifts in load spectrum 41–50	13.190	24.116
Load spectrum 51–60percentage counter	number	Number of lifts in load spectrum 51–60	9.833	17.099
Load spectrum 61–70percentage counter	number	Number of lifts in load spectrum 61–70	7.676	15.649
Load spectrum 71–80percentage counter	number	Number of lifts in load spectrum 71–80	4.699	10.615
Load spectrum 81–90percentage counter	number	Number of lifts in load spectrum 81–90	2.34	7.699
		Temperature		
Ambient temperature minimum	°C	Minimum ambient temperature during a given time period	10.940	8.045
Ambient temperature maximum	°C	Maximum ambient temperature during a given time period	20.770	9.290
Ambient temperature average	°C	Average ambient temperature during a given time period	16.190	8.371
Engine coolant temperature average	°C	Average engine coolant temperature during a given time period	78.312	11.117
Hydraulic temperature average	°C	Average hydraulic temperature average during a given time period	44.889	13.079
Transmission oil temperature average	°C	Average transmission oil temperature during a given time period	63.907	12.515
		Fuel-related Variables Per Time Unit		
Fuel used	Liter/day	The amount of fuel consumed by a vehicle during a specific time period (per day)	65.409	47.196
Fuel used per hour	Liter/hour	Average fuel consumption per engine hour	7.031	2.391
Fuel used per load	Liter/load	Average fuel consumption per load	1.604	7.398
Fuel used per ton	Liter/ton	Average fuel consumption per ton	0.691	4.925
Fuel used per ton-meter	Liter/ton-meter	Average fuel consumption per ton-meter	0.0216	0.264

Appendix B

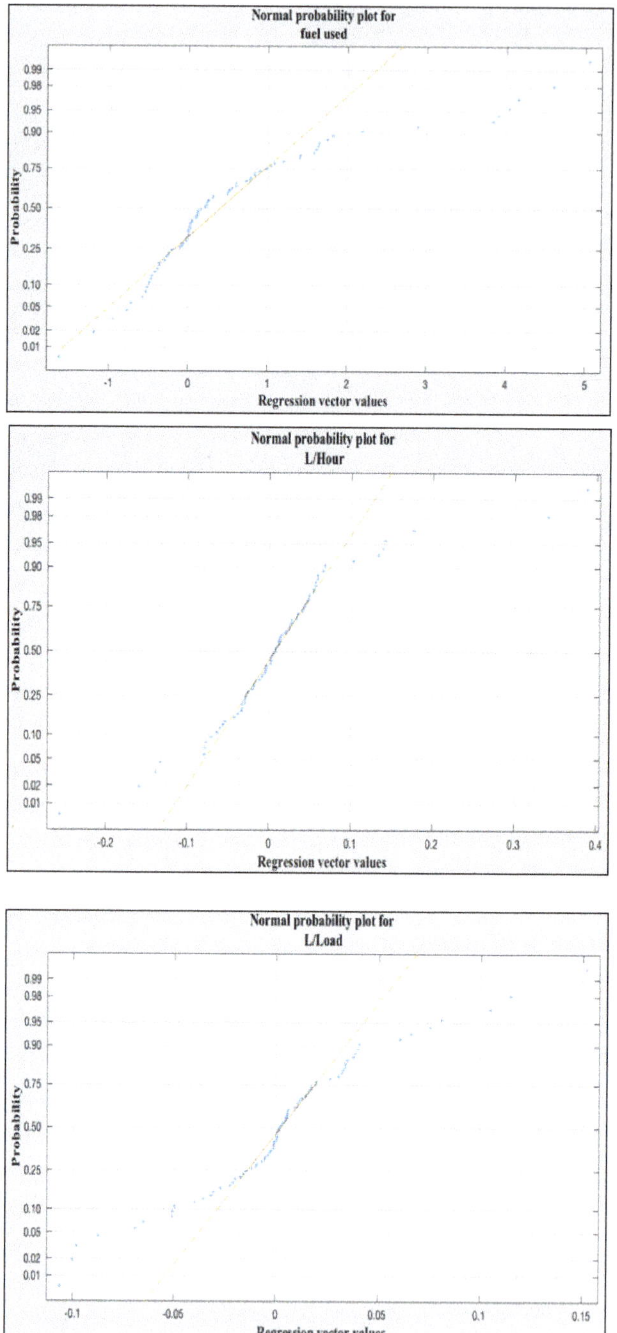

Figure A1. *Cont.*

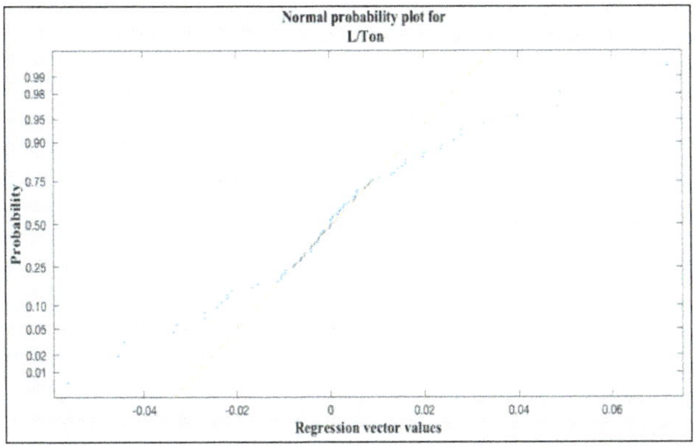

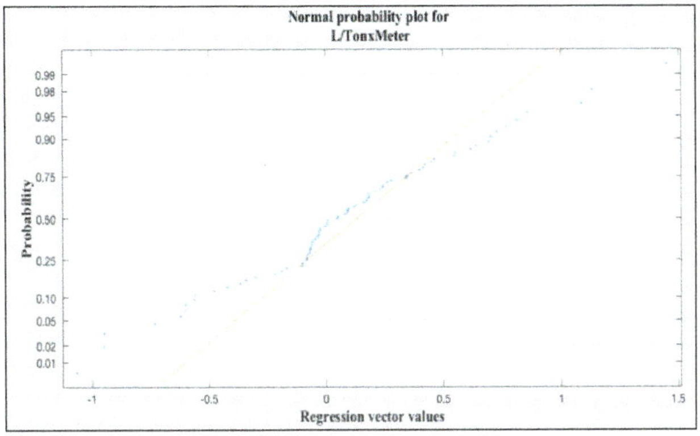

Figure A1. Normal probability plots of the most relevant variables for fuel consumption (liter/day, liter/hour, liter/load, liter/ton, liter/ton-meter). The data that did not follow the straight line were used to find cut-off limits in order to select important variables for fuel consumption.

Appendix C

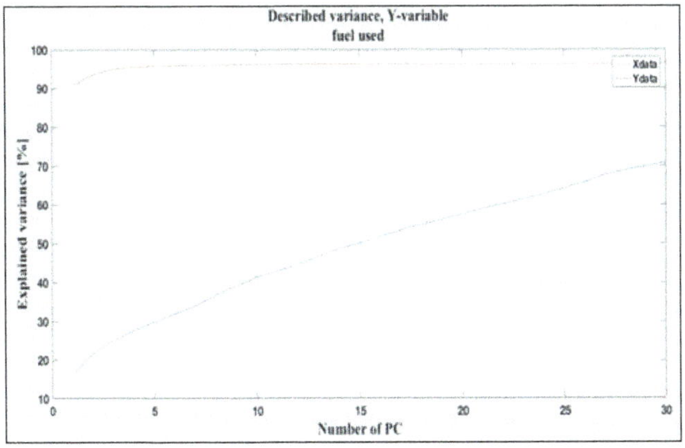

Figure A2. *Cont.*

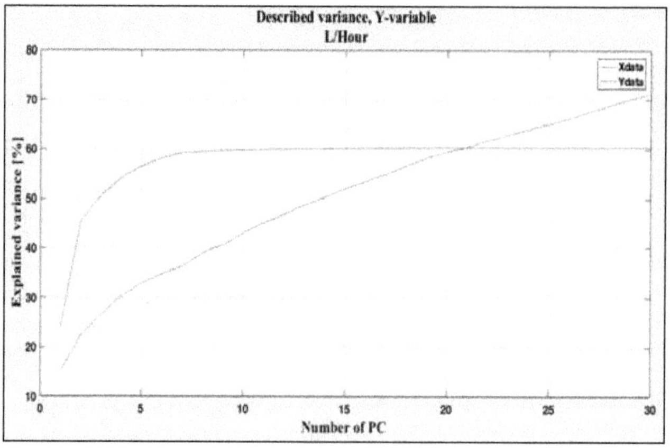

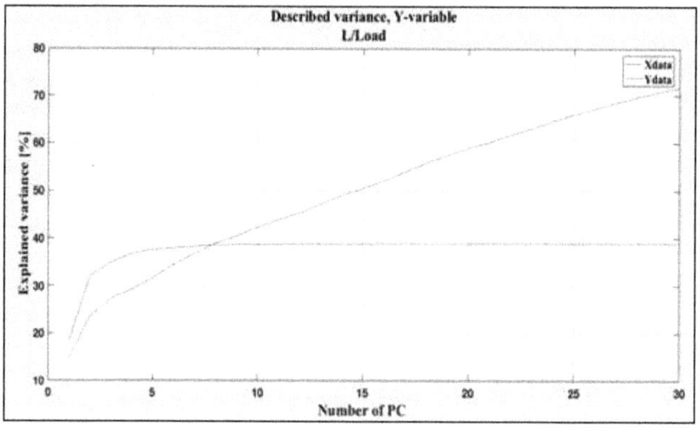

Figure A2. *Cont.*

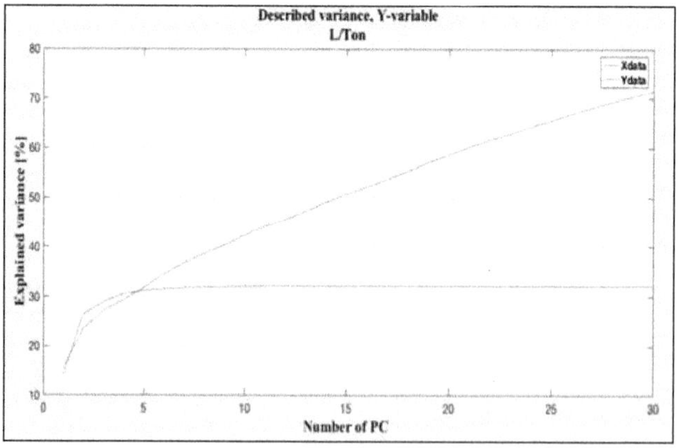

Figure A2. *Cont.*

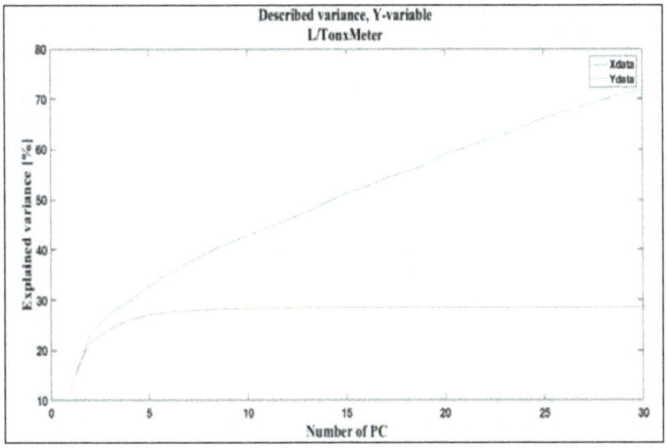

Figure A2. The choice of partial least-squares factors based on explained variance, preserving the essence of the original data (liter/day, liter/hour, liter/load, liter/ton, liter/ton-meter). Those factors that accounted for little variation were excluded from the analysis.

References

1. Ng, F.; Harding, J.A.; Glass, J. An eco-approach to optimise efficiency and productivity of a hydraulic excavator. *J. Clean. Prod.* **2016**, *112*, 3966–3976. [CrossRef]
2. Reşitoğlu, İ.A.; Altinişik, K.; Keskin, A. The pollutant emissions from diesel-engine vehicles and exhaust aftertreatment systems. *Clean Technol. Environ. Policy* **2015**, *17*, 15–27. [CrossRef]
3. Zhang, Y.; Yao, Z.; Shen, X.; Liu, H.; He, K. Chemical characterization of $PM_{2.5}$ emitted from on-road heavy-duty diesel trucks in China. *Atmos. Environ.* **2015**, *122*, 885–891. [CrossRef]
4. Tucki, K.; Mruk, R.; Orynycz, O.; Botwińska, K.; Gola, A.; Bączyk, A. Toxicity of exhaust fumes (CO, NOx) of the compression-ignition (diesel) engine with the use of simulation. *Sustainability* **2019**, *11*, 2188. [CrossRef]
5. Gola, A.; Kłosowski, G. Development of computer-controlled material handling model by means of fuzzy logic and genetic algorithms. *Neurocomputing* **2019**, *338*, 381–392. [CrossRef]
6. Lewis, P.; Fitriani, H.; Arocho, I. Engine variable impact analysis of fuel use and emissions for heavy-duty diesel maintenance equipment. *Transp. Res. Rec.* **2015**, *2482*, 8–15. [CrossRef]
7. Lewis, P.; Rasdorf, W. Fuel use and pollutant emissions taxonomy for heavy duty diesel construction equipment. *J. Manag. Eng.* **2016**, *33*, 04016038. [CrossRef]
8. Song, M.; Wu, N.; Wu, K. Energy consumption and energy efficiency of the transportation sector in Shanghai. *Sustainability* **2014**, *6*, 702–717. [CrossRef]
9. Osorio-Tejada, J.L.; Llera-Sastresa, E.; Hashim, A.H. Well-to-wheels approach for the environmental impact assessment of road freight services. *Sustainability* **2018**, *10*, 4487. [CrossRef]
10. Huo, H.; Yao, Z.; Zhang, Y.; Shen, X.; Zhang, Q.; He, K. On-board measurements of emissions from diesel trucks in five cities in China. *Atmos. Environ.* **2012**, *54*, 159–167. [CrossRef]
11. Harris, I.; Wang, Y.; Wang, H. ICT in multimodal transport and technological trends: Unleashing potential for the future. *Int. J. Prod. Econ.* **2015**, *159*, 88–103. [CrossRef]
12. Leviäkangas, P. Digitalization of Finland's transport sector. *Technol. Soc.* **2016**, *47*, 1–15. [CrossRef]
13. Kan, Z.; Tang, L.; Kwan, M.P.; Zhang, X. Estimating vehicle fuel consumption and emissions using GPS big data. *Int. J. Environ. Res. Public Health* **2018**, *15*, 566. [CrossRef]
14. Cho, W.; Choi, E. DTG Big data analysis for fuel consumption estimation. *J. Inf. Process. Syst.* **2017**, *13*, 285–304.
15. Holzleitner, F.; Kanzian, C.; Stampfer, K. Analyzing time and fuel consumption in road transport of round wood with an onboard fleet manager. *Eur. J. For. Res.* **2011**, *130*, 293–301. [CrossRef]

16. McGordon, A.; Poxon, J.E.; Cheng, C.; Jones, R.P.; Jennings, P.A. Development of a Driver Model to Study the Effects of Real-World Driver Behaviour on the Fuel Consumption. *Proc. Inst. Mech. Eng. Part D J. Automob. Eng.* **2011**, *225*, 1518–1530. [CrossRef]
17. Demir, E.; Bektaş, T.; Laporte, G. A review of recent research on green road freight transportation. *Eur. J. Oper. Res.* **2014**, *237*, 775–793. [CrossRef]
18. Li, Y.; Yu, Y. The use of freight apps in road freight transport for CO_2 reduction. *Eur. Transp. Res. Rev.* **2017**, *9*, 36. [CrossRef]
19. Boenzi, F.; Digiesi, S.; Facchini, F.; Mossa, G.; Mummolo, G. Sustainable Warehouse Logistics: A NIP Model for Non-Road Vehicles and Storage Configuration Selection. In Proceedings of the XX Summer School "Francesco Turco—Operational, Excellence, Experiences", Naples, Italy, 16–18 September 2015; pp. 263–270.
20. Boenzi, F.; Digiesi, S.; Facchini, F.; Mummolo, G. Electric and LPG Forklifts GHG Assessment in Material Handling Activities in Actual Operational Conditions. In Proceedings of the IEEE International Conference on Service Operations and Logistics, and Informatics, Bari, Italy, 18–20 September 2017; pp. 127–132.
21. Roodbergen, K.J. Storage assignment for order picking in multiple-block warehouses. In *Warehousing in the Global Supply Chain*; Springer: London, UK, 2012; pp. 139–155.
22. Gademann, N.; Velde, S. Order batching to minimize total travel time in a parallel-aisle warehouse. *IIE Trans.* **2005**, *37*, 63–75. [CrossRef]
23. Facchini, F.; Mummolo, G.; Mossa, G.; Digiesi, S.; Boenzi, F.; Verriello, R. Minimizing the carbon footprint of material handling equipment: Comparison of electric and LPG forklifts. *J. Ind. Eng. Manag. (JIEM)* **2016**, *9*, 1035–1046. [CrossRef]
24. Al-Shaebia, A.; Khader, N.; Daoud, H.; Weiss, J.; Won Yoon, S. The effect of forklift driver behavior on energy consumption and productivity. *Procedia Manuf.* **2017**, *11*, 778–786. [CrossRef]
25. Günther, W.A.; Mehrizi, M.H.R.; Huysman, M.; Feldberg, F. Debating big data: A literature review on realizing value from big data. *J. Strateg. Inf. Syst.* **2017**, *26*, 191–209. [CrossRef]
26. Hopkins, J.; Hawking, P. Big data analytics and IoT in logistics: A case study. *Int. J. Logist. Manag.* **2018**, *29*, 575–591. [CrossRef]
27. Mikalef, P.; Pappas, I.O.; Krogstie, J.; Giannakos, M. Big data analytics capabilities: A systematic literature review and research agenda. *Inf. Syst. E-Bus. Manag.* **2018**, *16*, 547–578. [CrossRef]
28. Sivarajah, U.; Kamal, M.M.; Irani, Z.; Weerakkody, V. Critical analysis of Big Data challenges and analytical methods. *J. Bus. Res.* **2017**, *70*, 263–286. [CrossRef]
29. Kecojevic, V.; Komljenovic, D. Haul truck fuel consumption and CO_2 emission under various engine load conditions. *Min. Eng.* **2010**, *62*, 44–48.
30. Demir, E.; Bektaş, T.; Laporte, G. An adaptive large neighborhood search heuristic for the pollution-routing problem. *Eur. J. Oper. Res.* **2012**, *2*, 346–359. [CrossRef]
31. Van Woensel, T.; Creten, R.; Vandaele, N. Managing the environmental externalities of traffic logistics: The issue of emissions. *Prod. Oper. Manag.* **2001**, *10*, 207–223. [CrossRef]
32. Bektaş, T.; Laporte, G. The pollution-routing problem. *Transp. Res. Part B Methodol.* **2011**, *45*, 1232–1250. [CrossRef]
33. Demir, E.; Bektaş, T.; Laporte, G. A comparative analysis of several vehicle emission models for road freight transportation. *Transp. Res. Part D Transp. Environ.* **2011**, *16*, 347–357. [CrossRef]
34. El-Shawarby, I.; Ahn, K.; Rakha, H. Comparative field evaluation of vehicle cruise speed and acceleration level impacts on hot stabilized emissions. *Transp. Res. Part D Transp. Environ.* **2005**, *10*, 13–30. [CrossRef]
35. Hari, D.; Brace, C.J.; Vagg, C.; Poxon, J.; Ash, L. Analysis of a Driver Behaviour Improvement Tool to Reduce Fuel Consumption. In Proceedings of the Connected Vehicles and Expo (ICCVE), 2012 International Conference, Beijing, China, 12–16 December 2012; pp. 208–213.
36. Lárusdóttir, E.B.; Ulfarsson, G.F. Effect of driving behavior and vehicle characteristics on energy consumption of road vehicles running on alternative energy sources. *Int. J. Sustain. Transp.* **2015**, *9*, 592–601. [CrossRef]
37. Zaabar, I.; Chatti, K. Calibration of HDM-4 models for estimating the effect of pavement roughness on fuel consumption for US conditions. *Transp. Res. Rec. J. Transp. Res. Board* **2010**, *2155*, 105–116. [CrossRef]
38. Baumgartner, M.; Leonardi, L. Optimierte disposition und telematik steigern effizienz im deutschen SGV. *Int. Verk.* **2004**, *56*, 197–201.
39. Leonardi, J.; Baumgartner, M. CO_2 efficiency in road freight transportation: Status quo, measures and potential. *Transp. Res. Part D Transp. Environ.* **2004**, *9*, 451–464. [CrossRef]

40. Baumgartner, M.; Léonardi, J.; Krusch, O. Improving computerized routing and scheduling and vehicle telematics: A qualitative survey. *Transp. Res. Part D Transp. Environ.* **2008**, *13*, 377–382. [CrossRef]
41. Wang, Y.; Sanchez Rodrigues, V.; Evans, L. The use of ICT in road freight transport for CO2 reduction – An exploratory study of UK's grocery retail industry. *Int. J. Logist. Manag.* **2015**, *26*, 2–29. [CrossRef]
42. Agar, B.J.; Baetz, B.W.; Wilson, B.G. Fuel consumption, emissions estimation, and emissions cost estimates using global positioning data. *J. Air Waste Manag. Assoc.* **2007**, *57*, 348–354. [CrossRef]
43. Hunt, S.W.; Odhams, A.M.C.; Roebuck, R.L.; Cebon, D. Parameter Measurement for Heavy-Vehicle Fuel Consumption Modelling. *Proc. Inst. Mech. Eng. Part D* **2011**, *225*, 567–589. [CrossRef]
44. Grubinger, T.; Wickström, N.; Björklund, A.; Hellring, M. Knowledge extraction from real-world logged data. *SAE Int. J. Commer. Veh.* **2009**, *2*, 64–74. [CrossRef]
45. Roberts, J. *The Modern Firm: Organizational Design for Performance and Growth*; Oxford University Press: Oxford, UK, 2007.
46. Caraman, D.; Constantin, I. Sustainable transport. In *Designing Mobility and Transport Services*; Routledge: Abingdon, UK, 2016; pp. 37–46.
47. Perego, A.; Perotti, S.; Mangiaracina, R. ICT for logistics and freight transportation: A literature review and research agenda. *Int. J. Phys. Distrib. Logist. Manag.* **2011**, *41*, 457–483. [CrossRef]
48. Nguyen, H.O. Critical factors in e-business adoption: Evidence from Australian transport and logistics companies. *Int. J. Prod. Econ.* **2013**, *146*, 300–312. [CrossRef]
49. Evangelista, P. Environmental sustainability practices in the transport and logistics service industry: An exploratory case study investigation. *Res. Transp. Bus. Manag.* **2014**, *12*, 63–72. [CrossRef]
50. Evangelista, P.; Sweeney, E. Information and communication technology adoption in the Italian road freight haulage industry. *Int. J. Logist. Syst. Manag.* **2014**, *19*, 261–282. [CrossRef]
51. Cramer, R.D.; Bunce, J.D.; Patterson, D.E.; Frank, I.E. Cross validation, bootstrapping, and partial least squares compared with multiple regression in conventional QSAR studies. *Quant. Struct. Act. Relatsh.* **1988**, *7*, 18–25. [CrossRef]
52. Peng, D.X.; Lai, F. Using partial least squares in operations management research: A practical guideline and summary of past research. *J. Oper. Manag.* **2012**, *30*, 467–480. [CrossRef]
53. Dindarloo, S.R.; Siami-Irdemoosa, E. Determinants of fuel consumption in mining trucks. *Energy* **2016**, *112*, 232–240. [CrossRef]
54. Wang, T.; Li, H.; Zhang, J.; Lu, Y. Influencing factors of carbon emission in China's road freight transport. *Procedia-Soc. Behav. Sci.* **2012**, *43*, 54–64. [CrossRef]
55. Zhang, M.; Mu, H.; Li, G.; Ning, Y. Forecasting the transport energy demand based on PLSR method in China. *Energy* **2009**, *34*, 1396–1400. [CrossRef]
56. Mevik, B.-H.; Wehrens, R. The PLS package: Principal component and partial least squares regression in R. *J. Stat. Softw.* **2007**, *18*, 1–23. [CrossRef]
57. Wold, S.; Sjöström, M.; Eriksson, L. PLS-regression: A basic tool of chemometrics. *Chemom. Intell. Lab. Syst.* **2001**, *58*, 109–130. [CrossRef]
58. Esposito Vinzi, V.; Chin, W.W.; Henseler, J.; Wang, H. *Handbook of Partial Least Squares: Concepts, Methods and Applications*; Springer: Heidelberg, Germany; Dordrecht, The Netherlands; London, UK; New York, NY, USA, 2010.
59. Ennen, E.; Richter, A. The whole is more than the sum of its parts—Or is it? A review of the empirical literature on complementarities in organizations. *J. Manag.* **2010**, *36*, 207–233. [CrossRef]

sustainability

MDPI

Article

Using Mobile Phones at Work in Personal and Professional Information Processes

Ștefan Andrei Neștian , Silviu Mihail Tiță and Elena-Sabina Turnea *

Faculty of Economics and Business Administration, Alexandru Ioan Cuza University of Iași, Bd. Carol I, nr. 22, 700506 Iași, Romania; nestian@uaic.ro (Ș.A.N.); silviutita@yahoo.com (S.M.T.)
* Correspondence: sabina.turnea@uaic.ro; Tel.: +40-744-951-559

Received: 2 December 2019; Accepted: 27 January 2020; Published: 29 January 2020

Abstract: Employees use mobile phones for several information processes at work, either in relation to their work or their personal life. This study uses descriptive statistics and regression analysis in order to identify which information processes are accessed by employees to reach their personal and professional goals when using mobile phones at work, using a sample of 368 professionals from different fields in Romania. The results of the study show that messaging applications (e-mail, sms, Messenger, Whatsapp, etc.) and searches for information on the Internet are the biggest time consumers for personal purposes, while telephone conversations (voice only) and searches for useful information on the Internet are the biggest consumers of working time for professional purposes. Based on the opinions of employees, we found that the most important effect of mobile phone use at work for personal purposes lies in the fact that it helps employees be more productive through a better work–life balance. The mobile phone was originally designed as a personal device, but today, since employers are allowing or requiring its use, during work, it is also used for professional purposes.

Keywords: mobile phone; information processes; personal information; professional information; employees

---

1. Introduction

The mobile phone can generate social capital, leading to economic, social and political opportunities [1]. Geser states that before the appearance of mobile phones, formal organizations had created sophisticated fixed telephone lines specifically for their structural and organizational purposes [2]. Today, mobile phones are substituting most of the fixed phones and are adding new functions for the users, such as activity recognition using cell phone sensors [3].

Information is especially useful for developing and sustaining a company's competitiveness in terms of its products and services on the market [4–6]. It is achieved by organizational control of information processes that involve information processing such as the acquisition, recording, organization, retrieval, display, or dissemination of information. Information processes have been considered from the information systems theories perspective. We considered the mobile phone as an instrument used by the individual to perform any generally recognized information processing: collect, organize, analyze, store (and retrieve), transmit (and receive), process and display. According to Encyclopedia Britannica, information processing is considered the acquisition, recording, organization, retrieval, display and dissemination of information [7]. The European Commission provides a definition of information processing as "any operation or set of operations such as collection, recording, organization, structuring, storage, adaptation or alteration, retrieval, consultation, use, disclosure by transmission, dissemination or otherwise making available, alignment or combination, restriction, erasure or destruction" [8] (p. 33). A similar definition of information processes can be extracted from Alter, who defines an information system as "a work system whose processes and activities are devoted to processing information, i.e., capturing, transmitting, storing, retrieving, manipulating, and displaying information" [9] (p. 6).

Smartphones are able to realize any of these information processing types. The focus of human behavior defines the purpose of the information processing, differentiating professional and personal purposes. Hence, this study considers two types of information processes involving the use of mobile phones: personal and professional information processes.

Mobile phones are processing information through different software, accessing many kinds of information from different information channels. Information processes connect the user with these channels by the information transmitted or accessed through them (e.g., information processes appear in the use of e-mail, sms, Messenger, Whatsapp, GPS, Waze, etc.). Therefore, it becomes obvious that information processes cannot be treated separately from their related information channels. Due to their various kind of processed information, different software and diverse information channels, this study considers the different practical use of mobile phones in different information processes: games, getting evidence through audio-video recordings for the work done (only for professional purposes), messaging applications (e-mail, sms, Messenger, Whatsapp, etc.), movies/videos viewing applications, music-listening applications (including on-line radio), online stores, orientation applications (maps, GPS, Waze, etc.), phone calls (voice only), search for useful information on the Internet, social networks (Facebook, Twitter, Instagram, etc.), specialized applications made available by the company, and video calls.

What kind of information processes will bring benefits to companies? Just ones used for professional purposes? Or could even the information processes used by employees for private matters sustain their working tasks? This study puts forward several reasons for using mobile phones for personal information processes at work and also stresses the positive and negative effects of mobile phone use at work for personal purposes. However, enterprises need to learn how information should be used in order to generate profitability and be competitive on the market [4], and how a culture of knowledge sharing could be promoted [10].

Today, mobile phones are replacing computers and are used to call, text, send e-mails, run video conferences, do micro-blogging, interact on social-networks, surf the Internet, watch and share videos and pictures, play video games, and utilize a tremendous array of software-driven applications. The main positive aspects of cell phone use (CPU) reported by other studies comprise the following:

- CPU is positively related to anxiety and satisfaction with life [11];
- CPU counts in positive use for organizations as it is important to have knowledge of market and share information and keep in touch with clients and superiors [12,13];
- CPU has positive impact on the experience of work and the ability to effectively solve problems on the spot [12];
- Smartphone promotes autonomy in a workplace, making employees feel better [13].

The main negative aspects to cell phone use (CPU) reported by previous studies include:

- CPU disrupts physical activity behaviour, causing high frequency users to be less physically active and more sedentary in comparison to low frequency users [14];
- Smartphone users are obsessed with their smartphones [15];
- CPU is negatively related to academic performance [11];
- CPU in the manufacturing sector may not positively contribute to productivity gains [13];
- CPU dependence on smartphones at work may increase workers' perception of their job performance and workplace social capital; however, on the negative side, it may lead to the emergence of smartphone addiction symptoms [15];
- CPU negatively affects attention as focus is on chatting, listening to music and other activities, while academic activities are neglected and left to suffer [16];
- Excessive use of smartphones separates people from realities [13];

- When employees use their smartphones to work on their projects from their work, sometimes they bring stress from their workplaces into their private lives at home, so they cannot separate their work and non-work lives [13].

Regarding the possible positive or negative influences when using mobile devices at work for personal purposes, in this study we outline the likely effects that may have an impact on individuals and organizations. These effects (either positive or negative) are related to productivity, efficiency, pace of work, work–life balance (WLB), colleagues from work and stress at work. Personal purposes are related to private life: communication with loved ones, interests regarding home-owning or other properties (e.g., car, personal goods, etc.), contact with friends and relatives, and also information regarding friends and relatives. These purposes have nothing to do with work tasks. Professional purposes are related to the work environment: work tasks, working with colleagues, working hours, deadlines for specific activities, etc. These purposes should not be related to personal issues. However, if we take into account that nowadays individuals work long hours every day and private matters are dealt with at the same time (and sometimes it becomes impossible to do so after working hours), then a work–life balance (WLB) is needed. The concept of WLB indicates to what extent the job allows employees to fulfill their personal life needs, considering their working hours. For WLB, mobile devices play a central role since they constantly provide workers with access to information, keeping them in touch with other people.

As these two issues recharge the engines of competitiveness—information and technology (mobile phone, the Internet, etc.), considering the return rates on digital investment [17]—it is important for managers to give proper importance to this mix if they wish to create a business-friendly, sustainable and value-added business.

The mobile phone has become a device that many of us cannot not live without, with many aspects of our daily life being influenced by its use [18]. Data included in the Human Development Index comprise a component on mobile phone subscription per 100 inhabitants, showing that the number of mobile subscriptions per 100 inhabitants in Romania between 2000–2010 grew by approximately 10.54 times, from 11.3 to 119.2, reaching a ratio of more than one subscription per inhabitant [19]. As the percentage of the population using the Internet on various devices grew from 3.6% in 2006 to 59.5% in 2016 [19], we can assume that the lives of Romanian workers have been influenced by the use of mobile phones and by Internet connectivity. Smartphone adoption by workers is similar all over the world; managers are facing the challenge of efficient integration of these new devices into the daily routine of their workers. It has been found that research is needed not only to determine how more mindful usage of technology influences employee engagement and effectiveness, but also to determine how the most effective norms around these practices could be created [20].

Given the large variety of apps available for today's smartphones, it is quite difficult to describe a complete taxonomy of areas in which these devices can be used. According to Yim and Gomez, mobile phones have three major intervention areas [21]:

- Communication with others, generating information, knowledge, emotional support, etc.;
- The process of focusing on information, which is connected to occupational practices and widening of knowledge, and enriching them;
- Flexibility in life at work.

The focus of our research is on the use of mobile phones at work, its main research question being how mobile phones are used by employees and for which purposes. We investigated several characteristics of the relationship between the use of mobile phones at work and which information processes are accessed by employees for personal and professional purposes, discovering that mobile phone use, as a knowledge-sharing instrument, is an important aspect at work. We consider that today, smartphones are the most used mobile devices on the market. In this study, we have not considered simple mobile phones, with no Internet connection, as nowadays these are rarely used. We also considered that any available use of a mobile phone involves the participation of an individual in an information process, since this device requires the user to acquire, record, organize, retrieve, display or disseminate information in relation to another individual or software. The phone calls, video calls, messaging, or use of any available apps involves the participation of an individual in an information process.

2. Theoretical Framework and Hypotheses

The access to information by means of smartphones is linked to learning processes. In a study involving students from Jamaica, it was found that when a mobile phone is used as a learning tool, there is pleasure when using it [22]. In addition, a mobile phone becomes an opportunity to rethink the higher education system, with students being always ready to use it in the classrooms for learning [22]. The communication function of these devices has consequences for the use of authority. In some cases, the use of mobile phones leads to the exclusion of authority's delegation to subordinates, as managers are always in touch with what is happening in the company [2], being able to call any subordinate on their mobile phone.

The unlimited access to worldwide sources of information changes the practical perspective of bounded rationality in decision-making. As Bratianu et al. assume, decision-makers should acknowledge the fact that good decisions rely on a manifold approach that simultaneously integrates various types of knowledge, intuition and bounded rationality [23]. From this perspective, the use of mobile phones at work expands the types of knowledge instantly available to a decision- maker, be it internal or external information.

This simple device (mobile phone) can also invade people's personal life. For example, in the case of doctors, who can be called at any time in their leisure moments, mobile phones bring a way for patients to notify them in case of urgent need [2]. Ultimately, a mobile phone is seen on the market as a marketing tool. This is due to the fact that the target audience is directly or indirectly contacted (either by voice calls or by text messages, etc.), based on the information that phone operators already have (age, marital status, occupation, domicile, number of children, etc.) [24].

2.1. Knowledge Management through Mobile Phones

The connection of mobile devices with the knowledge management field comes from the fact that the use of mobile phones expands knowledge-sharing [25]. High availability and ease of access, for practically any category of information, are basic conditions for knowledge sharing that are built into mobile phones. Access to social networks is, by its very nature, a knowledge-sharing activity. This wave of change affects the prospects of companies as regards the use of mobile phones in their information systems and knowledge management system. Pitichat states that, "every single company needs to work on a flow of information and knowledge in order to develop their employees to make them more productive" [13] (p. 5). This way, people can share information and knowledge easily for several purposes, whether personal or professional.

The use of smartphones, flows of information and knowledge in and out of an organization, without borders, creates a richer and potentially more effective information environment. Bratianu stresses that knowledge flows from individuals to groups of people and then to the whole organization [26], and, since organizations are open systems, knowledge flows across boundaries towards external business environments.

The adoption of smartphones at work has also been assessed by Ahmed et al. using a Technology Acceptance Model (TAM) [27]. Using this model, the author explains the perceptions of using new technologies, underlining their ease of use and usefulness that, in turn, affects the intention of adopting social media as a tool for knowledge sharing [27]. The TAM model has been widely applied in research on the use of social media for knowledge sharing as a means of looking into different scenarios for knowledge sharing, and for emerging Information Technology (IT) [27].

2.2. *Differetiating Personal and Professional Information Processes through Mobile Phones*

Mobile and smartphones, together with the Internet, digital television, and smart electronics, are new technologies that have brought about new e-business opportunities [28]. For instance, more and more Romanian users are accessing the Internet from their personal mobile phones [28]. This creates new opportunities for doing business in the online environment, removing several costs for companies. Chandramat et al. argue that communication barriers with anyone in the world have disappeared through voice calls, and multimedia messages have become increasingly important, being real engines of growth, alongside classical voice services [29]. In personal life, mobile phones are not only used for communicating with others. Smartphones have reached a much higher degree of utilization through such applications as calendar appointments, social networking, on-line radio, music, and games applications [30].

Problematic smartphone use is facilitated by such characteristics of technology as easy access, the possibility of escaping daily life, being able to remain anonymous online, and the frequency of alerts and messages. Popular apps such as Facebook are designed in such a way that the amount of time people spend on them increases [31]. The time spent each day (on average) at the workplace accessing different information channels has reached 1.55 h on social networking sites, and 1.44 h daily on seeking entertainment on the Internet (e.g., music, movies, videos, etc.), and 1.46 h on knowledge-related sites [32]. Whatsapp is the most used application, followed by Facebook and Gmail [32].

Mobile games are video games played online via a mobile device, being particularly popular when downloaded for free (e.g., "premium game"—games played for free and where customers can pay for extra features), and can be single-player or multiplayer games [33]. Moreover, the social elements of most mobile games are significant features in current digital gaming, as social networking sites (SNSs) are successfully integrated and used across many gaming platforms [34]. Earlier findings suggest smartphone gaming, specifically casual gaming, is one of the main activities users engage in, but it is not the most popular activity, as social networking (i.e., using Facebook) is more prevalent [34]. While games can be used during personal time, we believe that they should not be used during working hours since playing a game requires full visual attention to the game and the periodic use of hands for controlling behaviour in the game. For these reasons, we consider that spending time playing games on the mobile phone is highly unlikely to happen during work. That is why we consider that, in prioritising the time spent on the mobile phone at work, playing games should be one of the last choices—the main choices should be related to work needs, and the use of professional applications. Therefore, the following hypothesis has been formulated:

Hypothesis 1 (H1). *There is a negative correlation between the use of mobile phones in the workplace for professional purposes and the use of game applications.*

Even if mobile phones do not bring happiness, a recent study reported all respondents had confirmed that mobile phones make them happier and help them find a job more easily [1]. In another study, Yim and Gomez report that mobile phones helped respondents reduce their transport costs and improve their social relationships [21]. At the same time, mobile phones are more effective as they facilitate better communication for informal groups, beyond any control from organizations [35]. However, given that companies invest in specialized applications for mobile phones (used for professional purposes), Geser agrees that the use of mobile phones at work for personal purposes should be regulated by a constant procedure, which should be controlled [35].

According to Pitichat, there are three directions in the use of smartphones at the workplace: (i) autonomy—many companies have started using a Bring Your Own Device (BYOD) policy that can reduce costs and increase productivity; (ii) relationships—smartphones have been integrated into people's lives. Therefore, it would be counterproductive if companies prohibited employees from bringing their smartphones to work. Although there are some companies that totally prohibit their employees from using their own smartphones at work for security reasons, they provide to their employees a smartphone to be used at work; (iii) knowledge sharing—every single company needs to work on a flow of information and knowledge in order to develop their employees and make them more productive [13]. With the integration of smartphones and social network applications, people can share information and knowledge more easily [13]. Also, the "internal social networks have also experienced a rise in popularity, offering to employees and managers a knowledge-share opportunities and a virtual collaboration platform that keeps e-mail inboxes from being overwhelmed" [13] (p. 5). Companies have specialized applications, such as cloud computing, social-sharing sites like Facebook, video-sharing sites like Youtube, and document-sharing site like GoogleDocs [13].

Considering the benefits for the company, there are several acceptable uses of mobile phones in the workplace. Calling colleagues or partners is a natural use of any phone at the workplace. Text messaging, such as SMS, has been seen for a long time as a feature of mobile phones. However, the smartphone supplements classic mobile phone capabilities with computer capabilities. In order to understand the prevalence of one of the two different uses of smartphones at work, we decided to verify what kind of capability is most often used: the classic mobile phone (represented by calls and messaging) or the computer connected to the Internet. We consider the use of specialized applications made available by the company as most representative of the use of the computer capabilities of smartphones. Therefore, the second hypothesis has been formulated:

Hypothesis 2 (H2). *Most often, the mobile phone is used for professional purposes in the workplace through specialized applications made available by the company.*

The number of outgoing and incoming calls and their duration leads to a considerable amount of time that is lost through cell phone conversations. In this sense, Colbert et al. argue that research is needed to set up rules and practices for using technology at the workplace [20], even if there is a study confirming the discrepancies between what employees declare to be the time spent on phone calls for personal issues, and the real time spent on mobile phone calls [36].

Donya and Kumah reported that 47% of respondents need a mobile phone to carry out their working tasks, and by default, the rest of the 53% of respondents use their mobile phones for other purposes [37]. In another study, more than half of respondents admitted taking their mobile phone with them wherever they went [12]. Moreover, employees are expected at work to undertake individual responsibility concerning the use of their mobile phones for personal purposes, so it is advisable that they use their phones at lunch or tea breaks [12].

As social networks have invaded the virtual environment that employees are logging into every day, managers have begun to think about how these socialization applications should be integrated into the practices of companies [38].

Bakhuisen argues that the main categories of information exchange at the workplace are [39]:

- Task information related to tasks at hand, followed by information about the policy and plans of the organization (sharing vertically or top-down);
- Management information related to results, indicators, and monitoring (leaders need to know how an organization is performing);
- Social information, often given by the human resources department, covering such topics as trainings, pensions, or sick leave.

We should add to this list the information accessed from sources outside the organization, information from open sources or social networks. All these categories of information could be transferred (sent, uploaded or downloaded) using a mobile phone.

In a study conducted by Londhe et al., most respondents reported being compatible with listening to music and radio on their mobile phone at work, claiming it helps them reduce stress at the workplace [1]. At the same time, the use of the mobile phone is associated with a relaxed and positive working environment [1,40]. Similarly, Wahla and Awan underline that the use of mobile phones at the workplace for professional purposes has positive effects: it keeps the workers in touch with their managers and customers, while employees are kept up-to-date with the information on the market [12]. The findings of the same study point out that employees working in services had reported working more efficiently with a mobile phone and, therefore being more efficient [12]. Also, as people are responsible for their use of mobile phones, they do not disturb the work of other colleagues [12].

In addition, the study of Donya and Kumah reported that 26.7% of respondents used their mobile phone extensively to spread information related to working tasks, while 16.7% used their phones less intensely for the same purpose [37]. The same authors also reported that 46.7% of respondents do not use their mobile phone to spread or receive information related to working tasks [37].

According to Wahla and Awan, employees working in production are exposed to risks if they use their mobile phones while working, having a negative impact on their productivity [12]. Also, mobile phones distract the attention of employees and can lead to a lower labour productivity, disturbing the activity of other colleagues [12]. Therefore, it is important for employees to use cell phones only in cases of emergency during working hours, or for a limited time at lunch time or during other breaks [12]. The same authors state that text messages have been preferred by employees as they can hide from supervisors, and the overexploitation of the mobile phones for other than professional purposes should worry managers [12].

Summarising the arguments above, we can conclude that text messaging might be the first choice for using a smartphone for personal purposes for the following reasons:

- Employees can hide from supervisors when using their smartphone;
- Duration is considerably lower compared to cell phone conversations, with messaging distracting the attention of employees from work for shorter period of time;
- Personal interaction is not synchronous, compared to cell phone conversations which require synchronous interaction, giving the worker more freedom of choice as to when to detract attention from work;
- Messaging less disturbs the work of other colleagues, compared to phone calls;
- Several messaging applications are now available for social media.

Therefore, the following hypothesis has been formulated:

Hypothesis 3 (H3). *Most often, the mobile phone is used for personal purposes in the workplace through messaging applications (e-mail, sms, Messenger, Whatsapp, etc.).*

Nowadays, there are more and more discussions related to smartphone addiction [30,40–44]. In opposition, Ozkan and Solmaz deny this idea, in particular for Generation Z, saying that this generation is not addicted but has a habit of using smartphones as it is something usual [45]. This generation also wants to express its personality through social networks [45]. Kumar and Devi argue that most social media users are part of a homogeneous group, so the financial investments should follow their needs [46]. Finally, Potongsangarun et al. discuss the attitude towards mobile phone networks as being a function depending on three variables: personal factors, behavior and marketing [47]. Tan et al. admit that using mobile phones, and especially their applications, leads to less face to face interaction, and, ultimately, to loneliness [48]. As we can see from the previous arguments, social networks are characterised by a special feature when we look at the information processes. They allow multiple types of knowledge sharing: sharing thoughts, images and music. These networks enable people to express their personality and to feel a sense of group belonging. They create more context for information than simple Internet pages and generate more emotional reactions from users, leading to powerful emotional attractiveness. Compared to Internet pages, used for searching information, which are static and passive informational environments, social networks are vibrant, dynamic, emotional environments. People experience a feeling of connectivity with their friends and acquaintances and, at work, this need for connectivity can enter into conflict with the need to focus attention on the work to be done.

In analysing this conflict, we want to see if the propensity of employees to increase the time spent using smartphones at work brings an increase or a decrease in time spent on social networks. A decrease of time spent on social networks, when time spent on smartphone at work increases, will show that some restraining factors are manifested. In accordance to what has been stated above, this study hypothesizes that:

Hypothesis 4 (H4). *There is a positive correlation between the use of mobile phone at the workplace for personal purposes and access to social networks (Facebook, Twitter, Instagram, etc.).*

3. Research Methodology

3.1. Research Instrument, Data Collection and Sample

The aim of this study is to suggest two regression models to show which information processes are accessed by employees for personal and professional purposes when using mobile phones at work. It is a quantitative research that has been conducted using an online research questionnaire.

The questionnaire comprises 24 questions, with many sub-questions (items) that collected the ratings given by respondents on a 5-point Likert scale (1 = "never"; 5 = "very often" or 1 = "totally agree"; 5 = "totally disagree"), using rating names adapted to each question. Many of the items of this tool are related to information processes and information channels accessed through mobile phones, already discussed in the results of other studies [1,2,13,21,26,30,35,37,40,41,44,49], including perceptions of the behavior of managers related to the use of mobile devices at work, plus personal data covering nationality, age, gender, the highest level of education reached in a specific field. However, as this study focuses only on information processes used at work for personal or professional purposes, the additional collected data will be used in future research.

Along with the demographic variables, the whole questionnaire includes 95 items. The internal consistency of the items was tested only on 40 sub-questions in the questionnaire (those used for the current paper), excluding the items related to demographic variables. The Cronbach's α coefficient of these research sub-questions had a value of 0.868 (details in Table 1), higher than 0.600, which indicates that the internal consistency of the items has been reached.

Table 1. Reliability Statistics for the items used in the current paper.

Cronbach's α	Number of Items *
0.868	40

* The items related to demographic variables were excluded.

This instrument was pretested at the beginning of July 2018 and was subsequently modified. It was pretested using interviews with 10 specialists in such fields as marketing research, marketing analysis, engineering and education, who provided feedback and ideas for modifying it. The interviews were conducted in order to ensure that the items of the questionnaire are understandable and easy to complete. The participants made improvements, depending on the nature of their experience, both in terms of question formulation, type of variables and statistical analysis. The main improvements that have been made to the questionnaire in the pre-testing phase were: the informational channels were listed in order to clarify the items (for example: messaging applications (E-mail, sms, Messenger, WhatsApp, etc.), social networks (Facebook, Twitter, Instagram, etc.)); a distinction was made between telephone calls (voice only) and video calls (video calls) and the possibility of not using the mobile phone at work at all was also considered.

The questionnaire was distributed by e-mail and on social networks using a message that presented the study's aim, so as to stimulate the curiosity of potential respondents and invite them to take part in the research. The invitation to fill in the questionnaire also contained a questionnaire link, and was sent by the authors of this study. To complete the questionnaire, the respondents needed 15 min.

As all the potential respondents could not be counted (as we used such social networks as Facebook), we have not computed the response rate. Nonetheless, 368 valid responses from professionals working in Romania in different fields of activity were collected online between mid-July and December of 2018, using convenience sampling.

Sample respondents (N = 368, see details in Table 2) in the questionnaire included several socio-demographic characteristics, which can be summarized as follows: Romanian nationality; aged between 18 and over 48 (with the following distribution: 13% aged 18–23, 39% aged 24–29, 22% aged 30–35, 14% aged 36–41, 7% aged 42–47 and 5% aged over 48); gender (69% females and 31% males); highest level of education (with the following distribution: high school 5%, post-secondary 1%, undergraduate degree 42%, postgraduate degree 47% and phd degree 5%). The questionnaire was completed by people who work in organizations in various fields of production and services (see details in Table A7).

Table 2. Case Processing Summary.

Responses	N	%
Valid	368	100.0
Excluded(a)	0	0.0
Total	368	100.0

3.2. Developed Variables And Models and Calculation Of Information Processes Intensity

The proposed regression models are multiple and linear, which implies that the target link between the variables is proportional, with the occurrence of at least two independent variables. The general form of the multiple linear model is [50] (p. 90)

$$Y = \beta 0 + \beta 1 \times X1 + \beta 2 \times X2 + \ldots + \beta p \times Xp + \epsilon \tag{1}$$

where:

$\beta 0$ = constant
$\beta 1, \beta 2, \ldots, \beta p$ = regression coefficients for each independent variable
$X1, X2, \ldots, Xp$ = independent variables
Y = dependent variable
ϵ = residual variable

In order to design the regression model showing which information processes are accessed by employees for their personal purposes when using mobile phones at work, we have used the dependent variable—use of mobile phone at work for personal purposes (with possible answers "Yes/No")—and the independent variables—games, messaging applications (e-mail, sms, Messenger, Whatsapp, etc.), movies/videos viewing applications, music listening applications (including on-line radio), online stores, orientation applications (maps, GPS, Waze, etc.), phone calls (voice only), search for useful information on the Internet, social networks (Facebook, Twitter, Instagram, etc.), specialized applications made available by the company and video calls (with possible answers the using of these information processes on a scale from 1—minimum to 5—maximum).

For the regression model showing which information processes are accessed by employees for their professional purposes when using mobile phones at work, we have used the dependent variable—use of mobile phone at work for professional purposes (with possible answers "Yes/No")—and the independent variables—games, getting evidence through audio-video recordings for the work done, messaging applications (e-mail, sms, Messenger, Whatsapp, etc.), movies/videos viewing applications, music listening applications (including on-line radio), online stores, orientation applications (maps,

GPS, Waze, etc.), phone calls (voice only), search for useful information on the Internet, social networks (Facebook, Twitter, Instagram, etc.), specialized applications made available by the company and video calls (with possible answers the using of these information processes on a scale from 1—minimum to 5—maximum).

The dependent variables for both regression models were simple, in line with the aim of the study to confirm the action of using mobile phone at work for personal and/or professional purposes. As for the independent variables, these consist of the choices of respondents (in a declarative manner) in using mobile phones for specific information processes through their related channels.

We have selected the same independent variables as for dependent variables (the action of using mobile phone at work for personal/professional purposes) in order to maintain data comparability, except one independent variable—getting evidence through audio-video recordings for the work done—which is obviously specific only to professional purposes. To select the independent variables, we took two aspects into account: their discussion in previous studies, and whether they were realistic for the working environment in Romania.

In the analysis, we also have calculated the intensity of the use of information processes (in percentages), which represents an indicator related to the distance between minimum and maximum at which the mean of the use of information processes is located.

Using a scale with responses from 1 (minimum) to 5 (maximum) for using information processes, the distance between extremities is four intervals (therefore, it will result in the denominator value $5 - 1 = 4$). To normalize the numerator between 0–4, it is necessary to subtract a point (so it will result in the numerator value mean − 1). Therefore, the following formula was used

$$\begin{gathered}\text{Intensity of using an informational process P (\%)} = \\ (\text{Mean for using the informational process P} - 1)/(5 - 1) \times 100\end{gathered} \quad (2)$$

To present synthetic results other than the regression analysis, we have used specific items and responses in the questionnaire that are described in the results section.

4. Results

Respondents were asked to specify the percentage of time spent on using mobile phones at the workplace for personal and professional purposes. The results are shown in Table 3.

Table 3. Use of mobile phones for personal purposes at work.

Item	Answer	Total	Percentage
Use of mobile phone for personal purposes at work	No	62	16.85
	Yes	306	83.15
Total		368	100

On one hand, 83.15% of respondents declared using mobile phones at work for personal purposes. On the other hand, 16.85% denied it. More specifically, respondents in the second category work mainly in the following areas: public administration, defence and public order, commerce, construction, the manufacturing and extractive industry, engineering, education, health services, financial and insurance services, transport.

Being a fairly wide range of industries, we may consider that the use of mobile phones at work for personal purposes is largely based on individual choice, and is clearly influenced by the personal characteristics of each person [40]. Besides, the Pearson correlation coefficient between the use of mobile phones at work for personal purposes and field of activity (0.037) indicates a weak positive correlation (details in Table A1).

Respondents were also asked if their bosses prohibit and penalize the use of mobile phone for personal purposes during work. The question had five possible answers on a scale from 1—minimum to 5—maximum (1 = "never"; 2 = "rarely"; 3 = "sometimes"; 4 = "very often"; 5 = "always") and the results indicated an average of 1.71 with a standard deviation of 1.02. The distribution of the answers was: 61% never, 16% rarely, 18% sometimes, 3% very often, 2% always. As long as most of the respondents who are part of this research sample declared that their bosses do not prohibit or penalize the use of the mobile phone for personal purposes at work, the present study makes sense for using mobile devices for personal purposes at work.

A total of 68.75% of respondents declared using their mobile phone for work purposes, while 31.25% denied it (details in Table 4). In a further analysis, individuals in the first category are currently working in the following fields of activity: public administration, commerce, information and telecommunications (IT), extractive industry, engineering, education, energy production and distribution, health services, financial and insurance services, shows, cultural and recreational activities, tourism, hotels and restaurants, and other areas.

Table 4. Use of mobile phone for professional purposes at work.

Item	Answer	Total	Percentage
Use of mobile phone for professional purposes at work	No	115	31.25
	Yes	253	68.75
Total		368	100

According to the Pearson correlation coefficient (−0.133), there is a weak negative correlation between the field of activity and the use of a mobile phone for professional purposes correlation (details in Table A2). The ability to use phones at work for such purposes depends on company size, company policy, leadership, etc.

Most respondents (32%) reported using mobile phones at work, 80% for professional and 20% for personal purposes. Moreover, 19% admitted the opposite: the mobile phone is used by 20% of respondents for professional and by 80% for personal purposes. Finally, 16% of them use the mobile phone 60% for professional and 40% for personal purposes. Extremities indicate that 12% of respondents use their mobile phone strictly for personal purposes, and only 4% for professional purposes (see details in Figure 1).

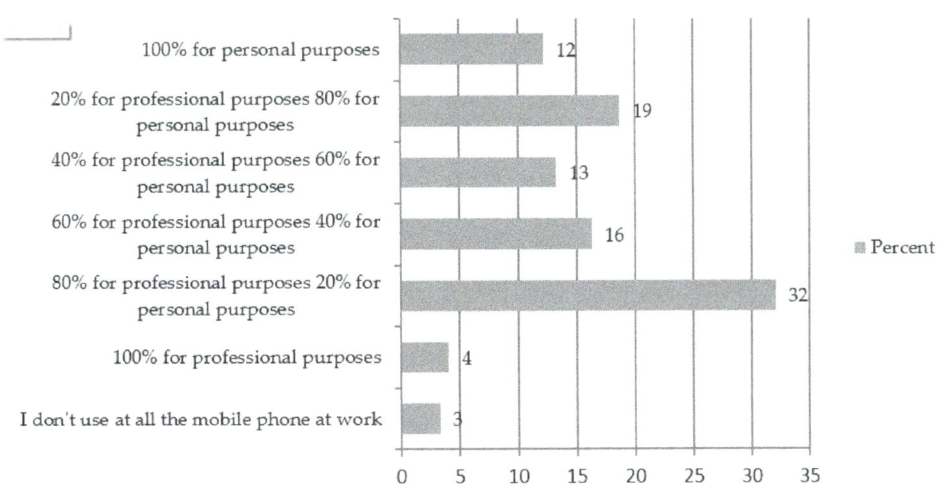

Figure 1. Percentages for personal/professional use of mobile phone at work.

It is natural for employees to use their mobile phone, depending on the nature of their work. For example, in the back office, it is normal for financial services to use mobile phone discussions in order to solve specific problems, while in the field of constructions, at the workplace, it is very important for the mobile phone to be used with caution when performing tasks in difficult working conditions. Finally, for the considered sample, the mobile phone shows its functionality, especially from a professional point of view.

4.1. Personal Use of Mobile Phone in Information Processes at Work

Respondents were asked to tick on a scale from 1 (never) to 5 (very often) how they use the mobile phone for personal purposes at work. This question does not go into personal details (how much time is dedicated to discussions, with whom are the discussions, what kind of information is being searched on the Internet, etc.). Instead, the item provides a global view of the types of information processes that are accessed at work and are not related to working tasks.

Table 5 shows the averages for each of the personal information processes taken into consideration and the significant differences between groups, considering the following demographic variables: gender, age and the highest level of education.

Table 5. Personal information processes at work through different information channels (ranked decreasingly) and significant differences between groups.

Personal Information Processes	Mean (N = 368)	Std. Deviation	*p* for Kruskal Wallis Test *		
			Gender	Age	Highest Level of Education
Messaging applications (e-mail, sms, Messenger, Whatsapp, etc.)	3.59	1.18	0.118	0.002	0.843
Search for useful information on the Internet	3.43	1.24	0.191	0.029	0.663
Phone calls (voice only)	3.34	1.10	0.771	0.986	0.958
Social networks (Facebook, Twitter, Instagram, etc.)	3.01	1.34	0.185	0.000	0.470
Orientation applications (maps, GPS, Waze, etc.)	2.45	1.39	0.058	0.634	0.721
Online stores	2.17	1.21	0.652	0.106	0.300
Music listening applications (including on-line radio)	2.11	1.38	0.408	0.002	0.224
Specialized applications made available by the company	1.96	1.30	0.234	0.639	0.368
Movies/videos viewing applications	1.88	1.20	0.128	0.007	0.032
Video calls	1.39	0.77	0.066	0.049	0.164
Games	1.35	0.77	0.011	0.000	0.001

* $p < 0.05$.

Most employees use text messaging applications (e-mail, sms, Messenger, Whatsapp, etc.) with an average of 3.59 out of five (intensity of use of 64.75%). The intensity of 64.75% was obtained as follows: $(3.59 - 1)/4 \times 100$. Therefore, hypothesis H3 "Most often, the mobile phone is used for personal purposes in the workplace through messaging applications (e-mail, sms, Messenger, Whatsapp, etc.)" has been validated.

In addition, employees search for useful information on the Internet with an average of 3.43 and a level of intensity of 60.75%. Finally, they use phone calls (voice only) with an average of 3.34 (intensity of use—58.5%). The lowest average was recorded for games: 1.35, with intensity of use of only 8.75%.

The distribution for the considered sample is not normal, so that, in order to test the significant differences between groups considering demographic variables, was used the nonparametric test Kruskal Wallis. With 95% confidence, it can be stated that there are significant differences between males and females regarding the use of games for personal purposes at work. The results indicate significant differences between the considered age groups for personal use of mobile devices at work for: messaging applications (e-mail, sms, Messenger, Whatsapp, etc.), the search for useful information on the Internet, social networks (Facebook, Twitter, Instagram, etc.), music listening applications (including online radio), movies/videos viewing applications, video calls and games. Also, there are significant differences between groups that have different levels of education for personal use of mobile phone at work for movies/videos viewing applications and games.

The first four highest averages indicate that employees want to communicate with other people either through text messages or voice calls. Further, they want to be aware of what is happening outside their working environment, accessing useful information from the Internet, but also by using social networks. While the personal information processes that employees choose at work have previously been reported, the reasons why employees use mobile phones for personal purposes at work are listed below. Respondents were asked to tick on a scale from 1 (totally disagree) to 5 (totally agree) for what reasons they use mobile phone for personal purposes at work (see details in Table 6).

Table 6. Reasons for using mobile phone for personal information at work (ranked decreasingly).

Reasons for Using Mobile Phone at Work for Personal Purposes	Mean (N = 368)	Std. Deviation
Phone helps me to find out if something bad happens to loved ones	4.39	0.89
The phone helps me to find out if there are critical issues with my home or property (car, home, etc.)	4.13	1.06
The phone helps me to schedule my time after work, by contacting friends and relatives	3.81	1.08
The phone helps me know more about relatives, friends, etc., through social networks	3.20	1.32

The most common reason respondents give for using the mobile phone at work for personal purposes, is the need to know that loved ones are safe. Secondly, the same need for safety is related to personal goods or properties. At the same time, the mobile phone is useful for work–life balance, helping employees schedule their time after work. Again, the need to get information about friends or relatives is important, so employees connect to social networking in order to keep up with the news. All the reasons checked by respondents have an intensity level of over 55%, with an average over 3.20 from 5.

When the mobile phone is used in the workplace for personal purposes, depending on the working conditions (how close employees are working, if there are possible recreational facilities, etc.), individual positive or individual/collective negative effects may occur.

For the results below, respondents were asked to tick on a scale from 1 (totally disagree) to 5 (totally agree) for how they use the mobile phone for personal purposes at work. We considered that using the mobile phone at work for professional purposes is a positive behavior, hence, we asked the respondents only about the positive or negative effects of the personal use of the mobile phone. We developed a scale of answers based on information from the pretesting phase.

The results from Table 7 show an interesting phenomenon: with an average of 3.17 out of 5 (54.25% intensity), employees have agreed that the mobile phone improves their efficiency, while with an average of 2.65 out of 5 (and intensity of 41.25%), they said they work more efficiently when they do not have the mobile phone next to them. Of course, there are many other negative effects that may occur at work when using mobile phone for personal purposes: slowing the pace of work, distracting attention, stress, and even disturbing other colleagues' activities. Finally, the best benefit of using a mobile phone in the workplace for personal purposes is having a work–life balance, resulting in better productivity (with a mean of 3.18 out of 5).

Table 7. Effects that come after using phone at work for personal purposes (ranked decreasingly).

	Effects	Mean (N = 368)	Std. Deviation
Positive	Phone helps me to be more productive because it keeps my work–life balance	3.18	1.18
	The mobile phone used in the workplace for personal purposes improves my efficiency	3.17	1.22
Negative	Message communication at work slows my pace of work	2.72	1.28
	The mobile phone used at work for personal reasons distracts me	2.69	1.27
	I work more efficiently when I do not have my mobile phone next to me	2.65	1.39
	Colleagues disturb the activity of other colleagues when they use the mobile phone for personal purposes	2.48	1.30
	Phone calls with family and friends at work reduce my productivity	2.48	1.22
	Using personal mobile for my personal purposes stresses me at work	1.89	1.07

The second hypothesis, related to personal purposes, H4 "There is a positive correlation between the use of mobile phone at the workplace for personal purposes and access to social networks (Facebook, Twitter, Instagram, etc.)", has been validated too.

Mobile phone use in the workplace for personal purposes, related to accessing social networks (Facebook, Twitter, Instagram, etc.), is positively and weakly correlated, with a correlation coefficient of 0.386 (details in Table 8). In other words, the more the mobile phone is used at work for personal purposes, the more social networks (Facebook, Twitter, Instagram, etc.) are among the information processes chosen by employees.

Table 8. Pearson coefficient for testing hypothesis H4.

Pearson Correlations Coefficient (N = 368)		
	Personal purposes	Social networks (Facebook, Twitter, Instagram, etc.)
Personal purposes	1	0.386 *
Social networks (Facebook, Twitter, Instagram, etc.)	0.386 *	1

* $p < 0.01$.

4.2. Professional Use of Mobile Phones in Information Processes at Work

The other hypothesis is related to professional purposes; H1 "There is a negative correlation between the use of mobile phone in the workplace for professional purposes and games applications" has been validated.

Mobile phone use in the workplace for professional purposes, related to accessing gaming applications, is negatively and very weakly correlated, with a correlation coefficient of −0.044 (details in Table 9). In other words, the more the mobile phone is used in the workplace for professional purposes, the less it will be used for gaming applications.

Table 9. Pearson coefficient for testing hypothesis H1.

Pearson Correlations Coefficient (N = 368)		
	Professional purposes	Games
Professional purposes	1	−0.044 *
Games	−0.044 *	1

* $p < 0.05$.

Respondents were asked to tick on a scale from 1 (never) to 5 (very often) what they use the mobile phone for when using it for professional purposes at work. This question does not go into too many professional details, but provides a general view regarding the types of information processes that are accessed at work and are related to the working tasks. Table 10 shows the averages for each of the professional information processes taken into consideration and the significant differences between groups considering the following demographic variables: gender, age and the highest level of education.

Table 10. Professional information processes at work through different information channels (ranked decreasingly) and significant differences between groups.

Professional Information Processes	Mean (N = 368)	Std. Deviation	p for Kruskal Wallis Test *		
			Gender	Age	Highest Level of Education
Phone calls (voice only)	3.56	1.45	0.211	0.000	0.458
Search for useful information on the Internet	2.91	1.45	0.084	0.111	0.314
Messaging applications (e-mail, sms, Messenger, Whatsapp, etc.)	2.83	1.46	0.092	0.007	0.835
Specialized applications made available by the company	2.14	1.36	0.106	0.075	0.692
Orientation applications (maps, GPS, Waze, etc.)	2.13	1.33	0.004	0.070	0.237
Social networks (Facebook, Twitter, Instagram, etc.)	1.90	1.20	0.922	0.316	0.705
Getting evidence through audio-video recordings for the work done	1.76	1.17	0.009	0.237	0.605
Video calls	1.60	0.97	0.275	0.110	0.371
Online stores	1.48	0.95	0.182	0.668	0.227
Movies/videos viewing applications	1.48	0.88	0.340	0.360	0.438
Music listening applications (including on-line radio)	1.39	0.85	0.290	0.934	0.175
Games	1.15	0.54	0.164	0.128	0.085

* $p < 0.05$.

Most employees use the mobile phone at the working place for phone calls (voice only), with an average of 3.56 out of 5 (an intensity of use of 64%). Moreover, they search for useful information on the Internet, with an average of 2.91 and level of intensity of use of 47.75%. They also use messaging applications (e-mail, sms, Messenger, Whatsapp, etc.) with an average of 2.83 (level of intensity of use of 45.75%). Finally, they use specialized applications, made available by the company, with an average of 2.14 (an intensity of use level of 28.5%). Therefore, hypothesis H2—"Most often, the mobile phone it is used for professional purposes in the workplace through specialized applications made available by the company"—has not been validated.

The lowest average was recorded for games: 1.15, with an intensity of use of only 3.75%. The first four highest averages indicate that employees need to communicate, either through voice calls or text messages, with professionals from the work environment. Also, they need to access useful information from the Internet and use specialized applications made available by the company.

Using the nonparametric test Kruskal Wallis, with 95% confidence, it can be stated that there are significant differences between males and females in personal use of mobile devices at work for: orientation applications (maps, GPS, Waze, etc.) and getting evidence through audio-video recordings for the work done. The results indicate significant differences between the considered age groups for personal use of mobile phones at work for: phone calls (voice only) and messaging applications (e-mail, sms, Messenger, Whatsapp, etc.).

4.3. *Personal versus Professional Use of Mobile Phone in Information Processes at Work*

Taking into account the same types of information processes, we present in Figure 2 a comparison between how often these processes are used for personal and professional purposes.

The biggest difference between the use of mobile phones in personal and professional information processes has been recorded for social networks (Facebook, Twitter, Instagram, etc.), which are most often used by employees for personal purposes. Then, there are big differences for messaging applications (e-mail, sms, Messenger, Whatsapp, etc.) and music listening applications (including on-line radio), which are more often used again for personal aims.

Regarding the specialized applications made available by the company, phone calls (voice only) and video calls, it seems that employees use them more for professional purposes at work. All the rest of the information processes analyzed are more intensely used for personal purposes.

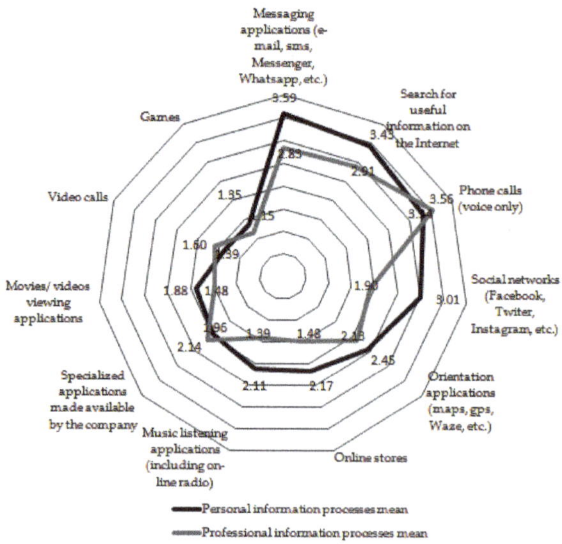

Figure 2. Information processes through different information channels: personal vs. professional.

4.4. Regression Analysis

4.4.1. A Model for Personal Use of Mobile Phones at Work and the Information Processes which They are Used for

Using backward regression analysis method, in the first version of the model, the use of the mobile phone in the workplace for personal purposes has been made for all the information processes that appear in the questionnaire (details in Table A3). The final model indicates that the use of a mobile phone for personal purposes at workplace is only for: social networks (Facebook, Twitter, Instagram, etc.), phone calls (voice only) and messaging applications (e-mail, sms, Messenger, Whatsapp, etc.) (details in Table A3). The best version of the model is the eighth, with an adjusted R^2 of 0.186 and an estimated standard error of 0.338 (details in Table A3). For all model variants, p values are 0 (details in Table A4), so the dependent variable are explained by the action of the independent variables. The eighth model has been chosen (details in Tables 11 and A4).

Table 11. Regression analysis for personal use of mobile phones at work and the information processes which they are used for.

Model *	Unstandardized Coeff.		Standardized Coeff.	t	p
	B	Std. Error	Beta		
(Constant)	0.500	0.065		7.668	0.013
Phone calls (voice only)	−0.048	0.019	−0.140	−2.483	0.000
Messaging applications (e-mail, sms, Messenger, Whatsapp, etc.)	0.091	0.022	0.286	4.096	0.000
Social networks (Facebook, Twitter, Instagram, etc.)	0.073	0.018	0.260	4.074	0.046
Specialized applications made available by the company	−0.028	0.014	−0.096	−2.005	−0.055

* Dependent Variable—Personal purposes.

The model for the considered sample (N = 368) for the use of the mobile phone at work for personal purposes has significance levels for the variables less than 0.05 (0.013; 0.000; 0.000; 0.046; −0.055), and is the following:

$$\text{Using mobile phone at work for personal purposes} = 0.500 - 0.048 \times \text{phone calls (voice only)} + 0.091 \times \text{messaging applications} + 0.073 \times \text{social networks} - 0.028 \times \text{specialized applications made available by the company} \quad (3)$$

The use of mobile phones in the workplace for personal purposes is very low (it achieves a score of 0.5 out of a maximum of 5), when employees do not use the mobile phone at all for: phone calls (voice only), messaging applications, social networking, and specialized applications made available by the company. This mobile phone use for personal purposes increases by 0.588 when employees are using mobile phone for: phone calls (voice only), messaging applications, social networking and specialized applications made available by the company—each of them growing by one unit ($0.500 - 0.048 \times 1 + 0.091 \times 1 + 0.073 \times 1 - 0.028 \times 1 = 0.588$). It is interesting that when employees use their mobile phones for voice calls and specialized applications made available by the company, the general trend of time spent on the phone for personal purposes decreases.

In other words, once personal interests have been resolved by phone calls (voice only) or through specialized applications made available by the company, the time spent on the phone for personal purposes should decrease. The model clearly indicates that the biggest productive time spent for personal purposes appears in messaging applications (e-mails, sms, Messenger, Whatsapp, etc.) and social networks (Facebook, Twitter, Instagram, etc.).

4.4.2. A Model for Professional Use of Mobile Phones at Work and the Information Processes Which They Are used for

The first version of the regression model obtained through the backward method links the use of the mobile phone at the workplace for professional purposes with all the information processes that appear in the questionnaire (details in Table A5). The final model indicates that the use of mobile phones at the workplace for professional purposes is only for: phone calls (voice only), online stores and search for useful information on the Internet (details in Table A5). The optimal version of the model is the tenth, with an adjusted R^2 of 0.331, and an estimated standard error of 0.380 (details in Table A5). For all model variants, p values are 0 (details in Table A6), so the dependent variable are explained by the action of the independent variables. Again, the analysis has confirmed that the tenth model is to be chosen (details in Tables 12 and A6).

Table 12. Regression analysis for professional use of mobile phones at work and the information processes which they are used for.

Model *	Unstandardized Coefficients		Standardized Coefficients	t	p
	B	Std. Error	Beta		
1 (Constant)	0.051	0.058		0.883	0.378
Phone calls (voice only)	0.160	0.015	0.502	10.371	0.000
Search for useful information on the Internet	0.056	0.017	0.177	3.341	0.001
Online stores	−0.066	0.023	−0.136	−2.846	0.005

* Dependent Variable—Professional purposes.

The model for the considered sample (N = 368) for the use of the mobile phone at work for professional purposes has significance levels for the variables less than 0.05 (0.378, 0.000, 0.001, 0.05), and is the following:

$$\text{Using mobile phone at work for professional purposes} = 0.051 + 0.160 \times \text{phone calls (voice only)} + 0.056 \times \text{search for useful information on the Internet} - 0.066 \times \text{online stores} \quad (4)$$

The use of mobile phones at the workplace for professional purposes is very low (with a score of 0.051 out of a maximum of 5), when employees do not use the mobile phone at all for: phone calls (voice only), and to search for useful information on the Internet and online stores. The use of the mobile phone at the workplace for professional purposes increases by 0.201 when the mobile phone is used by employees for: phone calls (voice only), and the search for useful information on the Internet and online stores, with each of them growing by one unit ($0.051 + 0.160 \times 1 + 0.056 \times 1 - 0.066 \times 1 = 0.201$). As employees use their mobile phone for online stores, the general trend of time spent on the phone for professional purposes decreases.

In other words, once the professional interests of searching for useful information about online stores have been resolved, the time spent on the phone for professional purposes should decrease. The model clearly indicates that the biggest consumers of work time for work purposes are telephone conversations (voice only) and the searches for useful information on the Internet.

5. Discussion and Conclusions

The use of mobile phones at work has two separate behavioural components. Employees use the devices for several information processes, some being related to work and others to their personal life. Most of them are involved in both personal and professional informational processes, during their working hours. The effects of the use of mobile phones/smartphones at work can be perceived as positive or negative, based on the resulting productivity [40,42]. The time spent on the use of mobile phones at work cannot be implicitly considered a waste. If it is spent on solving personal problems, social networks, personal leisure or comfort-related activities, it reduces working time, thus reducing productivity. However, that time can also be spent for professional purposes, thus having positive effects such as keeping the workers in touch with managers and customers, keeping employees up to date with information on the market and regarding the organizational environment, helping employees quickly access important information from public or specialized sources, using specialized software for doing their work. As our study has shown what information processes people access where they live and work, it contributes to possible future research on social sustainability [51]. We support this aspect, due to the fact that social sustainability promotes well-being at the workplace and information regarding the impact of technology on employees. Since this study shows what personal and professional information processes are accessed by employees at work, the results should be interesting for decision-makers in companies.

The aim of our research was to propose two regression models that capture what information processes are accessed by employees for personal and professional purposes when using the mobile phone at work.

In the first part of the quantitative analysis (mostly with descriptive statistics), we found that only 3% reported not using the mobile phone at work, with 4% using it only for professional purposes, and 12% only for personal purposes (details in Figure 1). Even if the time on the mobile phone is spent for personal interests, the overall effect might still be positive for the organization. We have found that employees reduce their level of stress related to personal issues by staying informed about their loved ones and their goods (see details in Table 6), thus creating a relaxed, less stressful, positive working environment. Results also stress that the biggest difference between the use of personal and professional information processes, in which the mobile phone is used at work, has been recorded for social networks (Facebook, Twitter, Instagram, etc.), which are most often used by employees for personal purposes. The biggest differences in favor of professional purposes have been found in the use of specialized applications made available by the company, phone calls (voice only) and video calls that employees use more for professional purposes at work.

The most unexpected result was the top positions of the two opinions regarding the positive effects of the use of mobile phones during work, with averages higher than the other six negative effects identified (details in Table 7). Employees say the most important effects of using mobile phones for personal interests are that they help them be more productive because they keep their work–life balance, and that phones used in the workplace for personal purposes improve their efficiency. A study based on the opinions of managers might show a different perspective.

The personal use of mobile devices was more intense than the professional use in eight application categories out of eleven, showing an imbalance between the personal and professional use of mobile phones at work (details in Figure 2). Yet, since the mobile phone was originally designed as a personal device, the fact that today it is used in a significant proportion for professional purposes is a beneficial fact, convincing many employers not to prohibit its use during work. Moreover, the study has shown that the possibility of using the mobile phone during working time for personal purposes reduces the stress of the employees related to personal life uncertainties and risks (details in Table 6), and creates a work environment based on trust, leading to increased employee performance.

In the second part of the quantitative analysis, we have analysed the two regression models. Summarizing the findings, the first hypothesis "There is a negative correlation between the use of mobile phone in the workplace for professional purposes and games applications", the third hypothesis "Most often, the mobile phone it is used for personal purposes in the workplace through messaging applications (e-mail, sms, Messenger, Whatsapp, etc.)", and the fourth hypothesis "There is a positive correlation between mobile phone use in the workplace for personal purposes and accessing Social networks (Facebook, Twitter, Instagram, etc.)", have been validated. The second hypothesis—"Most often, the mobile phone is used for professional purposes in the workplace through specialized applications made available by the company"—has not been validated. Both regression models provide empirical evidence for these hypotheses (validated or not): the biggest productive time consumers for personal purposes are messaging applications (e-mail, sms, Messenger, Whatsapp, etc.) and social networks (Facebook, Twitter, Instagram, etc.) and the biggest consumers of work time for work purposes are telephone conversations (voice only) and searches for useful information on the Internet.

Our results proved that preferences for using mobile phones for personal purposes through messaging and social networks (Facebook, Twitter, Instagram, etc.) remain somewhat stable [12,40,45,48]. The on-line stores, orientation applications (maps, GPS, Waze, etc.), music listening applications (including on-line radio), watching movies and videos, video calls and playing games were statistically excluded by the calculated regression model for personal use of mobile phones at work. Also, our study has proven that games are not used on the mobile devices at the workplace for professional purposes [30]. Regarding the use of mobile phones at work for professional purposes through specialized applications made available by the company, there is currently little emphasis on this, although there are opinions arguing that the use of mobile phones at work should be regulated by a constant procedure [35]. The study proved that the use of specialized applications made available by the company leads to a decrease in the time spent for personal purposes, but the regression model for the professional use of the mobile phone didn't reveal a significant impact of this kind of applications. In fact, the specialized applications made available by the company, messaging applications, orientation applications (maps, GPS, Waze, etc.), social networks (Facebook, Twitter, Instagram, etc.), getting evidence through audio-video recordings for the work done, video calls, movies/videos viewing applications, music listening applications (including on-line radio) and games were statistically excluded by the calculated regression model for professional use of mobile phones at work.

We consider that the use of mobile devices at work for personal interests, firstly, through the use of messaging applications, then for searching information on the Internet and, with a lower intensity, for voice-calls (details in Table 5), shows that the length of worktime interruption for the satisfaction of personal interests is important. The employees show they prefer uses that require shorter times, even if this reduces the consistency of the transferred information.

In using mobile devices for professional interests, the order of intensity of use is reversed. On the first place are voice-calls, followed by the search for information on the Internet. The use of messaging applications is in third place (details in Table 10). We consider that this order shows that, in the case of professional use of mobile devices, the quality of the information flow is more important and not the time invested in the transfer process.

Considering the limitations of this study, we must point out that respondents were only from Romania, without using a sampling scheme, hence the results are not relevant for other geographical areas. Yet, given the worldwide behavioral similarities in the use of smart phones, we expect that similar general studies in other countries could show similar results. We collected data on industries in which the respondents work, in order to be able to analyze their diversity, not for a sampling scheme. In the questionnaire, we used the Classification of Activities of the National Romanian Economy [52] to gain a global view of the fields of activities in which employees are currently working (details in Table A7). Hence, the resulting sample has no representativeness for each industry and the number of nominated industries (17) is very high relative to the total number of 368 respondents (with an average of 22 respondents/industry), which shows that no industry is predominant. This paper is limited regarding any influences from different industries on the usage of mobile phones and any significant differences between industries in terms of mobile phone usage. Thus, further research on specific industries might show different results, due to the specificity of potential uses of mobile phones in each industry or even in each type of job. Further lines of research on our topic could concentrate on analyzing the collected data on personal and professional information processes at work, taking into consideration the socio-demographic data of respondents.

Another limitation is the restriction of the applications of mobile phones to a classification of relevant categories, which we used during data collection. This classification covers most of the uses of smartphones but, given the versatility of applications that can be hosted by mobile devices, we cannot claim to have covered all their potential uses.

Author Contributions: The authors' contributions were equal. Conceptualization, Ș.A.N., S.M.T. and E.-S.T.; methodology, Ș.A.N., S.M.T. and E.-S.T.; statistical method and analysis, E.-S.T.; writing—original draft preparation, Ș.A.N. and E.-S.T.; writing—review and editing, Ș.A.N., S.M.T. and E.-S.T. All authors have read and agreed to the published version of the manuscript.

Funding: This research was funded by European Social Fund through Operational Programme Human Capital 2014-2020, grant number 15/30.09.2019.

Acknowledgments: This work was cofinanced from the European Social Fund through Operational Programme Human Capital 2014-2020, project number POCU/380/6/13/125015 "Development of entrepreneurial skills for doctoral students and postdoctoral researchers in the field of economic sciences".

Conflicts of Interest: The authors declare no conflicts of interest.

Appendix A

Table A1. Pearson coefficient for correlations between personal purposes and field of activity.

Pearson Correlations Coefficient (N = 368)		
	Personal purposes	Field of activity
Personal purposes	1	0.037 *
Field of activity	0.037 *	1

* $p < 0.05$.

Table A2. Pearson coefficient for correlations between professional purposes and field of activity.

Pearson Correlations Coefficient (N = 368)		
	Professional purposes	Field of activity
Professional purposes	1	−0.133 *
Field of activity	−0.133 *	1

* $p < 0.05$.

Table A3. Regression analysis for personal use of mobile phones at work and the information processes which they are used for—other results (1).

Model	R *	R^2	Adjusted R^2	Std. Error	Durbin-Watson
1	0.455 (a)	0.207	0.182	0.339	
2	0.455 (b)	0.207	0.185	0.338	
3	0.454 (c)	0.207	0.187	0.338	
4	0.454 (d)	0.206	0.188	0.338	
5	0.452 (e)	0.204	0.188	0.338	
6	0.449 (f)	0.201	0.188	0.338	
7	0.445 (g)	0.198	0.187	0.338	
8	0.442 (h)	0.195	0.186	0.338	2.024

Notes: * a Predictors: (Constant), Specialized applications made available by the company, Social networks (Facebook, Twitter, Instagram, etc.), Video calls, Games, Phone calls (voice only), Music listening applications (including on-line radio), Orientation applications (maps, GPS, Waze, etc.), Online stores, Search for useful information on the Internet, Messaging applications (e-mail, sms, Messenger, Whatsapp, etc.), Movies/videos viewing applications. b: Predictors: (Constant), Specialized applications made available by the company, Social networks (Facebook, Twitter, Instagram, etc.), Video calls, Phone calls (voice only), Music listening applications (including on-line radio), Orientation applications (maps, GPS, Waze, etc.), Online stores, Search for useful information on the Internet, Messaging applications (e-mail, sms, Messenger, Whatsapp, etc.), Movies/videos viewing applications. c: Predictors: (Constant), Specialized applications made available by the company, Social networks (Facebook, Twitter, Instagram, etc.), Video calls, Phone calls (voice only), Music listening applications (including on-line radio), Orientation applications (maps, GPS, Waze, etc.), Search for useful information on the Internet, Messaging applications (e-mail, sms, Messenger, Whatsapp, etc.), Movies/videos viewing applications. d: Predictors: (Constant), Specialized applications made available by the company, Social networks (Facebook, Twitter, Instagram, etc.), Video calls, Phone calls (voice only), Orientation applications (maps, GPS, Waze, etc.), Search for useful information on the Internet, Messaging applications (e-mail, sms, Messenger, Whatsapp, etc.), Movies/videos viewing applications. e: Predictors: (Constant), Specialized applications made available by the company, Social networks (Facebook, Twitter, Instagram, etc.), Video calls, Phone calls (voice only), Orientation applications (maps, GPS, Waze, etc.), Messaging applications (e-mail, sms, Messenger, Whatsapp, etc.), Movies/videos viewing applications. f: Predictors: (Constant), Specialized applications made available by the company, Social networks (Facebook, Twitter, Instagram, etc.), Phone calls (voice only), Orientation applications (maps, GPS, Waze, etc.), Messaging applications (e-mail, sms, Messenger, Whatsapp, etc.), Movies/videos viewing applications. g: Predictors: (Constant), Specialized applications made available by the company, Social networks (Facebook, Twitter, Instagram, etc.), Phone calls (voice only), Orientation applications (maps, GPS, Waze, etc.), Messaging applications (e-mail, sms, Messenger, Whatsapp, etc.). h: Predictors: (Constant), Specialized applications made available by the company, Social networks (Facebook, Twitter, Instagram, etc.), Phone calls (voice only), Messaging applications (e-mail, sms, Messenger, Whatsapp, etc.). Dependent Variable—Personal purposes.

Table A4. Regression analysis for personal use of mobile phones at work and the information processes which they are used for—other results (2).

Model *		Sum of Squares	df	Mean Square	F	p
1	Regression	10.667	11	0.970	8.443	0.000 (a)
	Residual	40.887	356	0.115		
	Total	51.554	367			
2	Regression	10.665	10	1.066	9.311	0.000 (b)
	Residual	40.889	357	0.115		
	Total	51.554	367			
3	Regression	10.649	9	1.183	10.355	0.000 (c)
	Residual	40.905	358	0.114		
	Total	51.554	367			
4	Regression	10.616	8	1.327	11.636	0.000 (d)
	Residual	40.939	359	0.114		
	Total	51.554	367			
5	Regression	10.510	7	1.501	13.169	0.000 (e)
	Residual	41.045	360	0.114		
	Total	51.554	367			
6	Regression	10.385	6	1.731	15.176	0.000 (f)
	Residual	41.170	361	0.114		
	Total	51.554	367			
7	Regression	10.231	5	2.046	17.925	0.000 (g)
	Residual	41.324	362	0.114		
	Total	51.554	367			
8	Regression	10.066	4	2.516	22.018	0.000 (h)
	Residual	41.489	363	0.114		
	Total	51.554	367			

Notes: * Predictors for Models 1–8 are the same as those specified in the notes a–h from Table A1. Dependent Variable—Personal purposes.

Table A5. Regression analysis for professional use of mobile phones at work and the information processes which they are used for—other results (1).

Model	R *	R^2	Adjusted R^2	Std. Error	Durbin-Watson
1	0.593 (a)	0.352	0.330	0.380	
2	0.593 (b)	0.352	0.332	0.379	
3	0.593 (c)	0.351	0.333	0.379	
4	0.593 (d)	0.351	0.335	0.379	
5	0.592 (e)	0.351	0.336	0.378	
6	0.591 (f)	0.350	0.337	0.378	
7	0.589 (g)	0.347	0.336	0.378	
8	0.586 (h)	0.344	0.335	0.379	
9	0.584 (i)	0.341	0.334	0.379	
10	0.580 (j)	0.336	0.331	0.380	1.807

Notes: * a: Predictors: (Constant), Games, Phone calls (voice only), Video calls, Social networks (Facebook, Twitter, Instagram, etc.), Getting evidence through audio-video recordings for the work done, Specialized applications made available by the company, Online stores, Music listening applications (including on-line radio), Orientation applications (maps, GPS, Waze, etc.), Movies/videos viewing applications, Search for useful information on the Internet, Messaging applications (e-mail, sms, Messenger, Whatsapp, etc.). b: Predictors: (Constant), Games, Phone calls (voice only), Video calls, Getting evidence through audio-video recordings for the work done, Specialized applications made available by the company, Online stores, Music listening applications (including on-line radio), Orientation applications (maps, GPS, Waze, etc.), Movies/videos viewing applications, Search for useful information on the Internet, Messaging applications (e-mail, sms, Messenger, Whatsapp, etc.). c: Predictors: (Constant), Games, Phone calls (voice only), Video calls, Getting evidence through audio-video recordings for the work done, Specialized applications made available by the company, Online stores, Music listening applications (including on-line radio), Movies/videos viewing applications, Search for useful information on the Internet, Messaging applications (e-mail, sms, Messenger, Whatsapp, etc.). d: Predictors: (Constant), Games, Phone calls (voice only), Getting evidence through audio-video recordings for the work done, Specialized applications made available by the company, Online stores, Music listening applications (including on-line radio), Movies/videos viewing applications, Search for useful information on the Internet, Messaging applications (e-mail, sms, Messenger, Whatsapp, etc.). e: Predictors: (Constant), Games, Phone calls (voice only), Getting evidence through audio-video recordings for the work done, Specialized applications made available by the company, Online stores, Music listening applications (including on-line radio), Movies/videos viewing applications, Search for useful information on the Internet. f: Predictors: (Constant), Games, Phone calls (voice only), Getting evidence through audio-video recordings for the work done, Specialized applications made available by the company, Online stores, Movies/videos viewing applications, Search for useful information on the Internet. g: Predictors: (Constant), Phone calls (voice only), Getting evidence through audio-video recordings for the work done, Specialized applications made available by the company, Online stores, Movies/videos viewing applications, Search for useful information on the Internet. h: Predictors: (Constant), Phone calls (voice only), Specialized applications made available by the company, Online stores, Movies/videos viewing applications, Search for useful information on the Internet. i: Predictors: (Constant), Phone calls (voice only), Specialized applications made available by the company, Online stores, Search for useful information on the Internet. j: Predictors: (Constant), Phone calls (voice only), Online stores, Search for useful information on the Internet. Dependent Variable—Professional purposes.

Table A6. Regression analysis for professional use of mobile phones at work and the information processes which they are used for—other results (2).

	Model *	Sum of Squares	df	Mean Square	F	p
1	Regression	27.801	12	2.317	16.045	0.000 (a)
	Residual	51.261	355	0.144		
	Total	79.063	367			
2	Regression	27.796	11	2.527	17.547	0.000 (b)
	Residual	51.266	356	0.144		
	Total	79.063	367			
3	Regression	27.788	10	2.779	19.348	0.000 (c)
	Residual	51.274	357	0.144		
	Total	79.063	367			
4	Regression	27.766	9	3.085	21.531	0.000 (d)
	Residual	51.296	358	0.143		
	Total	79.063	367			
5	Regression	27.724	8	3.466	24.234	0.000 (e)
	Residual	51.338	359	0.143		
	Total	79.063	367			

Table A6. *Cont.*

	Model *	Sum of Squares	df	Mean Square	F	p
6	Regression	27.637	7	3.948	27.638	0.000 (f)
	Residual	51.426	360	0.143		
	Total	79.063	367			
7	Regression	27.411	6	4.568	31.929	0.000 (g)
	Residual	51.652	361	0.143		
	Total	79.063	367			
8	Regression	27.196	5	5.439	37.962	0.000 (h)
	Residual	51.867	362	0.143		
	Total	79.063	367			
9	Regression	26.981	4	6.745	47.013	0.000 (i)
	Residual	52.082	363	0.143		
	Total	79.063	367			
10	Regression	26.596	3	8.865	61.505	0.000 (j)
	Residual	52.467	364	0.144		
	Total	79.063	367			

Notes: * Predictors for Models 1–10 are the same as those specified in the notes a–j from Table A5. Dependent Variable—Professional purposes.

Table A7. Field of activity in which respondents are currently working.

Field of Activity in Which Respondents are Currently Working *	Frecvency	%
Agriculture, forestry, fishing	3	0.82
Public administration	26	7.07
Defense and public order	5	1.36
Trade	35	9.51
Construction	6	1.63
Information and telecommunications (IT)	47	12.77
Manufacturing industry	12	3.26
Extractive industry	2	0.54
Engineering	20	5.43
Education	23	6.25
Energy production and distribution	3	0.82
Health	30	8.15
Financial and insurance services	52	14.13
Entertainment, cultural and recreational activities	4	1.09
Transport	3	0.82
Tourism hotels and restaurants	8	2.17
Another field of activity	89	24.18
Total	368	100.00

Note: * there was used the Classification of Activities in the National Romanian Economy [52].

References

1. Londhe, B.; Radhakrishnan, S.; Divekar, B.R. Socio economic impact of mobile phones on the bottom of pyramid population—A pilot study. *Procedia Econ. Financ.* **2014**, *11*, 620–625. [CrossRef]
2. Geser, H. *Towards a Sociological Theory of the Mobile Phone*; Online Publications University of Zurich: Zurich, Switzerland, 2004; pp. 1–47.
3. Akhavian, R.; Behzadan, A.H. Smartphone-Based construction workers' activity recognition and classification. *Autom. Constr.* **2016**, *71*, 198–209. [CrossRef]
4. Garifova, L.F. Infonomics and the value of information in the digital economy. *Procedia Econ. Financ.* **2015**, *23*, 738–743. [CrossRef]
5. Abueed, R.A.I.; Aga, M. Sustainable knowledge creation and corporate outcomes: Does corporate data governance matter? *Sustainability* **2019**, *11*, 5575. [CrossRef]

6. Zheng, X.; Li, L.; Zhang, F.; Zhu, M. The roles of power distance orientation and perceived insider status in the subordinates' Moqi with supervisors and sustainable knowledge-sharing. *Sustainability* **2019**, *11*, 1421. [CrossRef]
7. Encyclopedia Britannica. Information Processing. Available online: https://www.britannica.com/technology/information-processing (accessed on 21 January 2020).
8. EUR-Lex. Official Journal of the European Union. Regulation (EU) 2016/679 of the European Parliament and of the Council. Article 4. Available online: https://eur-lex.europa.eu/legal-content/EN/TXT/PDF/?uri=CELEX:32016R0679&from=EN (accessed on 21 January 2020).
9. Alter, S. Defining information systems as work systems: Implications for the IS field. *Bus. Anal. Inf. Syst.* **2008**, *22*, 1–43. [CrossRef]
10. Najam, U.; Inam, A.; Awan, H.M.; Abbas, M. The interactive role of temporal team leadership in the telecom sector of Pakistan: Utilizing temporal diversity for sustainable knowledge sharing. *Sustainability* **2018**, *10*, 1309. [CrossRef]
11. Lepp, A.; Barkley, J.E.; Karpinski, A.C. The relationship between cell phone use, academic performance anxiety, and satisfaction with life in college students. *Comput. Hum. Behav.* **2014**, *31*, 343–350. [CrossRef]
12. Wahla, R.S.; Awan, A.G. Mobile phones usage and employees' performance: A perspective from Pakistan. *Int. J. Acad. Res. Account. Financ. Manag. Sci.* **2014**, *4*, 153–165.
13. Pitichat, T. Smartphones in the workplace: Changing organizational behavior, transforming the future. *LUX J. Transdiscipl. Writ. Res. Claremont Grad. Univ.* **2013**, *3*. [CrossRef]
14. Lepp, A.; Barkley, J.E.; Sanders, G.J.; Rebold, M.; Gates, P. The relationship between cell phone use, physical and sedentary activity, and cardiorespiratory fitness in a sample of US college students. *Int. J. Behav. Nutr. Phys. Act.* **2013**, *10*, 79. [CrossRef] [PubMed]
15. Li, L.; Lin, T.T.C. Smartphones at work: A qualitative exploration of psychological antecedents and impacts of work-related smartphone dependency. *Int. J. Qual. Methods* **2019**, *18*, 1–12. [CrossRef]
16. Jumoke, S.; Oloruntoba, S.A.; Blessing, O. Analysis of mobile phone impact on student academic performance in Tertiary Institution. *Int. J. Emerg. Technol. Adv. Eng.* **2015**, *5*, 361–367.
17. Díaz-Chao, Á.; Sainz-González, J.; Torrent-Sellens, J. ICT, innovation, and firm productivity: New evidence from small local firms. *J. Bus. Res.* **2015**, *68*, 1439–1444. [CrossRef]
18. Distefano, A.; Me, G. An overall assessment of Mobile Internal Acquisition Tool. *Digit. Investig.* **2008**, *5*, S121–S127. [CrossRef]
19. United Nations Development Programme. Human Development Reports. *Human Development Index*. Available online: http://hdr.undp.org/en/data (accessed on 10 August 2019).
20. Colbert, A.; Yee, N.; George, G. The digital workforce and the workplace of the future. *Acad. Manag. J.* **2016**, *59*, 731–739. [CrossRef]
21. Yim, M.; Gomez, R. Examining capability enhancement through mobile phone use: The case of Southern Ghana. *E. J. Info. Sys. Dev. Ctries.* **2018**, *84*, e12013. [CrossRef]
22. Ahmad, T. Mobile phones as a learning tool: A lecturer's viewpoint. *Soc. Bus. Rev.* **2018**, *13*, 132–139. [CrossRef]
23. Bratianu, C.; Vătămănescu, E.M.; Anagnoste, S. The influence of knowledge dynamics on the managerial decision-making process. In Proceedings of the 19th European Conference on Knowledge Management (ECKM 2018), Padua, Italy, 6–7 September 2018; Bolisani, E., Di Maria, E., Scarso, E., Eds.; Curran Associates, Inc.: Red Hook, NY, USA, 2018.
24. Öztaş, Y.B.B. The increasing importance of mobile marketing in the light of the improvement of mobile phones, confronted problems encountered in practice, solution offers and expectations. *Procedia Soc. Behav. Sci.* **2015**, *195*, 1066–1073. [CrossRef]
25. Cugueró-Escofet, N.; Ficapal-Cusí, P.; Torrent-Sellens, J. Sustainable human resource management: How to create a knowledge sharing behavior through organizational justice, organizational support, satisfaction and commitment. *Sustainability* **2019**, *11*, 5419. [CrossRef]
26. Bratianu, C.; Orzea, I. Organizational knowledge creation. *Manag. Mark. Chall. Knowl. Soc.* **2010**, *5*, 41–62.
27. Ahmed, Y.A.; Ahmad, M.N.; Ahmad, N.; Zakaria, N.H. Social media for knowledge-sharing: A systematic literature review. *Telemat. Inform.* **2019**, *37*, 72–112. [CrossRef]
28. Apăvăloaie, E.I. The impact of the internet on the business environment. *Procedia Econ. Financ.* **2014**, *15*, 951–958. [CrossRef]

29. Chandramat, S.; Sekhar, N.C.; Adarsh, M.G.; Haomom, G.C.; Thirumalaivasan, K. A novel video surveillance system based on multimedia messaging service. *J. Comput. Sci.* **2005**, *1*, 244–248. [CrossRef]
30. Saidon, J.; Musa, R.; Harun, M.H.M.; Adam, A.A. The conceptual framework of pathological smartphone Use (PSU). *Procedia Econ. Financ.* **2016**, *37*, 426–431. [CrossRef]
31. van Velthoven, M.H.; Powell, J.; Powell, G. Problematic smartphone use: Digital approaches to an emerging public health problem. *Digit. Health* **2018**, *4*, 1–9. [CrossRef]
32. Shrivastava, A.; Sharma, M.; Marimuthu, P. Internet use at workplaces and its effects on working style in indian context: An exploration. *Indian J. Occup. Env. Med.* **2016**, *20*, 88–94.
33. Su, Y.S.; Chiang, W.L.; Lee, C.T.J.; Chang, H.C. The effect of flow experience on player loyalty in mobile game application. *Comput. Hum. Behav.* **2016**, *63*, 240–248. [CrossRef]
34. Lopez-Fernandez, O.; Männikkö, N.; Kääriäinen, M.; Griffiths, M.D.; Kuss, D.J. Mobile gaming and problematic smartphone use: A comparative study between Belgium and Finland. *J. Behav. Addict.* **2018**, *7*, 88–99. [CrossRef]
35. Geser, H. *Is the Cell Phone Undermining the Social Order?* Online Publications University of Zurich: Zurich, Switzerland, 2006.
36. Abeele, M.V.; Beullens, K.; Roe, K. Measuring mobile phone use: Gender, age and real usage level in relation to the accuracy and validity of self-reported mobile phone use. *Mob. Media Commun.* **2013**, *1*, 213–236. [CrossRef]
37. Donya, R.K.; Afari-Kumah, E. Cellular phone usage and productivity among employees in a Ghanaian SME: An Assessment. *Int. J. Comput. ICT Res.* **2011**, *5*, 21–34.
38. Georgescu, M.; Popescul, D. Social media—The new paradigm of collaboration and communication for business environment. *Procedia Econ. Financ.* **2015**, *20*, 277–282. [CrossRef]
39. Bakhuisen, N. Knowledge Sharing using Social Media in the Workplace. A Chance to Expand the Organizations Memory, Utilize Weak Ties, and Share Tacit Information? Master's Thesis, VU University, Amsterdam, The Netherlands, 2012.
40. Horwood, S.; Anglim, J. Personality and problematic smartphone use: A facet-level analysis using the Five Factor Model and HEXACO frameworks. *Comput. Hum. Behav.* **2018**, *85*, 349–359. [CrossRef]
41. Billieux, J. Problematic use of the mobile phone: A literature review and a pathways model. *Curr. Psychiatry Rev.* **2012**, *8*, 299–307. [CrossRef]
42. Duke, E.; Montag, C. Smartphone addiction, daily interruptions and self-reported productivity. *Addict. Behav. Rep.* **2017**, *6*, 90–95. [CrossRef]
43. Billieux, J.; Van der Linden, M.; Rochat, L. The role of impulsivity in actual and problematic use of the mobile phone. *Appl. Cogn. Psychol.* **2008**, *22*, 1195–1210. [CrossRef]
44. Billieux, J.; Van der Linden, M.; D'Acremont, M.; Ceschi, G.; Zermatten, A. Does impulsivity relate to perceived dependence and actual use of the mobile phone? *Appl. Cogn. Psychol.* **2007**, *21*, 527–537. [CrossRef]
45. Ozkan, M.; Solmaz, B. Mobile addiction of generation Z and its effects on their social lifes (an application among University students in the 18–23 age group). *Procedia Soc. Behav. Sci.* **2015**, *205*, 92–98. [CrossRef]
46. Kumar, K.S.V.; Devi, V.R. Social media in financial services—A theoretical perspective. *Procedia Econ. Financ.* **2014**, *11*, 306–313. [CrossRef]
47. Potongsangarun, R.; Worasesthaphong, T.; Taveechat, O.; Somkane, S. Factors influencing decision to subscribe mobile phone services. *Procedia Soc. Behav. Sci.* **2012**, *40*, 473–477. [CrossRef]
48. Tan, Ç.; Pamuk, M.; Dönder, A. Loneliness and mobile phone. *Procedia Soc. Behav. Sci.* **2013**, *103*, 606–611. [CrossRef]
49. Horsman, G.; Conniss, L.R. Investigating evidence of mobile phone usage by drivers in road traffic accidents. *Digit. Investig.* **2015**, *12*, S30–S37. [CrossRef]
50. Jemna, D.V. *Econometrie*; Sedcom Libris: Iaşi, Romania, 2009; pp. 1–246.
51. Colnar, S.; Dimovski, V.; Bogataj, D. Knowledge management and the sustainable development of social work. *Sustainability* **2019**, *11*, 6374. [CrossRef]
52. CAEN Codes from Romania. Classification of Activities in the National Economy. Available online: http://www.rocaen.ro/ (accessed on 1 March 2018).

sustainability

MDPI

Article

The Concept of Sustainability on Social Media: A Social Listening Approach

María Teresa Ballestar [1], Miguel Cuerdo-Mir [2,*] and María Teresa Freire-Rubio [1]

1. Academic Department of Economy and Finance, ESIC Business and Marketing School, Camino Valdenigriales, s/n, 28223 Pozuelo de Alarcón, Madrid, Spain; mariateresa.ballestar@esic.edu (M.T.B.); mariateresa.freire@esic.edu (M.T.F.-R.)
2. Department of Applied Economics I, Economic History, and Institutions, and Moral Philosophy – Applied Economics Area, URJC – Universidad Rey Juan Carlos, Paseo de los Artilleros s/n, 28032 Vicálvaro, Madrid, Spain

* Correspondence: miguel.cuerdo@urjc.es

Received: 31 January 2020; Accepted: 6 March 2020; Published: 9 March 2020

Abstract: The concept of sustainability has gone far beyond the issues of the sustainable management of natural and environmental resources. Nowadays, sustainability is part of the social sciences in a different way. The aim of this research was dual. Firstly, we analyzed the different contexts and areas of knowledge where this concept is used in society by using social listening on Twitter, one of the most popular social networks today. The sentiments of these conversations were rated to assess whether the feelings and perceptions of these conversations on the social network were positive or negative regarding the use of the concept. Also, we tested if these perceptions about the topic were attuned to other more formal fields, such as scientific research, or strategies followed nationally or internationally by agencies and organizations related to sustainability. The method used on this first part of the research consisted of an analysis of 15,000 tweets collected from Twitter using natural language processing (NLP) for clustering the main areas of knowledge of topics where the concept of sustainability was used, and the sentiment of these conversations on the social network. Secondly, we mapped the social network of users who generated or spread content regarding sustainability on Twitter within the period of observation. Social network analysis (SNA) focuses on the taxonomy of the network and its dynamics and identifies the most relevant players in terms of generation of conversation and also their referrers who spread their messages worldwide. For this purpose, we used Gephi, an open source software used for network analysis and visualization, that allows for the exploration and visualization of large networks of any kind, in depth. The findings of this research are new, not only because of the mix of technology and methods used for extracting data from Twitter and analyzing them from different perspectives, but also because they show that social listening is a powerful method for analyzing relevant social phenomena. Listening on social networks can be used more effectively than other more traditional processes to gather data that are more costly and time consuming and lack the momentum and spontaneity of digital conversations.

Keywords: sustainability; social media; social listening; natural language processing; social network

1. Introduction

Sustainability is the quality of the sustainable. This is expressed in the Cambridge Dictionary: "the quality of being able to continue over a period of time". Sustainability is therefore the quality of temporal continuity, without altering its specific properties, and can be associated with multiple natural, social, political, or economic phenomena. The most widespread and well-known concept associated with sustainability is "sustainable development", introduced by the UN in 1987 [1]. However, the idea of sustainability is much older. For instance, the concept was used in relation to Young's [2] discussion of the enclosure movement in the early 19th century [3], in which sustainability and productivity were associated with the development of private institutions and initiatives. Similarly, sustainability also appears as a novel criterion in the use of forest resources, through principles of sustainable management [4,5]. Sustainability also appeared as a when the term "maximum sustainable production" was coined in Schaefer's study of fisheries [6].

In addition to its use in the management of natural and environmental resources, the concept of sustainability has been used frequently in the social sciences. For instance, in the social science literature we found *sustainable competitive advantage*, corresponding to "an advantage that allows a business to be more successful than its competitors over a long period of time" (https://business_finance.enacademic.com/). Similarly, public debt is considered to be sustainable, and economists introduce sustainability rules to make it so. Very specific problems of economic policy, such as dollarization, are seen as a problem of "fiscal sustainability" [7]. With reference to the foreign sector of the economy, external sustainability is also required [8]. In the same way pension sustainability seeks to allow pensions to be maintained in the long run, just as the welfare state has to be sustainable in the long run, which in turn will require its own more general and complex rules [9].

However, since 1987, sustainability, in relation to businesses, has taken on the sense of being careful with the use of natural resources, beyond the relative scarcity expressed through prices [10]. There is also now a certain circularity in the use of these resources that refers to tasks not only of recycling but of transformation [11].

It is interesting to note, for example, how the processing industry has adapted to the concept, especially the one based on combustion processes, such as castings (metal casting). Thus, an editorial of the American sector journal referred to the speech of the president and CEO of ThyssenKrupp Waupaca at the 114th Metal Casting Congress in the United States, where we can read that the sustainability was already concerned not only with the survival of the planet, but also about the survival of the country and the sector, for which it proposed to strengthen the use and development of "green technologies". Similarly, in economics, we found the concept of sustainable finance that "emphasizes the environmental development and institutional aspects of the investment that promotes sustainable growth" [12].

We even found the development of indices such as those of the Dow Jones Sustainability Indices (DJSI), developed from 1999 in a collaboration between S&P Dow Jones and RobecoSAM (https://www.robecosam.com/csa/indices/djsi-index-family.html), which pointed out the extent to which a company will generate long-term value to the investor depending on the management of those resources that are more or less sustainable in terms not only economic, but also environmental and social. In a similar way, there is a growing concern in the economic world to turn the company's organizational culture into "sustainable sustainability" [13], in which the concrete proposal for sustainability is articulated as a central part of the strategy to differentiate itself from other organizations, forcing the reporting not only in financial terms but also in social and environmental terms.

There are many more examples of the increasing use of sustainability and the sustainable as elements of scientific research and social and economic behavior. However, there is little research, to our knowledge, on how people currently talk, perceive, and interact with the concept of sustainability on social networks and whether their behavior is oriented towards the type of action that we call sustainable.

In an attempt to understand these issues, the work that follows investigated how sustainability and sustainable terms are handled on social networks and what this entails. This research also tried to find out to what extent this perception on social media is aligned with what scientists do when they research sustainability and sustainable.

The second section is a literature review and states our hypotheses. We contrast the use of sustainability and sustainable terms in social networks with the world of scientific research. The third section provides a description of the Twitter data collection and the methods applied to analyze the tweets. In a fourth section, the empirical analysis of the results is carried out, followed by the conclusions.

2. Literature Review and Research Hypotheses

Sustainability is a complex, dynamic, and interdisciplinary problem. This forces the development of what is called a "transdisciplinary approach" [14]. It is important to understand how social and natural sciences must "embrace" [15] to advance the ultimate goals of this complex field of sustainability, but also to understand how society perceives these objectives and what behaviors it considers necessary to modify for this purpose.

A very positive step in this direction is seen in the work related to the scientometric review of the research that is being carried out throughout the world in relation to sustainability and sustainable development [16]. In this case, the research methodology has sought to map scientific knowledge and understand the structure and development that scientific researchers, faculties, countries, and scientific journals have followed with the choice of topics, terms, and trends in sustainability studies.

With 2094 bibliographic records, the approach followed by [16] is based on analysis of coauthorship, cocitation, or word use analysis, as well as performing clustering analyses based on geospatial analysis, generating networks of authors and scientific journals, from the Keyhole Markup Language (KML) files and the use of Google Earth.

This type of analysis, based on a broad semantic conception, or a network format, had already been used in other coauthoring analyses or publications in other areas, such as applied mathematics and physics [17], just as the art of "navigating" hypertexts had previously been introduced [18].

What is new in this scientometric analysis is their focus on sustainability and sustainable development, demonstrating that in international research on these topics, there are institutions that are intensifying this research area, such as the Chinese Academy of Sciences, with more than 65 articles in a brief interval of time. Also, there appeared to be a clear citations burst by country and periods, with a variable extension, between 1991, the initial moment, in the United Kingdom, and 2014 [16]. Likewise, using these citation bursts and some measures of centrality, fourteen keywords and themes were found to be the most referenced and influential in the realization of these articles. These themes included environment, climate change, design, policy, impact, sustainability indicator, energy or innovation. Also, the central and most impactful journals, from the *Journal of Cleaner Production* (impact factor of 5715) to the more general ones such as the *Current Opinion in Environmental Sustainability* (impact factor of 3954) allowed us also to analyze how the map of the most cited authors was formed.

No less important is the centrality study of the most influential documents, among which [10] stands out. In addition, the clustering exercise carried out in [16] allowed us to detect eleven fields of analysis with clear labels and reference documents in each of them. In short, the article provides a scientific visualization of a literature devoted to the study of sustainability and sustainable development, based on scientometric analysis based on coword, cocitation, or geospatial clustering and analysis.

As shown by the results of [16] in the literature of the social sciences, sustainability offer us an answer to diverse challenges in mankind's use of the natural resources. The extent to which sustainability is seen in seminal works as the need to find an appropriate institutional framework [19] and, in this sense, to find novel solutions (in the semantic field of "design", "policy", or "innovation") is clear. We see, too, that there is a feeling of the need to argue production and consumption models and to reflect on the limitations of substitutability between natural resources and resources generated in economic activity, in classical contributions [20,21], which are at the heart of the problems posed by "climate change" from "energy" uses. Similarly, sustainability forces a time-critical approach [22] and material well-being is only ensured on a long-term path, where important intergenerational issues are raised [23,24], focusing a lot of current research around "design", "sustainability indicators", or "impact" or "energy" use, again, or "policy", again and again.

Within this perspective, our approach reinforces and complements other lines of research using semantic techniques and network theory around research production containing sustainability and sustainable development terms, like [16]. Our contribution is dual. Firstly, we worked on a sentiment analysis of twitter data using natural language processing (NLP) techniques, and secondly, we drew the social network that generates, interacts, and spreads messages on Twitter regarding the topic of sustainability. We focused on two main hypotheses that were relevant for the analysis of the concept of sustainability on social media.

Our first hypothesis (H1) asked if there is a semantic map that allows us to systematize social expressions related to sustainability, extending the applications of NLP and clustering based on sentiment analysis methods from previous research such as [25–27]. To this end, two complementary hypotheses were raised. Firstly, (H1a) stated that social media is attuned to other more formal fields, such as scientific research or strategies followed nationally or internationally by agencies and organizations of a different nature related to any aspect of sustainability. Secondly, (H1b) stated that the terms sustainable and sustainability are also mainly used in a positive context on the Twitter social network. Users generate dialogue, look for information, and spread it among the network as a way of amplifying a particular message.

The contrasting instrument for this first hypothesis was an analysis of the tweets using natural language processing (NLP) for sentiment analysis. An analysis of the relative importance of the terms was carried out, already classified according to the feeling they generate, and analyzed based on some of the most widespread theories and evidence in social sciences that have as their object the study of sustainability or the sustainable.

As a second hypothesis (H2), we used graph theory to draw the network of accounts that generate content about sustainability and what accounts interact with them. For this purpose, some of the most relevant nodes and connections were studied, providing different measures of centrality and cohesion of the network built for this purpose [28,29].

3. Data Collection and Methods

The analysis performed in this research had two main objectives. The first one consisted of the analysis of the tweets that contain the words "sustainable" or "sustainability" on Twitter social network and understanding what are the main topics and feelings linked to them. With this purpose a sample of 15,000 tweets was collected within thirty days, from the 23th of November to the 22nd of December 2019, which contained either of these two keywords: "sustainable" or "sustainability". After a detailed inspection of the quality of the data to verify that the tweets met with the requirements to be used in this research, 14,029 (93.52%) were considered valid.

The second aim consisted of the analysis of the network of relationships among the accounts that interact with the gathered tweets, regarding the topic of sustainability. We identified who are the ones that create them and who are the ones who retweet them and become a referrer. In addition to this, we drew the structure and hierarchy of the social communities that share content and drive the conversation.

From a technical point of view, the extraction of data was made developing our own python script that connects to the premium search tweets 30-day API that provides a rolling 30 days of access to its historical data and also allows us to apply filters for the extraction, such as date, hashtag, user account, etc. In the extraction for this research we only applied a filter using the keywords "sustainable" and "sustainability".

The gathered tweets were stored in a json file that was processed and analyzed using our own python scripts that employ natural language processing (NLP) libraries for sentiment analysis and word cloud construction. Finally, the file was also processed with the Gephi software. Gephi is an open source software for exploring and manipulating networks that was developed by Bastian, Heymann, and Jacomy [28]. In our research we used this software for the identification of communities and relationships among users that generate and interact with tweets that contain the two keywords.

3.1. Sentiment Analysis

Once the extract, transformation, and load (ETL) process was finished, we used natural language processing to perform sentiment analysis and word cloud visual representations.

The sentiment analysis stage was performed using the lexicon-based sentiment analysis and classification, one of the most popular methods for measuring the polarity of sentiment of a collection of documents (Ahuja and Shakeel, 2017). In this particular case, we applied the Valence Aware Dictionary for Sentiment Reasoning (VADER), which is a rule-based model that is able to manage a wide variety of content generated in social media and compute its sentiment polarity. More than 7,000 items and their associated sentiments were handled by VADER. The quality of its measures was validated by humans before being incorporated to the sentiment lexicon dictionary [30,31]. The robustness of VADER is very high, it does not need to train the model in advance to make the classifications, and it is computationally efficient. These are the main reasons why it is widely used in the scientific community [32]. It was found to be able to outperform individual human raters [33].

The VADER NLP method evaluates each lexical feature of a tweet written in English and calculates a metric score for the sentiment of the tweet. Later, it applies five different rules that are based on general syntactic and grammatical conventions to adjust the initial metric score. The final score ranges the sentiment's tweet from −1 (strongly negative sentiment) to 1 (strongly positive sentiment) [26].

In this research we have applied the following criteria to classify the sentiment of the tweets into two clusters: Tweets with scores ranking from −1 to −0.05 are considered negative and tweets with scores ranking from 0.05 to 1 are considered positive. Neutral tweets have scores from −0.05 to 0.05, but they are not the main focus of our research. This classification criteria avoids the bias involved in assigning the tweets with scores very close to 0 a positive or negative sentiment, minimizing the false positives and negatives [26,27].

Hence, we were able to score whether the conversations that contained the words "sustainable" and "sustainability" happened in a positive or negative context in the social network community.

According to Figure 1, the distribution of tweets by their sentiment score shows that 8,813 tweets (62.82%) had a positive sentiment, 3,061 tweets (21.82%) were considered neutral, and 2,155 tweets (15.36%) had a negative sentiment. Therefore, we can see that the conversation about sustainability (no matter what the terms "sustainable" or "sustainability" are referring to) happens in a positive or neutral context most of the time (84.64% of the tweets).

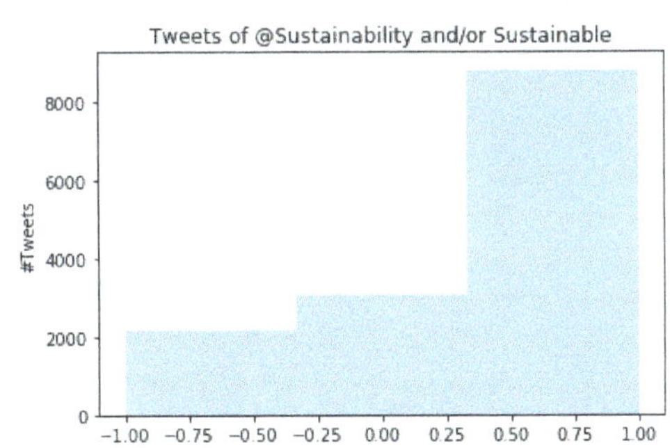

Figure 1. Distribution of tweets by their sentiment score.

3.2. Word Cloud Analysis and Segmentation

A word cloud is a visual representation of text that is developed based on the frequency of the usage of each word in the data collection. Word clouds are an increasingly popular method as they are very efficient in summarizing large amounts of data, in this case tweets from Twitter, and depict the ideologies behind a textual discourse [34,35]. In this research, the aim of the word cloud analysis was to understand the most relevant topics and concepts linked to the two keywords—"sustainable" and "sustainability"—in the conversations that take place on social media.

In addition to this, we applied a clusterization consisting of the conjunction of the word cloud analysis and the sentiment analysis NLP performed in the previous stage of this research. As a result, we obtained a word cloud that identified the most relevant topics that raise positive feelings (with a weight of the 62.82% of the tweets in the sample) and another one that identified the most relevant topics that raise negative feelings among the contributors on the social network (with a weight of 15.36% of the total sample of tweets). For this purpose, we used in our python code several existing python libraries, such as matplotlib, pandas, and wordcloud, that are well known among the scientific and data science communities [36]

We designed the word clouds to show the one hundred most repeated words and word phrases for the two clusters of positive (Figure 2a) and negative sentiment (Figure 2b) tweets, obtaining two different word clouds, and enriching the existing literature on word cloud segmentation [37,38].

(a) (b)

Figure 2. (**a**) Word cloud of the one hundred most frequently used terms in positive sentiment tweets; (**b**) word cloud of the one hundred most frequently used terms in negative sentiment tweets.

The larger the size of the word or word phrase in the word cloud the greater its frequency. The different colors are simply for facilitating the visualization of the content.

The following bar diagrams in Figure 3 show the quantitative representation of the top words or word phrases in terms of absolute frequencies for both positive (Figure 3a) and negative (Figure 3b) word clouds. Hence, these are the words with the highest frequencies in the tweets when we segmented them by their sentiment.

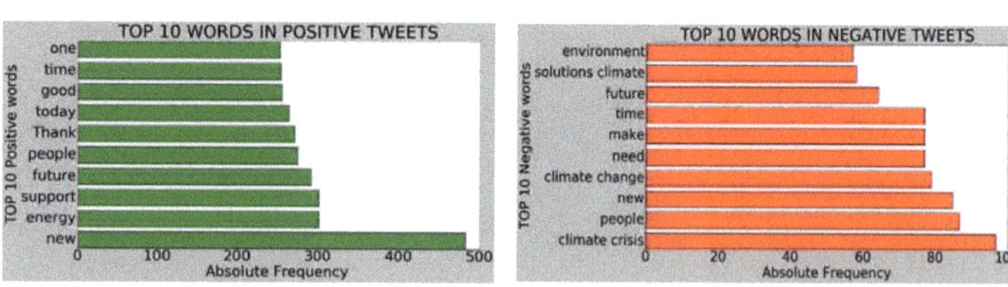

(a) (b)

Figure 3. (**a**) Top 10 words absolute frequencies in positive tweets; (**b**) top 10 words absolute frequencies in negative tweets.

3.3. Social Network Analysis

Gephi is an open source software used for network analysis and visualization. This powerful software allows for the exploration and visualization of large networks of any kind, providing features such as high-quality layout algorithms, clustering, and sample filtering by specific characteristics of the network and statistics of the network as a whole, but also the nodes, edges, and its dynamic [28].

Feeding Gephi software with the sample of tweets collected in the first stage of this research, we have analyzed the dynamics of the accounts that contributed with tweets that contained at least one of the two words (sustainable, sustainability) and also the accounts that acted as prescribers and retweeted these contents within the period of observation (from 23th of November to the 22th of December). Hence, this network representation is focused on the activity of the accounts that generated tweets or interacted as prescribers of these tweets (retweeting) that contain one of the two words "sustainable" or "sustainability".

For this purpose, we used the ForceAtlas2, a continuous graph layout algorithm provided by Gephi. "ForceAtlas2 is a force directed layout: it simulates a physical system in order to spatialize a network. Nodes repulse each other like charged particles, while edges attract their nodes, like springs. These forces create a movement that converges to a balanced state. This final configuration is expected to help the interpretation of the data." [39]. This network allowed us to understand how the communities interact, and their taxonomy [40].

The description of the topology of the directed network in Figure 4 is as follows: The number of nodes was 15,666 and the number of edges was 5,215. Nodes are both accounts that create the tweets and accounts that interacted with these tweets, acting as referrers, spreading the message in form of a retweet. This means that the average degree of the network, measure of connectivity among the accounts, was 0.524, proving that the structure of the network consisted of many different communities, many of them really small (grey dots in the Figure 4) and some others more relevant (large colored dots in Figure 4), having conversations about the sustainability topic but not really connected among them. This was also validated by the average clustering coefficient of the single nodes, which was 0.001, which is very low but an expected figure as we were working with a network where the interactions among users consist of retweets.

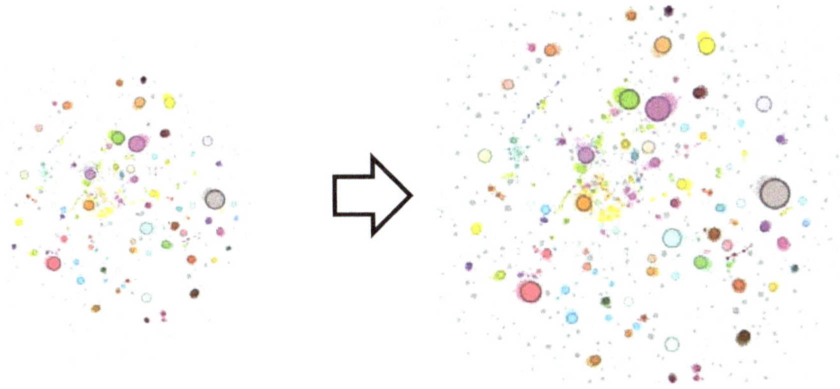

(a) (b)

Figure 4. (**a**) Overall view of the network with all its nodes and edges. Network colored by modularity and size of the nodes by out-degree. (**b**) Zoom in the core of the network: nodes with the highest modularity and out-degree.

According to this, the average path length of the edges that connects the nodes was 1.027, meaning that one account that acts as referee and retweet contents from a specific account, will spread the message to their own portfolio of followers but not much further in terms of length. This was also validated by the network diameter of 3, that is the shortest distance between the most distant accounts in the network.

In the directed network, betweenness centrality, closeness centrality, and eccentricity were calculated using Brandes algorithm [41]. *Betweenness centrality* represents how often a node appears on shortest paths between nodes in the network (Table 1); closeness centrality is the average distance from a given starting node to all other nodes in the network and eccentricity is the distance from a given starting node to the farthest node from it in the network.

Table 1. Top 10 accounts by betweenness centrality.

Accounts	Betweeness Centrality	Account's Short Description
mvollmer1	22	Tech influencer.
SDG2030	12	SDG2030
HaroldSinnott	11	Tech influencer
EarthAccounting	10	Sustainable Consumption
AdamRogers2030	9	Activist and Strategic Coms Advisor
enricomolinari	8	innovation manager
erinbiba	7	Freelance Science Journalist
ASteiner	7	Administrator - United Nations Development Programme
thewebbix	6	Influencer
Dragofix	6	Naturalist

The highest *betweenness centrality* of an account in this network is 22. This node (mvollmer1) is the one that has the most control over the network as it is the one that the most information passes through. The ten accounts with the highest figures are as follows:

Closeness centrality provides us the information about the accounts that are able to spread the information in a very efficient way through the network.

Network diameter is the maximum eccentricity among the nodes. There were just five nodes that had an eccentricity equal to 3.

Finally, the modularity, with a value of 0.996, allows us to identify the different communities in the network. They are represented by the different colors in Figures 4 and 5. We used the Louvain method [42] for community detection, created where modularity ranges from –1 to 1 and measures the density between the edges inside the communities and edges outside the community. The modularity is represented in Figures 4 and 5 by the different colors.

The size of the node/accounts are represented by their out-degree centrality—number of links established with other accounts that retweeted their content that contained the two keywords under investigation. GreenpeaceJP had the highest out-degree with 75 links, followed by MikeHudema with 62, XR_NYC with 51, and WEF with 49.

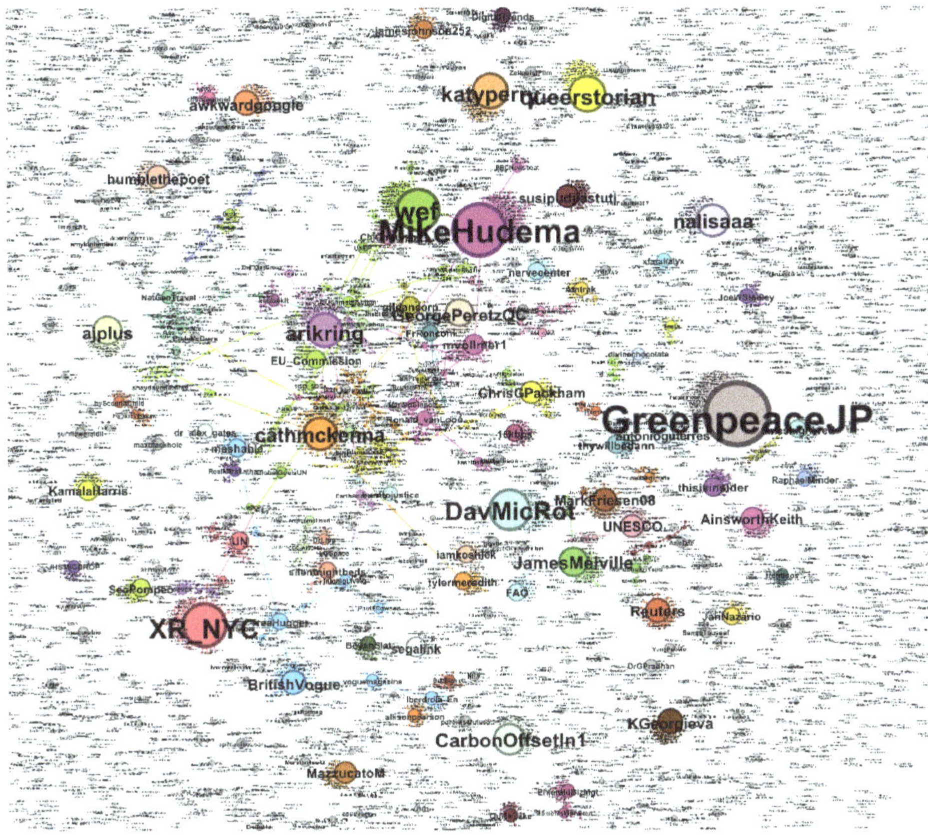

Figure 5. Zoom into the core of the network: nodes with the highest modulatity and out-degree. Nodes are labeled by Twitter account.

4. Empirical Analysis and Results

What was observed in the sampling of tweets and retweets made was that the term sustainability is now clearly associated with environmental sustainability. When the 100 most common words were taken from tweets scored as positive or negative, we found that at least 15 of the 50 most frequent terms shared conversation both from the positive and negative ("new", "future", "people", "time", "way", "good", "environment", "like", "want", "world", "climate change", "business", "development", "long term"). Therefore, beyond the negative or the positive feeling of the tweet where the term was used, there was a set of signifiers that were used interchangeably and that, in some way, strengthened the understanding of the concept. However, in the application of the method explained above, the definitive thing here is how, through an accurate process of clustering, those words and others are used on tweets with a positive or negative feeling.

4.1. Positive Sentiment Cluster

When we deconstructed some of these relationships (Figure 2a), we saw that the use of "new" in tweets associated with a positive feeling (the most prominent term by absolute frequency according to Figure 3a), may indicate that the term "sustainability" is new in terms of its social use. It is used in accordance with the idea that, socially, the current *modus vivendi* is not sustainable in the UN's sense of environmental sustainability, when it was defined in 1987, and as the ability to cope with desire satisfaction through the present consumption of goods and services without jeopardizing the well-being of future generations.

From a social point of view, what is new is the emergence, in the individual and collective preference map, of 'environmental sustainability', with its own identity and strength, and its influence on decisions about the use and consumption of goods and services that the population makes.

No previous generation has had before it, with obvious concern, an environmental problem such as what we know as climate change, caused by past and present generations. What is new is that there was a set of natural and environmental goods and services, which, being an obvious part of the real well-being of people, did not need to be defined with regard to property rights about them. This is a good reason to underline a keyword in Olawumi and Chan—"environment" [16]. However, it is not new to the social sciences, since Hardin had already defined it as "the tragedy of the commons" [19]. In an excellent work, never well known, Georgescu-Roegen also made this clear, pointing out that perhaps social scientists and, especially economists, did not raise these issues earlier because of the "absence of difficulties" in the supply of raw materials by the most advanced countries, even when in the past, wars for its control were unleashed [21]. The growing scarcity of natural resources threatens the stability of our *modus vivendi* itself and this, combined with climate change forces us to consider the situation differently.

In the positive sense, it is also new that "sustainability" and "sustainable" are presented in the conversations as something closely related to the use of 'energy'. "Energy" is also a key word in Olawumi and Chan, in that that the new uses of energy require immediate support [16]. In addition, with a high frequency, "sustainable" and "sustainability" are being related to the future of "the people". On a second level of frequency, terms have a logical value that only extends to the first idea, in the sense of associating with a problem of time, causing us to seek a way that allows us to see something good in what we call 'the environment', that we want to keep in some certain levels of quality and quantity. To do this, the dimensions of such a project have a world scope.

The project started well in that social networks considered sustainability based on energy use to be of the utmost importance, since the current pattern of fossil fuel-based energy consumption is the main anthropogenic source of climate change. So, sustainable energy is seen as a positive solution. In the current scenario the world renewable electricity generation will reach only a little more than 17,000 TWh in 2040, and we need more than 25,000 TWh by that date to be in line with the Sustainable Development Scenario [43]. It is clear that an effective fight against climate change requires us to act on the patterns of energy evolution.

When social networks like Twitter use the words "future", "time", and "way", in relation to environmental sustainability, they are understood in the same sense as in the field of sciences. This is something that concerns time and the future and, therefore, there cannot be an approximation that is not essentially dynamic. In this sense, the importance of the term "way" in this context is underlined, since from a social point of view the key to sustainability requires a concrete way of doing things and designing the future [22].

Here, the question of whether this clashes with the mainstream and more ingrained current conceptions in the field of social sciences arises, and especially with the economic analysis of natural and environmental resources. For some illustrious economists, this concept of sustainability is "essentially vague" [24]. According to Solow, the question in terms of material well-being is whether we can assure future generations of the same level of well-being as present generations. For this, a sustainability rule is needed that ensures the highest level of well-being, updated for the present and for the future [23]. If welfare is expressed through the consumption of goods and services, the maximization of the same requires a trade-off between goods of the present and goods of the future. The well-being of the present requires a more intensive use of natural resources that will eventually become, in the best case, capital goods for the future. This new capital will make the future more productive, although with a smaller allocation of natural resources, higher man-made physical capital, higher human capital, and higher technological capital, which will compensate in terms of well-being with the loss of future natural capital.

In these terms, the concept of sustainability is associated with an opportunity cost of the future [43]. The future appears as an untouchable horizon in terms of present well-being and, therefore, as an obligation on the present that restricts the current framework of opportunities for decision-making that has intertemporal effects. However, what has to be sustainable in the long term is well-being [24] and, to that extent, it may be represented by different proportions of natural capital, manufactured capital, human capital, and technical capital. In this regard, it is very useful to study the analysis by Hartwick [44] to see the conception that underpins this sustainability rule. In another order of things, we should always remember the seminal article of Hotelling [23], in which a dynamic and long-term approach is given to any issue related to the management of natural resources, even if in that case the study was related to the intertemporal optimal allocation of nonrenewable resources, such as those of mining.

However, if likely combinations entail irreversibility costs and increasing uncertainty about the same level of well-being in the future, a strategy of natural capital conservation would have an obvious economic point [45]. To the extent that one accepts a greater number of combinations, one can speak of weak sustainability, and to the extent that substitutability between the components of possible combinations is expressly limited, while retaining the initial allocation of natural capital or by significantly restricting the use of this initial natural capital, there is talk of strong sustainability [46]. This is the basis on which the paradigm of the so-called ecological economy takes turns out [47,48].

The question of the future is not only about whether a critical mass of natural capital should be left at all times in order to ensure environmental sustainability, but, as has been said, the debate on time and sustainability often revolves around cost opportunity for that future [43]. To do this we must look at the real interest rate and the discount rate, that is, know what is the remuneration which is being waived in the present for making available resources for the future or, alternately, what is the cost to us in the present for the preservation of resources for those who belong to the future. This is where it is noted that the issue of environmental sustainability or, most specifically, the fight against climate change is not disputed as to whether it needs to be addressed as a dynamic long-term problem, but precisely because the long term is involved, what should be the discount rate to apply, since one value or another is a crucial thing to know—whether to incur costs today or defer the solution to deal with resources generated in the future [49–51]. The importance of this literature has been a point of debate for more than twenty years in regards to what should be the discount rate to use in the updated calculations of the values of future welfare losses caused as a result of effective climate change.

If we now go to the following most frequent terms in our word cloud, we found "people". The word refers to a very inclusive, obviously popular social basis and the foundation of the democratic regime. It should be remembered, for instance, that in a typical democratic political constitution like that of the US of 1787, the text begins with a "We the people..." and it has a lot of weight in defining the concept of democracy. This perception is very consistent with some relevant contributions in the field of social sciences [45], when the hypothesis of whether democracies as forms of political organization imply a greater commitment to quality international cooperation in this area. The results in Neumayer are conclusive, since the estimators have the expected sign and are significant statistically, but are equally significant and relevant when the democracies of the most advanced countries are excluded from the samples.

Similarly, the term "people" connects with "future". On one hand, there is a perception that it is the youngest people who have taken the lead in the fight for environmental sustainability. Thus, the young Greta Thunberg, born in 2003, is an influencer of this social movement who, because of her age and her likely level of education, is unlikely to have any advantage in terms of knowledge and experience over other generations. This movement gains an advantage in its use of social media, since we cannot ignore that they are already a generation of people born to digital society. In any case, for purely probabilistic reasons, the future will affect them more than any other population cohort.

Moreover, they are joined by a longer-term vision, since they are less concerned about their lives at their present time than in the future. In relation to this issue, one issue that is not a minor one is the claim of young people requesting the right to political choice, which would involve lowering the voting age to 16, which in many developed countries is the age that marks the ability to access the labor market. In short, this clear reference to people in general and not to specific groups greatly universalizes the use of sustainability. That is, it makes it a very cross-cutting term from a social point of view.

In this way we reach a fourth frequency level in the conversations, in which it is clear that the fundamental issue is climate change and that solutions are associated with both the microeconomic (business) and the macroeconomic, needing a long term approach in which industry and agriculture become"green" and "better" and can be actioned through communities in the local realm, using for this purpose both innovation and investment. Every word tweeted is very closely related to the aforementioned issues.

4.2. Negative Sentiment Cluster

From a negative perspective (Figures 2b and 3b), "sustainability" is associated with many terms similar to those already seen in the positive sentiment; even though with a much lower frequency in all cases. "Sustainable" and "sustainability" are terms that allow us to overcome an increasingly overwhelming "climate crisis", asociated to other key words like "climate change" [16]. In other words, from a social point of view, the 'climate crisis' is considered a new concern about the lack of sustainability in the way of life that we follow today. As before, it is something new that involves a climate change that affects "people", where the future is at stake.

Now, with a negative perspective, the time is limited, so we need to find (make) "climate solutions", to attack in concrete fashion the "problem" of the environment, which is seen with a long-term perspective and that has to accompany "development". In this area, the most negative term is diagnosed as a 'climate emergency', in which "economy", "waste", "food waste", and "growth" are involved. These occur always in a "world environment", involving ("want", "like") a "climate action" that affects "business" and, no less important, "cost", so that "money" is seen as part of the problem.

What was most surprising in the results of this word cloud analysis was the similarity of terms, including the importance given to them, when comparing these social networks with the word cloud taking the sample of scientific research conducted in recent years in different fields [16]. It is the words "climate change", "impact", "innovation", "policy", "design" that dominate those professions, while social media conversations move in the same semantic territories.

4.3. Social Networks Analysis

Social networks will have different characteristics depending on the topics and the relationships that are studied [39]. Our network was made up of accounts with tweets that contained the words "sustainable" or "sustainability" and also the accounts that acted as prescribers retweeting this content (Figure 5). The network shows how content regarding sustainability spreads within the Twitter social network. There are many micro-communities, but they are not closely connected. We used centrality measures to describe how this network works.

4.3.1. Out-Degree Centrality Measure

Using the results of out-degree centrality (Figure 5 and Table 2), we observed that, in general, there were many communities of accounts interacting with a main contributor, but there were few connections among these communities.

Table 2. Accounts distribution by Closeness centrality.

Closeness Centrality	%
1	27.17%
0–1	0.59%
0	72.24%

We found that nodes closer to active militancy for environmental sustainability had a higher out-degree. Among them, is that of Greenpeace Japan, echoing the Climate Action Network platform, which included an active participation of outstanding Greenpeace Members International Committee. This organization maintained a deep skepticism regarding possible COP25 agreements at its meeting in Madrid and claimed a "Climatestrike", which in that month meant a mobilization, according to its own sources, of more than 7 million people all over the world. Something similar can be noted from the node representing the Twitter activity of Mike Hudema, an environmental activist from Greenpeace Canada, one of the most influential figures of the Canadian State of Alberta, and some of his campaigns. Hudema has more than 120,000 followers on this network.

These two nodes make evident the importance to the network of *Action on Climate*, the "climate crisis", "green jobs", and the so-called *Green New Deal*. Other nodes, such as @XR_NYE, appear, with a major impact from a British movement called *Extintion Rebellion*, which in December 2019 was throwing a party to raise funds to campaign for the emergency through a New Year's Eve party in London, promoted through the network.

Similarly, there were nodes of obvious importance in social networks, according to their out-degree centrality measure, for which "sustainability" or "sustainable" are key terms for more general objectives. This is the case of the @WEF node, referring to the World Economic Forum, which in December pointed towards sustainability as a fundamental element, favoring a "civil society prepared" for what they call the fourth industrial revolution.

More focused on the vision and strategy of sustainable development, though less important than those mentioned above in relation to the out-degree centrality measure, came very notable nodes, such as @UNESCO and United Nations Secretary-General, @Antonio Gutierres. The first, with more than 3 million followers, was able to enforce the insertion of sustainable development into the Global Goals. The second, with 733,000 followers, pointed out within our dates that "sustainable development is seriously off-track" and that sustainable development is "more than just a goal". The @EU_Commission node, with more than 400 retweets stressing that "sustainability is part of Europe's DNA" and calling for the so-called "The European Green Deal" is also of note.

On the other hand, there were nodes of manifest importance, from the out-degree centrality measure of the social network, that responded to the call to sustainable development or sustainability, but based on a political agenda or simple topicality. This is not to say that the matter is not relevant to the community of users to which they are central. This would be the case of nodes such as @DavMicRot, economist, consultant, very active on the topic of differentiating political formations according to their "sustainable capitalism", with more than 200 retweets and a project called "Threader", which generates more than 500,000 visits a month on the internet. The @JamesMelville node, in which a Scottish consultant in sustainable development of the same name responds, then draws on his position to discuss international progress in sustainable development and the barriers he sees for its progress, in a context of reflection on British general issues, particularly Scottish, has more than 140,000 followers.

Something similar can be noted from a node like @GeorgePeretz, with more than 15,000 followers, dealing with different current affairs, from the point of view of a London lawyer. Other relevant nodes respond to these same characteristics, including the Arik Ring. Further away in terms of the issues dealt with on a daily basis, we can also point to influencers who at some point have regarded the issue of environmental sustainability as an element to take into account in the way of life of them and their followers. This would be the case of @Nalisaaa, with almost 30,000 followers. In this area we should also point out the highlight of the @queerstorian node, as an influencer that supports the collection of money for the construction of a "sustainable" house of a transgender Colombian woman. This Twitter account, with a little under 500 followers gets retweets of almost 1000. In another order of magnitude, from the combined world of music and musicians, appears the node @katyperry, a singer who, with more than 108 million followers, tweets that she feels "proud to be part of the January Sustainability by Vogue Magazine", retweeted more than 600 times.

4.3.2. Betweenness Centrality Measure

The *betweenness centrality measure* allows us to measure not only the number of connections of a node, as is the case of out-degree, but the importance of that node as others go through it. This measure allows us to know, in terms of retweets, who are the ones who actually spread conversations, ideas, and suggestions on social networks about how to deal with issues related to sustainability and the sustainable. In our network, only the first two reached a value of betweenness well away from the rest. Everyone else took a value of half or less than the first.

The first thing of note is that the relationship of tweet-generating nodes (Table 3) has little to do with those who are transmitters of conversations, messages, and news through retweets (Table 1). Thus, the node that achieved the most betweenness was @mvollmer1, who could be considered as a technological influencer, positioned as head of innovation of a major company, Celonis. This Twitter account has been able to accumulate more than 45,000 followers, and devotes special attention to digital supply chains in their most sustainable versions. In this case the connection with @mikehuddema, one of the most meaningful nodes from the point of view of the out-degree, is interesting, and allows us to think about the importance of its connection with the environmental movement and the challenges it poses for innovation, robotics, or artificial intelligence. Thereafter, other nodes are receiving all this information not in a straight line from Huddema but from Vollmer.

Table 3. Top 10 accounts by out-degree centrality.

Accounts	Out Degree	Account's Short Description
GreenpeaceJP	75	Greenpeace Japan
MikeHudema	62	Climate campaigner
XR_NYC	51	Extinction Rebellion NYC
wef	49	world economic forum
DavMicRot	47	Economist
queerstorian	41	others
katyperry	40	singer; artist
arikring	39	Expert consultant. Innovation. Energy
cathmckenna	37	Politician
nalisaaa	37	others

Something similar resulted from some of the highest betweenness. An example is @haroldsinnott, a technology influencer recognized in Florida as one of the most influential professionals in business intelligence, with more than 65,000 followers.

Other nodes, such as the Californian @earthaccounting, with more than 21,000 followers promoting sustainable products and producers, have a manifest interest in spreading the culture of sustainability to the fullest and retweeting everything that involves its dissemination and reinforcement.

The node with the second highest *betweenness* was @sdg30 account, managed from the United Nations and focused on the organization's strategy for disseminating the organization's 2030 sustainable development goals. This node continuously retweeted any news that had to do with the seventeen objectives of the sustainable development strategy. It was therefore a continuous dissemination of the terms sustainable and sustainability associated with very different topics.

4.3.3. Other Network Centrality Measures

The *closeness centrality measure* gives us a measure of how fast the tweets spread from one account to other accounts, in the form of retweets. In our case (Table) it was observed that just over a quarter of the nodes (27.17%) achieved a level of efficiency in the transmission of messages, while almost three quarters of the nodes (72.24%) in the network were unable to connect with the rest. The network was therefore not only structured around communities of nodes that were very consistent and relatively isolated, but a good part of the nodes were simple prescribers, retweeting from other accounts' content, without no diffusion capability.

In regards to *modularity centrality measure*, we noted that there is a strong community structure, where the accounts of the different communities are strongly connected with the main contributor, but later the different communities are almost unconnected amongst themselves. High modularity is a characteristic of biological and other real-world networks.

5. Discussion and Implications

In general, sustainability is an issue of current importance and fashion, a fact which is reflected in the conversations generated on social networks, mainly linked to environmental sustainability. In order to contrast certain hypotheses about the sustainability concept and its use on social media, we used a social listening method. This method avoids biases as it analyzes a representative sample of tweets gathered from Twitter, in which the researchers have not mediated in any way. Analyzing these conversations and messages achieves a momentum effect, difficult to appreciate by other means. It also is relevant because of the cost-effectiveness achieved with its application.

As a result of the research, the findings supported H1, showing that the use of social listening in Twitter can build a map that systematizes the feelings, opinions, and characteristics of the messages issued by users of the social network in relation to a particular topic, such as 'sustainability'. The investigation also confirmed H1a, as the social media approach to the environmental sustainability dialogue coincides fundamentally with what is said in other more formal settings, such as academia, national or international agencies, etc. confirming that social listening is a useful and a complementary tool for research for this topic and in the current context. It also serves to evaluate, not only in this topic, but also in others, if there are dissonances between what society thinks and what science and experts think.

In relation to the hypothesis raised about the sentiment generated by the conversation, it was shown that it was mainly positive, confirming H1b. Thus, 62.82% of tweets have positive sentiment and dialogue ensues for the construction, improvement, and search of solutions. Conversations developed in a context of positive feeling focused on social issues. Central to the groups are people in search of renewal and the construction of a different future, based on different behaviors, mainly related to, and with the goal of achieving, greater well-being in a long-term perspective.

The negative focus in the dialogue focused on the lack of sustainability in an environmental framework. They show concern and discontent about how sustainability is at risk. The conversations developed in the negative context focused on concern about climate change, confirming the hypothesis that society believes we are already facing a climate crisis and that it will have an irreparable impact on the future.

Our research also confirmed that Twitter is a valuable source of information for researchers and organizations. We showed that it is possible to gather a sample of tweets about a specific topic and develop a robust social network map of accounts according to their activity and the interactions among them, confirming H2. The network can be designed as a characterization of participants on social networks, both those who generate the content and those who disseminate and spread it. We confirmed that the "sustainability" concept is part of many global conversations in micro-communities almost not connected among themselves. There are a few communities that are relevant and led by important players, and they are mainly institutional, such as Greenpeace, Mike Hudema, Extinction Rebellion NYC, or the World Economic Forum, etc., but the greater part of the conversations happens in thousands of small communities without any relevant leader and little capacity for the dissemination of their message. This is a sign that this topic is global in nature, not monopolized by anybody, and it can be considered a trending topic nowadays.

We also identified the role of some accounts that are influencers and act as message amplifiers from the main accounts that contribute about sustainability. These influencers are able to disseminate a specific message very widely through their followers. The main characteristic of these accounts is that they are linked to the world of science, technology, and activism, such as Dr Marcell Vollmer, SDG2030, or Harold Sinnott, etc. This means that in the composition of the most relevant communities, there are accounts with very different roles that contribute not only to generate content, messages, and conversation, but also to spreading them among the audience.

6. Conclusions

This research represents a novelty as, to our knowledge, it is the first investigation that analyzed the concept of sustainability in depth using social listening on Twitter, one of the most relevant social networks today.

We used the advantages of the Twitter social network to gather a representative sample of data without interfering in the activities or conversations of the individuals, minimizing the sample bias issue of other traditional methods.

Applying a bunch of different technologies and methods, such as natural language processing (NLP), clustering, and social network analysis (SNA), we have fulfilled two different objectives. On the one hand, we analyzed the different context and areas of knowledge where the concept of "sustainability" was used, and the feelings that these conversations produced among the users on the social network. Using natural language processing (NLP) for sentiment analysis we have seen that the concept of sustainability is used mainly in a positive way in conversations on social media. From the whole sample of tweets, 84.64% of them were scored as positive or neutral, while only 15.36% were scored as having a negative sentiment. This research also provides an overview of the different topics to which the concept of "sustainability" is linked nowadays when generating both positive and negative sentiment.

Positive feelings associated with sustainability are linked to the topic of "new", while the negative is linked to the topic of "climate crisis". Hence, in this research we extended the application of NLP and clustering based on sentiment analysis methods from previous research [26,27,33].

In addition, we drew the social network of users that generate content about sustainability or spread it using Gephi software, showing that sustainability is, in fact, a trending topic on social media with thousands of micro-communities having conversations about it, but without anybody leading or guiding these conversations [28]. We also identified the different kind of accounts that play a key role in the generation and spreading of messages on social networks.

Thus, we have confirmed that social media listening is a powerful tool to complement more formal fields of research with the additional benefit of providing real time information on many topics of interest in the social sciences. In this sense, this paper complements previous literature about concept of "sustainability" [16], bridging a gap and paving the way for new lines of research based on data analysis on social media that can be readily implemented for the benefit of both researchers and also organizations.

Despite its strength, the study has some limitations that indicate directions for future research. Firstly, the large data sample of tweets was gathered within a month, December 2019. Future research should validate that there is no seasonal bias and the results and conclusions remain stable using a new data sample of tweets gathered in a different period of time. In addition to this, we would like to go deeper into the understanding of the dynamics of the social network around the concept of "sustainability" and see how the relationship among accounts evolves over a period of time, providing a longitudinal view of the network.

Secondly, our gathered sample of tweets only contained searchable public contents published by the users on the social network. It means that there is content that cannot be accessed if their owners choose to keep it private.

Finally, we deliberately limited the sample of tweets to those written in the English language. Hence, this analysis applies to the concept of "sustainability" used by English speakers and it would be interesting to replicate the same analysis for other languages, such as Spanish, to understand if different cultures may interpret and use the concept in a different way.

Author Contributions: Conceptualization, M.C.-M.; Data curation, M.T.B.; Formal analysis, M.T.B.; Investigation, M.T.F.-R.; Methodology, M.C.-M.; Project administration, M.C.-M.; Resources, M.T.F.-R.; Software, M.T.B.; Supervision, M.C.-M.; Validation, M.C.-M.; Writing – original draft, M.T.B. and M:C.-M.; Writing – review & editing, M.T.F.-R. All authors have read and agreed to the published version of the manuscript.

Funding: This research received no external funding.

Conflicts of Interest: The authors declare no conflict of interest.

References

1. World Commission on Environment and Development (WCED). *Our Common Future*; Oxford University Press: London, UK, 1987.
2. Young, A. *General View of Agriculture of Hertfordshire*; G. and W. Nicol: London, UK, 1804.
3. Kula, E. *History of Environmental Economic Thought*; Routledge: London, UK, 1998.
4. Chow, N.; Chow, K.L. Sustainable pensions and retirement schemes in Hong Kong. *Pensions Int. J.* **2005**, *10*, 137–143. [CrossRef]
5. Von Thunen, J.H. *Isolated State*; P. Hall, Pergamon Press: London, UK, 1826.
6. Faustmann, M. Gasrechnung des Wertes Welchen Waldbaden Sowie Noch nicht Haubare Holzbestänce für die Waldwirtschaft Besitzen. *Allgemeine Forst un Vagd-Zeitung* **1849**, *25*, 441–445.
7. Schaefer, M.B. Some aspects of the dynamics of populations important to the management of commercial marine fisheries. *Bull. Inter-Am. Trop. Tunna Community* **1954**, *1*, 25–56.
8. Marí Del Cristo, M.L.; Gómez-Puig, M. Fiscal sustainability and dollarization: The case of Ecuador. *Appl. Econ.* **2016**, *48*, 2139–2155.
9. Kouparitzas, M. Is the U.S. Current Account Sustainable? *Chic. Fed Lett.* **2005**, *215*, 1–4.
10. Stern, N. The Economics of Climate Change. *Am. Econ. Rev. Pap. Proc.* **2008**, *98*, 1–37. [CrossRef]
11. Pesci, M.; Tamai, I.; Guo, D.; Critto, A.; Brombal, D.; Wang, X.; Cheng, H.; Marcomini, A. Circular Economy in China: Translating Principles into Practice. *Sustainability* **2020**, *12*, 832. [CrossRef]
12. Cheng, C.; Hua, Y.; Tan, D. Spatial dynamics and determinants of sustainable finance: Evidence from venture capital investment in China. *J. Clean. Prod.* **2019**, *232*, 1148–1157. [CrossRef]
13. Galpin, T.; Whittington, J.L.; Bell, G. Is your sustainability strategy sustainable? Creating a culture of sustainability. *Corp. Gov.* **2015**, *15*, 1–17. [CrossRef]
14. Komiyama, H.; Takeuchi, K. Sustainability science: Building a new discipline. *Sustain. Sci.* **2006**, *1*, 1–6. [CrossRef]
15. McMichael, A.J.; Campbell-Lendrum, D.H.; Corvalan, C.F.; Ebi, K.L.; Githeko, A.K.; Scheraga, J.D.; Woodward, A. *Climate Change and Human Health*; World Health Organization: Geneva, Switzerland, 2003; pp. 145–186.
16. Olawumi, T.O.; Chan, D.W.M. A scientometric review of global research on sustainability and sustainable development. *J. Clean. Prod.* **2018**, *183*, 231–250. [CrossRef]
17. Newman, M.E.J.; Girvan, M. Finding and evaluating community structure in networks. *Phys. Rev. E* **2004**, *69*, 026113. [CrossRef] [PubMed]
18. Nielsen, J. The art of navigating through hypertext. *Commun. ACM* **1990**, *33*, 296–310. [CrossRef]
19. Hardin, G. The Tragedy of the Commons. *Science* **1968**, *162*, 1243–1248. [PubMed]
20. Hartwick, J.M. International Equity and the Investing of Rents from Exhaustible Resources. *Am. Econ. Rev.* **1977**, *66*, 972–974.
21. Georgescu-Roegen, N. *The Entropy Law and the Economic Process;* Harvard University Press: Cambridge, MA, USA, 1971.

22. Hotelling, H. The Economics of Exhaustible Resources. *J. Political Econ.* **1931**, *39*, 137–175. [CrossRef]
23. Solow, R.M. Sustainability: An Economist's Perspective. In *Economics of the Environment*, 3rd ed.; Selected Readings; Dorfman, R., Dorfman, N.S., Eds.; Norton: New York, NY, USA, 1993; pp. 179–187.
24. Solow, R.M. Intergenerational Equity and Exhaustible Resources. *Rev. Econ. Stud.* **1974**, *41*, 29–45. [CrossRef]
25. Mohanty, A.K.; Misra, M.; Drzal, L.T. Sustainable bio-composites from renewable resources: Opportunities and challenges in the green materials world. *J. Polym. Environ.* **2002**, *10*, 19–26. [CrossRef]
26. Dahal, B.; Kumar, S.A.P.; Li, Z. Topic modeling and sentiment analysis of global climate change tweets. *Soc. Netw. Anal. Min.* **2019**, *9*, 24. [CrossRef]
27. Manning, C.D.; Raghavan, P.; Schütze, H. *Introduction to Information Retrieval*; Cambridge University Press: Cambridge, UK, 2008.
28. Jacomy, M.; Venturini, T.; Heymann, S.; Bastian, M. ForceAtlas2, a continuous graph layout algorithm for handy network visualization designed for the Gephi software. *PLoS ONE* **2014**, *9*, e98679. [CrossRef]
29. Bastian, M.; Heymann, S.; Jacomy, M. Gephi: An open source software for exploring and manipulating networks. In Proceedings of the 3rd International AAAI Conference on Weblogs and Social Media, San Jose, CA, USA, 17–20 May 2009.
30. Becken, S.; Stantic, B.; Chen, J.; Alaei, A.R.; Connolly, R.M. Monitoring the environment and human sentiment on the Great Barrier Reef: Assessing the potential of collective sensing. *J. Environ. Manag.* **2017**, *203*, 87–97. [CrossRef] [PubMed]
31. Ribeiro, F.N.; Araujo, M.; Goncalves, P.; Goncalves, M.A.; Benevenuto, F. A benchmark comparison of state-of-the-practice sentiment analysis methods. *EPJ Data Sci.* **2016**, *5*, 1e29. [CrossRef]
32. Yadav, M.; Raskar, S.; Waman, V.; Chaudhari, S.B. Sentimental Analysis on Audio and Video using Vader Algorithm. 2019. Available online: https://s3.amazonaws.com/academia.edu.documents/60339127/IRJET-V6I64120190819-54847-980qtp.pdf?response-content-disposition=inline%3B%20filename%3DIRJET-_Sentimental_Analysis_on_Audio_and.pdf&X-Amz-Algorithm=AWS4-HMAC-SHA256&X-Amz-Credential=AKIAIWOWYYGZ2Y53UL3A%2F20200308%2Fus-east-1%2Fs3%2Faws4_request&X-Amz-Date=20200308T180734Z&X-Amz-Expires=3600&X-Amz-SignedHeaders=host&X-Amz-Signature=08146dfec1675db56f2e7b1c02c15fcd39a42db58a6eddee07f195794db0ccba (accessed on 8 March 2020).
33. Hutto, C.J.; Gilbert, E. Vader: A parsimonious rule-based model for sentiment analysis of social media text. In Proceedings of the 8th International AAAI Conference on Weblogs and Social Media, Ann Arbor, MI, USA, 1–4 June 2014.
34. Ahuja, V.; Shakeel, M. Twitter presence of jet airways-deriving customer insights using netnography and wordclouds. *Procedia Comput. Sci.* **2017**, *122*, 17–24. [CrossRef]
35. Singla, Z.; Randhawa, S.; Jain, S. Statistical and sentiment analysis of consumer product reviews. In *2017 8th International Conference on Computing, Communication and Networking Technologies (ICCCNT), Delhi, India, 3–5 July 2017*; IEEE: Piscataway, NJ, USA, 2017; pp. 1–6.
36. Katre, P.D. Text Mining and Comparative Visual Analytics on Large Collection of Speeches to Trace Socio-Political Issues. In *Proceedings of the 2019 IEEE 9th International Conference on Advanced Computing (IACC), Tiruchirappalli, India, 13–14 December 2019*; IEEE: Piscataway, NJ, USA, 2019.
37. Shahid, N.; Ilyas, M.U.; Alowibdi, J.S.; Aljohani, N.R. Word cloud segmentation for simplified exploration of trending topics on Twitter. *IET Softw.* **2017**, *11*, 214–220. [CrossRef]
38. Hidayatullah, A.F.; Ma'arif, M.R. Road traffic topic modeling on Twitter using latent dirichlet allocation. In Proceedings of the 2017 International Conference on Sustainable Information Engineering and Technology (SIET), Batu, Indonesia, 24–25 November 2017; pp. 47–52.
39. Grau-Carles, P.; Cuerdo-Mir, M. Using Network Theory to Detect Dominant Cartel Firms. *J. Compet. Law Econ.* **2016**, *12*, 541–556. [CrossRef]
40. Ballestar, M.T.; Sainz, J.; Torrent-Sellens, J. Social networks on cashback websites. *Psychol. Mark.* **2016**, *33*, 1039–1045. [CrossRef]
41. Brandes, U. A faster algorithm for betweenness centrality. *J. Math. Social.* **2001**, *25*, 163–177. [CrossRef]
42. Blondel, V.D.; Guillaume, J.L.; Lambiotte, R.; Lefebvre, E. Fast unfolding of communities in large networks. *J. Stat. Mech. Theory exp.* **2008**, *2008*, P10008. [CrossRef]
43. Siebert, H. *Economics of the Environment (Theory and Policy)*, 5th ed.; Springer: Berlin, Germany, 1998.
44. World Energy Agency. World Energy Outlook. November 2019. Available online: https://www.iea.org/reports/world-energy-outlook-2019/ (accessed on 8 March 2020).

45. Neumayer, E. *Weak Versus Strong Sustainability: Exploring the Limits of Two Opposing Paradigms*, 4th ed.; Edward Elgar Publishings: Cheltenham/Northampton, UK, 2013.
46. Pearce, D.W.; Atkinson, G.D. Capital Theory and the Measurement of Sustainable Development: An Indicator of "Weak" Sustainability. *Ecol. Econ.* **1993**, *8*, 103–108. [CrossRef]
47. Daly, H. Toward some operational principles of sustainable development. *Ecol. Econ.* **1990**, *2*, 1–6. [CrossRef]
48. Ehrlich, P.R. The limits to substitution: Meta resource depletion and new economic-ecological paradigm. *Ecol. Econ.* **1989**, *1*, 10. [CrossRef]
49. Nordhaus, W.D. *Managing the Global Commons: The Economics of Climate Change*; MIT Press: Cambridge, MA, USA, 1994.
50. Weitzman, M.L. Gamma Discounting. *Am. Econ. Rev.* **2001**, *91*, 260–271. [CrossRef]
51. Freeman, L.C. Centrality in Social Networks I: Conceptual Clarification. *Soc. Netw.* **1978**, *1*, 215–239. [CrossRef]

sustainability

MDPI

Article

Sustainable Knowledge Investment Increases Employment and GDP in the Spanish Agricultural Sector More Than Other Investments

Carolina Cosculluela-Martínez

Applied Economics I Department, Law and Social Sciences Faculty, University Rey Juan Carlos, 28032 Madrid, Spain; carolina.cosculluela@urjc.es; Tel.: +34-620-630-299

Received: 31 January 2020; Accepted: 8 April 2020; Published: 13 April 2020

Abstract: Investment in every type of asset increases GDP and net employment differently. This paper compares the effect produced by a permanent unitary shock in Sustainable Knowledge for the Primary Sector (SKPS) on the Spanish employment and GDP growth with the effect produced by the other fourteen capital stock types. The methodology used is a Vector Error Correction Model (VECM), where the complementary capital can affect SKPS instantaneously. The results suggest that SKPS produces the second-highest, short and long-term effects on both labor and production, per Euro invested; moreover, the investment of 4.3 thousand euros is retrieved in the first year and increases net employment in one person after four years. Accordingly, the 5 million Euro Budget to invest in sustainable machinery and processing techniques increases net employment by 827 employees.

Keywords: sustainable knowledge; sustainable development; productivity; Gross Domestic Product; social labor; macroeconomic tool; investment policies

---

1. Introduction

Aschauer's research [1,2] focused on quantifying the effects of capital investment on the economy. In recent years there has been a significant number of papers on the critical topic of estimating the productivity of the agricultural sector [3–7]. In the meantime, in Spain, the percentage of GDP invested in machinery for the primary sector has decreased from 46.22% (1982–1986) to 17.57% (2002–2005). However, the change has come, the Spanish Government has increased the quantity for the sector by 1.3%, and there are 5 million euros for investment in sustainable machinery and processing techniques [8]. Spain is an agricultural country, the second in Europe. The agricultural, fishing, and farmer sector produces more than 10%, directly or indirectly, of the GDP [9]. The agricultural sector is one of the economic engines affecting exports and employment.

The first goal of this paper is to calculate the effects of a structural unitary shock in sustainable knowledge for the primary sector capital stock (SKPS) on the growth of GDP and net employment. Is knowledge, advances in technology towards the Agenda 2030, productive for the sector? The second objective is to compare these effects with those of other types of capital stock. The aim is to provide answers to the following questions: Is investment in SKPS productive in Spain, or does the primary sector show signs of having technological obsolescence? If so, are EU funds for investment sufficiently productive in Spain to contribute to the so-called European Cohesion?

Until the year 2000, when Pereira [10] itemized five different types of public investment, not considering all existing capitals, there had been no research on the effects of investment on different types of public capital.

This paper compares the effects of SKPS capital stock with 14 types of capital stocks, considering former capitals. The other capitals analyzed are (1) housing capital stock, (2) aggregated construction, (2.1) road infrastructures, (2.2) public water infrastructures, (2.3) railways, (2.4) airports, (2.5) port infrastructures, (2.6) civil infrastructures, (2.7) other constructions, (3) aggregated transport, (3.1) motor vehicles, (3.2) other vehicles, (4) aggregated machinery capital stock, and (4.2) metal machinery capital stock.

Determining whether investing is productive in terms of GDP and employment has been a matter of academic interest for some time (Tables 1–3 provide the results obtained in previous studies and the types of data and methodologies used). The contribution of this paper to the field is the use of a particular Vector Error Correction Model in a meticulous disaggregated analysis.

Table 1. Results compared with others obtained in the previous empirical literature.

Methodology	Author	Year	Elasticity		Scope	Data	
			α_Y	α_L		Series	Type
U-f(Y)	(Aschauer) [1,2]	1989	0.39		National USA	1949–1985	(St)(P)(I: transport)
U-f(Y)	(Munnell) [11]	1990	0.34		National USA	1948–1987	(St)(PI)(I: transport)
U-f(Y)	(Munnell, Cook) [12]	1990	0.15		States USA	1970–1986	(St)(PI)(I: transport)
U-f(Y)	(Tatom) [13]	1991	0.146		National USA	1974–1987	(St)(P)(I: transport and prices of energy)
U-f(Y)	(Eberts) [14]	1997	0.15		States USA	1988–1992	(St)(P)(I: transport)
VAR	(Pereira, Roca-Sagalés) [15]	2003	0.523		National SP	1970–1995	(St)(P)(I: transport: roads and highways, ports, airports and railways, communications)
VAR	(Pereira, Flores de Frutos) [16]	1999	0.63	0.04	National USA	1956–1989	(St)(P)(I: core infrastructure, buildings and equipment, road infrastructure, transport, airport infrastructure, gas and electricity, water and sewage systems, educational buildings, police, justice, administration, etc.)
VAR	(Pereira) [10]	2000	0.005	0.004	National USA	1956–1997	(PI)(I: conservation structures, development structures, and civilian equipment)
VAR	(Pereira) [10]	2000	0.02	0.003	National USA	1956–1997	(PI)(I: education buildings, hospital buildings, and other buildings (industrial, general office, police and fire stations, etc.)
VAR	(Pereira) [10]	2000	0.009	−0.01	National USA	1956–1997	(PI)(I: sewage and water supply systems)
VAR	(Pereira) [10]	2000	0.02	0.01	National USA	1956–1997	(PI)(I: electric and gas facilities, transit systems, airfields, etc.)
VAR	(Pereira) [10]	2000	0.006	−0.006	National USA	1956–1997	(PI)(I: highways and streets)
VAR	(Pereira) [10]	2000	0.04	0.007	National USA	1956–1997	(PI)(I: core infrastructure)
VAR/EC	Pereira [17]	2001	0.26	0.13	OECD (12 countries) National USA	Differs from each country 1960s to 1980s	(PI)(I: public capital)
VAR/EC	Pereira [17]	2001	0.04	0.035	OECD (12 countries) National SP	Differs from each country 1960s to 1980s	(St)(PI)(I: core infrastructures, residential and non-residential buildings, road and highway infrastructure, transport, airport infrastructure, gas and electricity infrastructure, sewage and water supply systems, buildings for the police, justice, administration, education, etc.) (6)
VECM	(Flores de Frutos, Gracia-Díez et al.) [18]	1998	0.43	0.02	National SP	1964–1992	(St)(P)(I: transport and communications)
VECM	Cosculluela		1.08	2.20	National SP	1977–2005	(St)(I: public capital) (1)
VECM	Cosculluela		0.91	1.88	National SP	1977–2005	(St)(I: transport and communications) (2)
VECM	Cosculluela		0.74	1.50	National SP	1977–2005	(St)(I: transport) (3)
VECM	Cosculluela		0.04	0.08	National SP	1977–2005	(St)(I: road infrastructure)
VECM	Cosculluela		0.20	0.42	National SP	1977–2005	(St)(I: other non-housing constructions) (4)
VECM	Cosculluela		0.12	0.25	National SP	1977–2005	(St)(I: sewage and water supply systems)
VECM	Cosculluela		0.55	1.11	National SP	1977–2005	(St)(I: Transit and airfields) (5)

Table 1. *Cont.*

Methodology	Author	Year	Elasticity	Scope	Data
Source: Adapted from Munnell (1990) [11]					

Notes:

(1) includes road infrastructure, public water infrastructures, railway infrastructures, airport infrastructures, port infrastructures, civil infrastructures, other transport material (goods and passengers) and education buildings, warehouses, hospitals, churches and other ecclesiastical buildings, etc.

(2) includes road infrastructure, railway infrastructures, airport infrastructure, port infrastructure, other transport material (goods and passengers), and non-specialized machinery (hardware and software).

(3) includes road infrastructure, railway infrastructures, airport infrastructure, port infrastructure, other transport material (goods and passengers).

(4) includes education buildings, warehouse, hospitals, churches and other ecclesiastical buildings, etc.

(5) includes road infrastructure, airport infrastructure, other transport material (goods and passengers).

(6) As they used Argimón et al. computed capital stock data in first differences of log levels, they assumed data correspond to real net investment.

Keys: (U) static relations; (PI) public investment; (f(Y)) Production function; (α_Y) Output elasticity to capital; (α_L) Labor elasticity to capital; (I: transport) core investment infrastructure in transportation systems; (USA) United States; (SP) Spain; (St) capital stock; (P) Public; (VAR) Autoregressive Vector; (EC/VEC) Vector Error Correction Model.

- The estimated elasticity of output to other constructions and transportation in Spain (1.08) is higher than its USA counterpart (0.63) estimated by Pereira and Flores [16] (0.63) using capital stock series and by Pereira [10,15] 0.04 and 0.26, respectively, using investment series.
- The estimated elasticity of output to capital stock of road, port, air, railway and communication networks (0.91) is higher than that obtained by Pereira and Roca-Sagales [15] (0.52), and the one estimated by Flores et al. [4] (0.43) in Spain. Pereira and Roca-Sagales [15] omit possible presence of co-integration relations between the variables without testing it.
- The estimated elasticity of output to capital stock of road, port, air and railway networks (0.74) is higher in Spain than that obtained in different countries and regions around the world. The highest estimated elasticity of those countries and regions found in the literature is (0.71).
- The estimated elasticity of output to road network in Spain (0.04) is higher than the one obtained by Pereira [10] (0.006) using investment series of USA.
- The estimated elasticity of output to non-residential constructions in Spain (0.2) is higher than the one obtained by Pereira (2000) [10] (0.02) using investment series of USA.
- The estimated elasticity of output to sewage and water supply systems in Spain (0.12) is higher than the one obtained by Pereira (2000) [10] (0.009) using investment series of USA.
- The estimated elasticity of output to transit systems and airfields in Spain (0.51) is higher than the one obtained by Pereira (2000) [10] (0.02) using investment series of USA, including gas, electricity, and transit systems and airfields investment.

Table 2. Marginal productivity and return rates in Spain and the USA.

Author	Year	Investment	Marginal Productivity	Return Rate
Pereira	2000	Public capital	$4.46	7.8%
		Core infrastructures (highways and streets)	$1.97	3.4%
		Core infrastructures (electric and gas facilities, transit systems, airfields …)	$19.79	16.1%
		Core infrastructures (sewage and water supply systems)	$6.35	9.7%
		Education buildings, hospital buildings, and other buildings (industrial, general office, police and fire stations, etc.)	$5.53	8.9%
		Conservation structures, development structures, and civilian equipment	$4.06	7.2%
Pereira and Flores	1999	Core infrastructure, buildings and equipment, transportation vehicles, road and airport networks, gas electricity, sewage and water supply systems, education buildings, hospital buildings, and other buildings (industrial, general office, justice, administration, police and fire stations, etc.).	$0.65	
		SPAIN		
Pereira and Roca-Sagales	2003	Transportation (roads, ports, airports, and railroads) and communications owned by national, regional administrations.	2.892€	5.5%
Cosculluela	2009	Core infrastructures, buildings and equipment, transportation vehicles, road and airport networks, gas electricity, sewage and water supply systems, education buildings, hospital buildings, and other buildings (industrial, general office, justice, administration, police and fire stations, etc.). (1)	15.34€	15.15%
		Public capital (1)	15.34€	15.15%
		Core infrastructures (highways and streets)	1.34€	15.82%
		Core infrastructures (transit systems, airfields) (2)	30.28€	14.81%
		Core infrastructures (sewage and water supply systems)	13.54€	16.63%
		Education buildings, hospital buildings, and other buildings (industrial, general office, police and fire stations, etc.)	1.59€	16.21%
		Road transportation, ports, airfields and railways and communications (3)	15.93€	14.93%

Table 2. *Cont.*

Author	Year	Investment	Marginal Productivity	Return Rate

Marginal productivity is computed following Pereira [10] as the total added product obtained by the investment of one monetary unit along the ten first periods of time, in order to compare the results. That is, the total added production of the first 10 periods (caused by an increase in one transitory percentage point in the rate of growth) divided by the effect that the increase of one percentage point has produced in the capital series. The rate of return associated to this marginal productivity is an indicator of profitability, considering the effects in previous periods. It has been calculated as the rate of return that converges to that marginal productivity.

(1) Includes road infrastructures, public water infrastructures, railway infrastructures, airport infrastructures, port infrastructures, civil infrastructures, other transport material (goods and passengers) and education buildings, warehouse, hospitals, churches and other ecclesiastical buildings, etc.

(2) Includes road infrastructures, airport infrastructures, other transport material (goods and passengers).

(3) Includes road infrastructures, railway infrastructures, airport infrastructures, port infrastructures, other transport material (goods and passengers).

- Road networks and buildings for public services have the lowest marginal productivities in Spain and in the USA.
- Investment in public capital stock—non-residential buildings and transportation of people and goods—is much more productive in Spain than in the USA; during the 10 first periods, one euro in Spain produces €15,35 while one dollar produces $4.46, according to Pereira [10], and $0.65 according to Pereira and Flores (1999). Thus, the rate of return of public capital in Spain is 15.15% while in the USA it is 7.8%.
- On the one hand, transit capital and airfields are the investment with the highest marginal productivity in Spain (€30.28, base year 2000) and in the USA ($19.79), with corresponding rates of return of 14.81% and 16.1%, respectively. On the other hand, road transportation networks have the lowest marginal productivity, €1.34 (base year2000) and $1.97, respectively. Thus, the results in this paper for marginal Spanish productivity in road, port, air, train, and communication networks suggest €15.93 (base year 2000), while the result in Pereira and Roca-Sagales is €2.89 (base year 1986).
- Sewage and water supply systems have a marginal productivity of €13.54 (base year 2000), and its corresponding rate of return is 16.63% in Spain, while in the USA the marginal productivity is $6.35, and its corresponding rate of return is 9.7%.
- A one euro investment in construction, buildings for public services, in Spain produces, along 10 periods, €1.59 (base year 2000) of GDP, with an associated rate of return of 16.21%; on the other hand, in the USA, one dollar produces $5.53 of marginal production, with an associated rate of return of 8.9%.

Table 3. Long-term accumulated elasticity of private-sector variables with respect to public investment in the USA (Pereira, [10]).

Investment	Rate of Return	Marginal Productivity	Elasticity		
			Output	Employment	Investment
Aggregated Public Investment	7.8%	$4.46	0.04253	0.00735	0.22909
			(0.025,0.045)	(−0.062,0.014)	(0.004,0.229)
Core infrastructures (streets and highways)	3.4%	$1.97	0.0055	−0.0057	0.01154
			(0.002,0.006)	(−0.008,−0.004)	(−0.036,0.012)
Core infrastructures (electric and gas facilities, transit systems, airfields, etc.)	16.1%	$19.79	0.02103	0.01143	0.09455
			(−0.0008,0.021)	(−0.005,0.011)	(−0.047,0.104)
Core infrastructures (sewage and water supply systems)	9.7%	$6.35	0.00856	−0.01159	0.01239
			(−0.0058,0.01)	(−0.012,−0.005)	(−0.058,0.017)
Education buildings, hospital buildings, and other buildings (industrial, general office, police and fire stations, etc.)	8.9%	$5.53	0.01732	0.00285	0.02174
			(0.0049,0.017)	(−0.008,0.0029)	(−0.12,0.025)
Conservation structures, development structures, and civilian equipment	7.2%	$4.06	0.00491	0.00392	0.06874
			(0.002,0.0056)	(0.0024,0.0056)	(0.021,0.069)

Pereira computes the marginal productivity multiplying the output to public investment ratio for the last ten years by the elasticity of private output with respect to public investment. The rates of return that converge to that marginal productivity are calculated as the estimated profit of the investment taking into account the effects of those profits in the 20 previous periods. In parentheses are the estimated confidence bounds.

Table 3. *Cont.*

Investment	Rate of Return	Marginal Productivity	Elasticity		
			Output	Employment	Investment

- The estimated elasticity of labor to non-residential constructions and transportation network in Spain (2.20) is higher than the one estimated by Pereira and Flores [16] (0.04) using capital stock series and by Pereira [10,15], 0.13 and 0.007, respectively, using investment series. It is also higher if it is compared to the one estimated by Pereira [10,15] (0.035) using capital stock series of the Spanish economy.
- The estimated elasticity of labor to transportation network (road, port, air, railway) and communications (1.88) in Spain is higher than the one obtained by Flores et al. [18] (0.02).
- The estimated elasticity of labor to road network in Spain (0.08) is higher than the one obtained by Pereira [10] (−0.006) using USA investment series.
- The estimated elasticity of labor to non-residential constructions in Spain (0.42) is higher than the one obtained by Pereira [10] (0.003) using USA investment series.
- The estimated elasticity of labor to sewage and water supply systems in Spain (0.25) is higher than the one obtained by Pereira [10] (−0.01) using USA investment series.
- The estimated elasticity of labor to transit systems and airfields in Spain (1.11) is higher than the one obtained by Pereira [10] (0.01) using investment series of USA, including gas, electricity, and transit systems and airfields investment.

This paper answers the following questions:

First, is an investment in SKPS productive compared with other capitals? Furthermore, how many periods are needed to retrieve the quantity invested?

Second, which types of investment have the highest short-, medium-, and long-term effects on employment? How much it is needed to increase net employment by one employee? Last, are there complementary effects found between employment and SKPS?

The analysis follows the methodology proposed by Cosculluela-Martínez and Flores de Frutos [19] to measure the effect of investing in housing in Spain and also partially used to find the weights in the Life Expectancy Index [20]. Other authors have either used this methodology or based analyses on its results [21–25].

The contribution of this paper lies in its comparison of the economic effects of different investment distributions, allowing the isolation of responses to shocks in the capital stock type studied and/or in the complementary capital stock. This isolation of responses makes it possible to study the effects, on labor and production, of different investment distributions at different periods. Therefore, the results obtained provide a useful macroeconomic policy instrument to quantify the effects of investment in SKPS capital stock compared with other capital stock types, information which may be helpful towards the goals of the Agenda 2030. The results provide enough evidence to determine that investment in SKPS is retrieved in the first period and increases net employment by one person after four years per investment of 4.3 thousand euros.

Section 2 of this paper (Materials and Methods) describes the version of the methodology used. Section 3 (Estimation of the Theoretical Model) presents the time series used, their statistical properties, and the empirical estimation of the theoretical model. Section 4 (Results) discusses the step response functions (SRFs) of output and employment. Section 5 (Discussion) presents a brief critical analysis of previous literature on the subject and provides a comparative analysis with the results obtained in previous papers. Section 6 concludes with a proposal on the results obtained and points out the limitations of the analysis.

2. Materials and Methods

Although the data of the Spanish economy available cover the timespan 1977- 2012, the data timespan was from 1977 to 2005. The worldwide crisis in 2008 changed the model adjustment completely, and there were not enough data from 2008 to 2012 to leave enough degrees of freedom to estimate two different models. This intervention analysis concluded not to modify the time series so the data would be accurate.

Y_t: Gross Domestic Product (GDP) obtained from the World Bank. Thousands of euros, the base year 2000.

L_t: Total employment (The employment of Ceuta and Melilla are not considered due to missing data in the first time periods.), measured in thousands of workers and obtained from the Spanish Labor Force Survey published by the National Statistics Institute (2006).

K_{i_t}: Capital stock data computed by the Instituto Valenciano de Investigaciones Económicas (IVIE) and published by the Banco Bilbao Vizcaya BBVA Foundation (Mas et al. 2007), where i = 1-4.3, according to BBVA-IVIE's second level classification. Thousands of euros, the base year 2000.

$\overline{K}_{i_t}$: Capital stock data computed by IVIE and published by the BBVA Foundation (Mas et al. 2007), excluding the isolated Capital Stock K_{i_t}. Thousands of euros, the base year 2000.

The main goal is to estimate the responses of Y_t, L_t, and $\overline{K}_{i_t}$ to an increase of K_{i_t}. Thus, the vector of variables which are used in this research is $\mathrm{W_t} = \left(Y_t,\ L_t,\ K_{i_t},\ \overline{K}_{i_t}\right)'$. As the variables of $\mathrm{W_t}$ are stationary in the second differences of the variables I(2), lowercase variables $\mathrm{w_t} = \left(y_t,\ l_t,\ \overline{k}_{i_t}, k_{i_t}\right)'$ represent the vector of first-differenced logged variables of $\mathrm{W_t}$. The objective is to estimate the impulse response functions (IRFs) of y_t and l_t to a permanent unitary shock in k_{i_t} ; the SRFs are computed by adding the IRFs.

In $\mathrm{w_t}$ there are two types of variables: the vector of variables of fast reaction, vector $\mathrm{z_t} = (y_t,\ l_t)'$ and vector $\mathrm{k_t} = \left(k_{it},\ \overline{k}_{it}\right)'$, which are the more rigid ones. The variables of $\mathrm{z_t}$ react faster than those of $\mathrm{k_t}$. It seems reasonable to think that a shock in $\mathrm{k_t}$ (in period t) would have both instantaneous and lagged effects on the variables in $\mathrm{z_t}$. However, a shock in period t in any variable of $\mathrm{z_t}$ would only cause lagged responses in $\mathrm{k_t}$ variables. This means that $\mathrm{k_t}$ variables need time to react to changes in y_t or l_t. Thus, $\mathrm{k_t}$ levels are determined by past values of $\mathrm{z_t}$, while $\mathrm{z_t}$ values are determined by past and present values of $\mathrm{k_t}$.

Formally, the behavior of vectors $\mathrm{z_t}$ and $\mathrm{k_t}$ can be represented as follows:

$$\begin{array}{c} \mathrm{z_t} = \mathrm{v_z(B)k_t} + \mathrm{N_{z_t}} \\ \pi_\mathrm{z}(\mathrm{B})\mathrm{N_{z_t}} = \alpha_{\mathrm{z_t}} \end{array} \tag{1}$$

$$\begin{array}{c} \mathrm{k_t} = \mathrm{v_k(B)z_t} + \mathrm{N_{k_t}} \\ \pi_\mathrm{k}(\mathrm{B})\mathrm{N_{k_t}} = \alpha_{\mathrm{k_t}} \end{array} \tag{2}$$

where $\mathrm{v_z(B)}$ and $\mathrm{v_k(B)}$ are (2×2) matrices of stable transfer functions:

$$\mathrm{v_z(B)} = \begin{pmatrix} \mathrm{v}_{y_{\overline{k}it}}(\mathrm{B}) & \mathrm{v}_{y_{kit}}(\mathrm{B}) \\ \mathrm{v}_{l_{\overline{k}it}}(\mathrm{B}) & \mathrm{v}_{l_{kit}}(\mathrm{B}) \end{pmatrix} \text{and } \mathrm{v_K(B)} = \begin{pmatrix} \mathrm{v}_{\overline{k}_{iy_t}}(\mathrm{B}) & \mathrm{v}_{\overline{k}_{il_t}}(\mathrm{B}) \\ \mathrm{v}_{k_{iy_t}}(\mathrm{B}) & \mathrm{v}_{k_{il_t}}(\mathrm{B}) \end{pmatrix}$$

$\pi_\mathrm{z}(\mathrm{B}),\ \pi_\mathrm{k}(\mathrm{B})$ are polynomial matrixes in B, with the lag operator:

$\pi_\mathrm{z}(\mathrm{B}) = \pi_{\mathrm{o_z}} - \pi_{1_\mathrm{z}}\mathrm{B} - \pi_{2_\mathrm{z}}\mathrm{B}^2$ whose elements are a (2×2) coefficient matrix.

Each function in $\mathrm{v_z(B)}$ represents the response function of each variable y_t and l_t to shocks in $\mathrm{k_t}$.

Together, $\mathrm{k_t}$ variables have diverse yields. Complementary infrastructures $\overline{k}_{it}$ other than k_{i_t} take longer to react than the infrastructure k_{i_t} isolated.

It is worth noting that the empirical analysis shows significant contemporaneous correlations between some types of the capitals studied. The isolated infrastructure k_{i_t} reacts immediately (in the same period) to variations in other infrastructures $\overline{k}_{it}$ and will continue reacting to those changes along several periods. However, other infrastructures $\overline{k}_{it}$ only show lagged effects to changes in the infrastructure studied and do not react in the same period. Thus, shocks in SKPS or in any other capitals produces delayed changes, from the second year onwards, in other infrastructures such as houses, roads, etc.

Mathematically this is expressed in Equation (3) as follows:

$$\mathrm{E}(\alpha_{\mathrm{k}t}\alpha_{\mathrm{k}t}') = \Sigma_\mathrm{k} = \mathrm{P_k}\Sigma_\mathrm{k}^*\mathrm{P}_\mathrm{k}' \tag{3}$$

where $P_K = \begin{pmatrix} 1 & 0 \\ -\beta & 1 \end{pmatrix}$ is the diagonalization matrix of Σ_k and β represents the slope in Equation (4).

$$\alpha_{kt} = \beta \alpha_{\overline{k}_t} + \alpha^{*}_{k_t} \tag{4}$$

Introducing this assumption, Equation (2) is represented as

$$P_k \Pi_k(B) k_t = P_k \Pi_k(B) \nu_k(B) z_t + \left[P_k \alpha_{k_t} = \alpha^{+}_{k_t} \right]$$

with

$$E\left(\alpha^{+}_{k_t}, \alpha^{+\prime}_{k_t}\right) = \Sigma^{+}_{k} \tag{5}$$

as the diagonal.

Compacting Equations (1) and (5) results in

$$\begin{bmatrix} \Pi_z(B) & -\Pi_z(B)\nu_z(B) \\ -P_k\Pi_k(B)\nu_k(B) & P_k\Pi_k(B) \end{bmatrix} \times \begin{bmatrix} z_t \\ k_t \end{bmatrix} = \begin{pmatrix} \alpha_{z_t} \\ \alpha^{+}_{k_t} \end{pmatrix} \tag{6}$$

with

$$E\left[\begin{pmatrix} \alpha_{z_t} \\ \alpha^{+}_{k_t} \end{pmatrix} \begin{pmatrix} \alpha'_{z_t} & \alpha^{+\prime}_{k_t} \end{pmatrix}' \right] = \begin{bmatrix} \Sigma_z & 0 \\ 0 & \Sigma^{+}_{k} \end{bmatrix}$$

where:

- Σ_z non-diagonal;
- Σ^{+}_{k} diagonal;
- $E\left[\begin{pmatrix} \alpha_{z_t} \\ \alpha^{+}_{k_t} \end{pmatrix} \begin{pmatrix} \alpha'_{z_t} & \alpha^{+\prime}_{k_t} \end{pmatrix}' \right]$ block diagonal.

Model (6) is represented as

$$\Pi^{+}(B) w_t = \alpha^{+}_{t} \tag{7}$$

with

$$E\left(\alpha^{+}_{t} \alpha^{+\prime}_{t}\right) = \Sigma^{+} \tag{8}$$

as the block diagonal.

Since $\Pi^{+}(0) = \begin{bmatrix} I & -\nu_{z0} \\ 0 & P_k \end{bmatrix} \neq I$, the stochastic Model (8) is not normalized in the sense of Jenkins and Alavi [26]. However, it can be normalized by pre-multiplying (8) by $\left[\Pi^{+}(0)\right]^{-1}$:

$$\left(\Pi(B) = \left[\Pi^{+}(0)\right]^{-1} \Pi^{+}(B)\right) w_t = \left(\left[\Pi^{+}(0)\right]^{-1} \alpha^{+}_{t} = a_t\right) \tag{9}$$

- a_t is a (4×1) vector of structural shocks, which follows a white-noise vector process, with a diagonal contemporaneous covariance matrix Σ.

where (9) is the theoretical Model (10). The difference between them is that Σ_z is not diagonal, which is the dependence of the variables in α_{z_t}. Nevertheless, it permits estimating the response functions of each one of the elements of z_t to a shock in k_{i_t} .

$$\Pi(B) w_t = a_t \tag{10}$$

Estimating (10) and its corresponding instant covariance matrix permits consistent estimation of the parameters in (7) and (8) (all mathematical details can be provided under request); i.e., $\left[\Pi^{+}(B)\right]$

and Σ^+, and from them, the IRFs. Positions (1,4) and (2,4) of the polynomial elements in (12) will give the response functions of y_t and l_t, respectively.

$$w_t = \Psi^+(B)\alpha_t^+ \tag{11}$$

with

$$\Psi^+(B) = \left[\Pi^+(B)\right]^{-1} = \Psi_0^+ + \Psi_1^+ B + \Psi_2^+ B^2 + \ldots \tag{12}$$

In the following section, Equations (9) and (12) are estimated.

3. Estimation of the Theoretical Model

Before estimating the multivariate theoretical model, a univariate analysis is done. The software used to carry out the univariate analysis is called E-Views 9.

Univariate Analysis. All variables are I(2) according to the values of the Augmented Dickey-Fuller (ADF) test [27,28] (the Autoregressive Integrated Moving Average (ARIMA) univariate estimated models suggest that none of the series seems to be over differenced, and no MA terms are present) for a unit root in first and second differenced series. The analysis shows that no intervention analysis was needed (all ARIMA univariate analyses and ADF tests can be provided under request via email). No important outliers were present.

Co-integration. Methods from Johansen [29,30] were used to study whether there were co-integration relationships among the variables $\left(y_t,\ l_t,\ \overline{k}_{i_t}, k_{i_t}\right)$.

Results suggest that there was one co-integration equation ξ_{1t}, which involves GDP and employment growth rates isolating every type of capital stock. (Methods from Engle and Granger [31] were used to check Johansen results. All regressions, including all the variables and constant terms, have been estimated. The ADF test indicates that for every w vector isolating every type of capital stock, the residuals of the regression of y_t on l_t, k_{i_t}, and $\overline{k}_{i_t}$ are I(0), according to Phillips and Ouliaris [32] critical values (95% critical value, −4.11). There are also I(0) when each capital series is not considered in the regression (95% critical value, −3.77) or when both of them are excluded (95% critical value, −3.37). Thus, when l_t is not included in the regression of y_t on each capital series, or on both of them, the ADF test indicates that residuals are I(1). The ADF test indicates that the residuals of the regressions of l_t, k_{i_t}, and $\overline{k}_{i_t}$ on the other variables in each set of variables that isolate every type of capital stock series are I(1), except when airport infrastructures is the isolated capital.)

$$\xi_{1t} = y_t - 0.47_{(0.05)} l_t - 0.02_{(0.001)}$$

Co-integration equation ξ_{1t} can be interpreted as a stable, positive relationship between GDP and employment growth rates, where the disequilibrium in each period t is measured by ξ_{1t}.

If airport infrastructure capital stock $\left(k_{24_t}\right)$ is isolated, another co-integration equation ξ_{2t} is found between variables of w vector. (When airport infrastructures is the isolated capital, the ADF test indicates that the residuals of the regression of l_t on y_t, k_{24_t}, and $\overline{k}_{24_t}$ are I(0). In fact, in the regression of l_t on y_t, k_{24_t}, and $\overline{k}_{24_t}$, the ADF value is −5.72, while in the regression of l_t on k_{24_t} and $\overline{k}_{24_t}$, of l_t on y_t and $\overline{k}_{24_t}$, of l_t on y_t, and of l_t on $\overline{k}_{24_t}$, the ADF values are respectively −2.30, −3.64, −3.10, and −2.17. Then, by isolating every type of capital, one co-integration relationship including $\nabla \ln Y_t$ and $\nabla \ln L_t$ is found, and when airport infrastructures is the isolated capital, another co-integration relationship that must include $\nabla \ln L_t$, $\nabla \ln Y_t$, and $\nabla \ln K_{24t}$ is found.)

$$\xi_{2_t} = l_t - 1.39_{(0.15)} y_t - 0.27_{(0.06)} k_{24_t} + 0.04_{(0.01)}$$

where ξ_{2_t} measures the volatility in the stable, positive relationship between employment, GDP, and airport infrastructure growth rates.

4. Results

Estimation of the Multivariate Model

The software used for the multivariate analysis is J-Multi 4.15.

Akaike information criterion (AIC) (AIC values can be provided under request via email) suggests that the variables follow a VAR(3). Therefore, VEC(2), on twice differenced variables, was estimated by Generalized Least-Squares (GLS). All non-significant parameters were set to be zero. AIC applied to the residuals of the model showed that a_t followed a multivariate white noise process (all diagnoses of the estimated models can be provided under request via email). From $\widehat{\Sigma^+}$ the instant correlation matrix $\hat{\rho}$ is calculated, and $\hat{\Pi}^+(0)$ is estimated. $\hat{\Pi}^+(0)$ permits the estimation of (10) from (9). Model (10) will be calculated by pre-multiplying (9) by $\hat{\Pi}^+(0)$. Table 4 shows the resulting Model (10) adjusted to data. The compact model is presented in Table 4 as

$$\hat{\Pi}^+_w(B)w_t + c = \hat{a}^+_t$$

Table 4. Orthogonalized Reduced Forms.

$\hat{\Pi}^+_w(B)w_t = \hat{a}^+_t$.		
$\hat{\Pi}^+_w(B)$	w_t	$\hat{a}^+_t$
$\begin{bmatrix} \hat{\Pi}^+_{w_{11}}(B) & \hat{\Pi}^+_{w_{12}}(B) \\ \hat{\Pi}^+_{w_{21}}(B) & \hat{\Pi}^+_{w_{22}}(B) \end{bmatrix}$	$\begin{pmatrix} y_t \\ l_t \\ \bar{k}_{it} \\ k_{it} \end{pmatrix} + \begin{pmatrix} c_1 \\ c_2 \\ c_3 \\ c_4 \end{pmatrix}$	$\begin{pmatrix} \hat{a}_{y_t}^+ \\ \hat{a}_{l_t}^+ \\ \hat{a}_{\bar{k}_i t}^+ \\ \hat{a}_{k_i t}^+ \end{pmatrix}$
Agricultural, Farm, and Fishing Machinery ($k_{4_1 t}$)		
$\hat{\Pi}^+_{w_{11}}(B)$		$\hat{\Pi}^+_{w_{12}}(B)$
$\begin{bmatrix} 1-0.29B & -0.34B \\ 0 & 1-1.17B+0.40B^2-0.23B^3 \end{bmatrix}$		$\begin{bmatrix} 6.04B-2.07B^2-0.29B^3-3.68 & 0 \\ 9.12B-3.12B^2-0.44B^3-5.56 & 0.06B-0.06 \end{bmatrix}$
$\hat{\Pi}^+_{w_{21}}(B)$		$\hat{\Pi}^+_{w_{22}}(B)$
$\varnothing$		$\begin{bmatrix} 1-1.64B+0.56B^2+0.08B^3 & 0 \\ 0 & B \end{bmatrix}$
$\hat{\Pi}^+_{0,w}$	$\hat{\rho}$	$\hat{\Sigma}^+$
$\begin{pmatrix} 1 & 0 & -3.68 & 0 \\ & 1 & -5.56 & -0.06 \\ & & 1 & 0 \\ & & 0 & 1 \end{pmatrix}$	$\begin{pmatrix} 1 & 0.81 & 0.80 & -0.07 \\ & 1 & 0.85 & 0.15 \\ & & 1 & -0.05 \\ & & & 1 \end{pmatrix}$	$\begin{pmatrix} 1.30\times10^{-4} & 1.50\times10^{-4} & 2.29\times10^{-5} & -4.04\times10^{-5} \\ & 2.62\times10^{-4} & 3.43\times10^{-5} & 1.30\times10^{-4} \\ & & 6.23\times10^{-6} & -6.56\times10^{-6} \\ & & & 2.85\times10^{-3} \end{pmatrix}$

This is presented together with their corresponding $\widehat{\Sigma^+}$, $\hat{\rho}$, and $\hat{\Pi}^+(0)$ matrix, where c is a vector of constant terms.

The relations among all the variables are shown in Table 4. As explained in Section 2, IRFs can be found from the reduced form of Model (10) in Table 4. By adding up the IRFs, the SRFs are computed, as mentioned in the following section. The elasticity is calculated by dividing the SRFs of production, employment, or complementary capital by the SRFs of the capital of the shock.

Table 5 shows the calculated reactions of production, employment, complementary capital stock, the 70% confidence level Bootstrap bounds, and also the feedback effects, in percentage points, for each of the following 20 periods, to an increase in the level of the aggregated and disaggregated capital stock of one percentage point.

Table 5. Response functions (%) of each variable level to a shock in agricultural, farm, and fishing machinery capital stock.

Period	LB	ln Y	UB	LB	ln L	UB	LB	$\ln \bar{K}_{4-1}$	UB	LB	$\ln K_{4-1}$	UB
1	0.00	0.00	0.00	0.03	0.06	0.11	0.00	0.00	0.00	0.77	1.00	1.42
2	0.01	0.02	0.04	0.04	0.07	0.13	0.00	0.00	0.00	0.77	1.00	1.42
3	0.02	0.03	0.05	0.04	0.06	0.10	0.00	0.00	0.00	0.77	1.00	1.42
4	0.02	0.03	0.05	0.03	0.05	0.10	0.00	0.00	0.00	0.77	1.00	1.42
5	0.01	0.02	0.05	0.03	0.05	0.10	0.00	0.00	0.00	0.77	1.00	1.42
6	0.01	0.02	0.05	0.03	0.05	0.10	0.00	0.00	0.00	0.77	1.00	1.42
7	0.01	0.03	0.05	0.03	0.05	0.10	0.00	0.00	0.00	0.77	1.00	1.42
8	0.01	0.03	0.05	0.03	0.05	0.10	0.00	0.00	0.00	0.77	1.00	1.42
9	0.01	0.03	0.05	0.03	0.05	0.10	0.00	0.00	0.00	0.77	1.00	1.42
10	0.01	0.03	0.05	0.03	0.05	0.10	0.00	0.00	0.00	0.77	1.00	1.42
11	0.01	0.03	0.05	0.03	0.05	0.10	0.00	0.00	0.00	0.77	1.00	1.42
12	0.01	0.03	0.05	0.03	0.05	0.10	0.00	0.00	0.00	0.77	1.00	1.42
13	0.01	0.03	0.05	0.03	0.05	0.10	0.00	0.00	0.00	0.77	1.00	1.42
14	0.01	0.03	0.05	0.03	0.05	0.10	0.00	0.00	0.00	0.77	1.00	1.42
15	0.01	0.03	0.05	0.03	0.05	0.10	0.00	0.00	0.00	0.77	1.00	1.42
16	0.01	0.03	0.05	0.03	0.05	0.10	0.00	0.00	0.00	0.77	1.00	1.42
17	0.01	0.03	0.05	0.03	0.05	0.10	0.00	0.00	0.00	0.77	1.00	1.42
18	0.01	0.03	0.05	0.03	0.05	0.10	0.00	0.00	0.00	0.77	1.00	1.42
19	0.01	0.03	0.05	0.03	0.05	0.10	0.00	0.00	0.00	0.77	1.00	1.42
20	0.01	0.03	0.05	0.03	0.05	0.10	0.00	0.00	0.00	0.77	1.00	1.42

Notes: (*) Response functions of natural logarithms of each variable. LB and UB represent the lower and upper Bootstrap Bounds at a 70% confidence level, respectively.

The results can be summarized as follows:

1. Output responded with a lag of one year to a shock in SKPS, as well as housing capital stock, road, airport and railway networks, public water infrastructures, and civil infrastructures. A shock in other types of capital stock produced contemporaneous effects on output. These results were also obtained in previous literature [10]. The elasticity was not constant over time in most capitals, although the SKPS elasticity was (0.3) from the third period onwards.
2. Employment reacted quicker than output and did so instantaneously; it decreased its elasticity to SKPS over the time from 0.062 to 0.051, according to the natural decrement evolution of labor.
3. Results did not show feedback effects, with the exceptions of housing, other aggregated construction capital, and non-specific infrastructures. Thus, SKPS capital stock and the rest of the capital types studied remained at equilibrium just 1 percentage point over their initial level or less (airport infrastructures).
4. Effects on the complementary capital stock were not detected in SKPS only when the non-specific infrastructures and non-specialized machinery and software, and consequently also in aggregated machinery other than housing construction, received a shock. The weights on the total capital stock of the studied capital, in most cases, was too small to produce effects on its complementary capital.

5. Discussion

This section compares the results obtained with those in previous literature, whether estimating elasticity in static or in a dynamic framework.

From Aschauer's research in 1989 [1,2], until the beginning of the 21st century, there had been no research on the effects of investment on different types of public capital. Pereira [10] itemized five different types of public investment, but the investment time series applied did not allow considering all existing capitals, and he used investment series. It is worth noting that Pereira's breakdown of public capital into five categories, although excluding capital stock series, provided the most detailed results at that moment in time. Before Pereira [10], they divided the capital into only two types. He found that all variables were I(1) and, using Engle and Granger's method [31], tested the possible presence of co-integration equations, without finding any. The main conclusion was that the slowdowns of the production in the United States during the 1970s was the reduction of public investment in infrastructures.

Table 1 shows the methodology, data, and the estimated elasticity to both production and employment obtained in the empirical literature on the subject. In Table 2, the first column shows the rate of return corresponding to the marginal productivity (column 2) of ten periods (long-term) to the monetary increase of output for a one-dollar investment in every type of public capital. The corresponding rate of return is the yield that converges to marginal productivity. The last three columns show the estimated elasticity, together with their corresponding confidence bounds. Table 4 also contains the marginal productivity and the return rates associated with the marginal productivities, i.e., the investment profit and the effect generated by the previous investment. Previous literature shows that elasticity of output to any investment estimated using USA data is lower than the elasticity of output using Spanish data, including the results obtained in this paper. Thus, according to the elasticity estimated, the investment profit of any asset is higher in Spain than in the USA. However, capital series and investment series are different in every country; therefore, some authors show the marginal productivity. Marginal productivity is typically computed as the total added product obtained from the investment of one monetary unit throughout the ten first periods. That is the total added production of the first ten periods, caused by a one transitory percentage point increase of the growth rate, divided by the effect that that increase has produced on the capital series. Therefore, this marginal productivity does not coincide with the marginal productivity of economic theory, so some authors also calculate the rate of return associated with it as an indicator of profitability. The "modified" rate of return becomes the estimated profit of the investment, taking into account the effects produced by the previous investment.

Table 2 shows a comparative analysis with the results obtained by and Pereira [10] Pereira and Flores de Frutos [16] in the USA, and by Pereira and Roca-Sagalés [15] in Spain. The highest marginal productivity is produced by an investment in the same type of capital in Spain using capital stock series than in the USA using investment series. Thus, the most and least productive capitals are the same in the USA and Spain. The rates of return show that investment in physical capital is more productive in Spain than in the USA.

Table 3 shows the estimated elasticity of labor to public capital in the range of 0.007–0.04. Thus, labor elasticity is lower than output elasticity. The results obtained in this paper suggest that the elasticity of labor is lower than the elasticity of output.

The estimated elasticity of labor to public capital (all types of capital included in the aggregated other constructions and transportation network) is 2.20. Thus, additional investment increases employment, so public capital and labor are complementary inputs in the production function.

From this vast amount of literature, we can conclude that the investment in SKPS has not been analyzed, and the Agenda 2030 places it as the second objective. As pointed out in the results section, the main conclusion is that, although during the first years other types of investment produce and increase net employment instantaneously, SKPS is the second most productive and employee-hiring investment from the second period onwards.

The literature does not estimate the effects of investment in SKPS compared with other capitals. More important is the number of periods needed to retrieve the quantity invested. Moreover, the types of investment that have the highest short-, medium-, and long-term effects on employment were not identifyed. When unemployment increases and public policies can turn around the curve, it is essential to know how much investment is needed to increase net employment in one employee in as many types of assets as possible to weigh the National Budget conveniently.

Comparing the capital stock types, the investment of 1 million euros of 2000 in SKPS increases net employment after 4 years by 229 people, nearly doubling the investment in railway infrastructures that leads to an increase by 128 people. Indeed, per 1 million euros in 2020 invested in sustainable machinery and processing techniques, net employment increases by 166 employees. While SKPS produces 11.91€ per euro (base 2000) invested in 4 years and 24.73€ in 8 years, railway infrastructures only produce half as much, 6.28 and 12.15€, respectively, per euro (base 2000) invested.

The methodology used in this paper contributes to the field in that the two-step orthogonalization allows to affect the complimentary capital instantaneously, and that it considers the highest disaggregation of capital stock types for the Spanish economy to compare the effects of SKPS.

6. Conclusions

Applying the methodology proposed by Cosculluela-Martínez and Flores de Frutos [19] to data from the Spanish economy, it is possible to conclude that SKPS 1€ investment yields are €11.91 in the first four years (short-run), €24.73 after eight years (medium-run), and €47.32 after twenty years (long run).

Additionally, SKPS, together with airport infrastructures and other transport equipment, provides the highest employment (per euro invested) in every considered period.

SKPS, as well as investments in airport infrastructures, other transport equipment, railway infrastructures, and public water infrastructures, takes one period to be productive. Metal machinery, motor vehicles, or other constructions (non-specific), i.e., education buildings, warehouses, hospitals, churches, and other ecclesiastical buildings, produce instantaneous results.

Answering the second question, the investment required in SKPS to reduce the number of unemployed people by one person is almost 30 times less than the investment in non-specific constructions. Indeed, the investment needed to increase net employment by one employee after four periods varies from €3566.58 for investment in airfield infrastructures to €4372.77 for investment in SKPS or €6690.37 for other transport equipment, reaching €102,758.42 in non-specific construction infrastructures. To increase net employment by one employee after 20 periods, the investment needed in airport infrastructures is €3052, in SKPS €51,664.34, while in housing it is €93,690, in other aggregated constructions €63,800, and non-specific constructions €112.932,09, twice the investment needed in SKPS.

The answer to the third question—Do complementary effects exist between capital and employment when investing in SKPS?—is yes; investment in SKPS increases employment. Is there crowding in the effect of other types of capital? Externalities are present in the investment in other aggregated constructions and non-specific construction from the second period onwards and after one period in the investment in other machinery and software, but not in SKPS. These increase the effect on output and labor.

To summarize, SKPS is one of the two most productive and employee-hiring capitals of the 14 capitals analyzed in any timespan. It produces instantaneous effects on employment, although it needs one period to increase output. Thus, the results support the importance of the Spanish primary sector and the need for new technology to stimulate it. SKPS investment continues to be very productive, both in terms of output and in terms of employment. The sector does not show signs of saturation; in fact, it is the second most productive type of investment (per euro invested) after investment in airports. Therefore, according to the results of this paper, a 5 million euro investment after 4 years will increase net employment by 827 employees. Thus, it would be recommended to promote this type of investment.

Thus, the SKPS sector does not seem to be overinvested, and its productivity and capacity to employ people seem to be far from the inflection point. The results reveal that EU funds supporting the SKPS sector and encouraging European cohesion are productive and create employment, with 259 employees per million euros invested (the base year 2000). Results asses the second objective (2.a) of the Agenda 2030 to invest in technological development and agricultural infrastructure.

This paper contributes to the field in two ways; first the results of this paper could be expanded to countries with similar characteristics, and second, the methodology used to carry out the study can be used with data from any other country or region. The main limitation is that is not taking into account the effects of the period in which a global crisis can occur, so the results of the model can be extended when the country is recovering from a crisis such as the 2008 economic crisis or the 2020 COVID-19 crisis.

Funding: No funding for the article.

Acknowledgments: I am grateful to anonymous referee and the editors for their useful comments. I am responsible for all the remaining errors.

Conflicts of Interest: The author declares no conflict of interest.

References

1. Aschauer, D.A. Does public capital crowd out private capital? *J. Monet. Econ.* **1989**, *24*, 171–188. [CrossRef]
2. Aschauer, D.A. Is public expenditure productive? *J. Monet. Econ.* **1989**, *23*, 177–200. [CrossRef]
3. Gasques, J.G.; Bastos, E.T.; Bacchi, M.R.P.; Valdes, C. Produtividade total dos fatores e transformações da agricultura brasileira: Análise dos dados dos censos agropecuários. In *A Agricultura Brasileira: Desempenho, Desafios e Perspectivas*; Brasília Ipea: Brasilia, Brazil, 2010; pp. 19–44.
4. Capalbo, S.M.; VO, T. A review of the evidence on agricultural productivity. In *Agricultural Productivity: Measurement and Explanation*; Routledge, Abingdon-on-Thames: England, UK, 2015; pp. 96–129.
5. Wang, S.L.; Heisey, P.; Schimmelpfennig, D.; Ball, V.E. *Agricultural Productivity Growth in the United States: Measurement, Trends, and Drivers*; Economic Research Service: Washington, DC, USA, 2015.
6. Shiferaw, B.; Hellin, J.; Muricho, G. Markets access and agricultural productivity growth in developing countries: Challenges and opportunities for producer organizations. In *Cooperatives, Economic Democratization and Rural Development*; Edward Elgar Publishing: Cheltenham, UK, 2016; p. 103.
7. Orea, L.; Wall, A. A Parametric Approach to Estimating Eco-Efficiency. *J. Agric. Econ.* **2017**, *68*, 901–907. [CrossRef]
8. Ministerio de Agricultura, "El Real Decreto 147/2014, de 7 de marzo, por el que se regula la concesión directa de ayudas del Plan de Impulso al Medio Ambiente para la renovación de tractores agrícolas 'PIMA Tierra'", Madrid. 2014. Available online: https://www.boe.es/diario_boe/txt.php?id=BOE-A-2014-4382 (accessed on 23 November 2019).
9. Ministerio de Agricultura, Análisis y prospectiva-Serie INDICADORES, Madrid. 2018. Available online: https://www.mapa.gob.es/es/ministerio/servicios/analisis-y-prospectiva/informe_anual_indicadores2018__tcm30-513683.pdf (accessed on 23 November 2019).
10. Pereira, A.M. Is all public capital created equal? *Rev. Econ. Stat.* **2000**, *82*, 513–518. [CrossRef]
11. Munnell, A.H. Why has productivity growth declined? Productivity and public investment. Federal Reserve Bank of Boston. *New Engl. Econ. Rev.* **1990**, 3–22.
12. Munnell, A.H.; Cook, L.M. How does public infrastructure affect regional economic performance? *New Engl. Econ. Rev.* **1990**, 11–33.
13. Tatom, J. Public capital and private sector performance. *Fed. Reserve Bank St.Louis Rev.* **1991**, *73*, 3–15. [CrossRef]
14. Eberts, R.W. *Highway Infrastructure: Policy Issues for Regions*; Federal Reserve Bank of Chicago: Chicago, IL, USA, 1997; Available online: http://research.upjohn.org/externalpapers/38 (accessed on 23 November 2019).
15. Pereira, A.M.; Roca-Sagalés, O. Spillover effects of public capital formation: Evidence from the Spanish regions. *J. Urban Econ.* **2003**, *53*, 238–256. [CrossRef]
16. Pereira, A.M.; De Frutos, R.F. Public capital accumulation and private sector performance. *J. Urban Econ.* **1999**, *46*, 300–322. [CrossRef]
17. Pereira, A. International evidence on public investment and private sector performance. *Public Financ. Manag.* **2001**, *1*, 261–277.
18. Flores De Frutos, R.; Gracia-Díez, M.; Perez, T. Public capital stock and economic growth: An analysis of the Spanish economy. *Appl. Econ.* **1998**, *30*, 985–994. [CrossRef]
19. Cosculluela-Martínez, C. And Flores De Frutos, R. Housing investment in Spain: Has it been the main engine of growth? *Appl. Econ.* **2013**, *45*, 1835–1843. [CrossRef]
20. Cosculluela-Martínez, C.; Ibar-Alonso, R.; Hewings, G.J.D. Life Expectancy Index: Age Structure of Population and Environment Evolution. *Soc. Indic. Res.* **2019**, *142*, 507–522. [CrossRef]

21. de La Paz, P.T.; Pablo-Martí, F. Building Activities in Barcelona and Madrid Metropolitan Areas. In *European Metropolitan Commercial Real Estate Markets*; Springer: Berlin, Heidelberg, 2014; pp. 71–101.
22. Cosculluela-Martínez, C.; Flores De Frutos, R. The macroeconomic impact of transportation investment on the Spanish economy. *EJTIR* **2015**, *15*, 376–395.
23. Martínez Guirao, J.E. Desarrollo Inmobiliario y Turismo. Un Estudio Sociológico Sobre las Consecuencias de la Crisis en la Vega Baja del Segura. Ph.D. Thesis, Universitat d'Alacant-Universidad de Alicante, Alicante, Spain, 2016.
24. León Navarro, M.; Tejera Martín, I. Evaluación de la política de expansión del stock de capital como motor de crecimiento económico y convergencia entre CCAA: Los casos de Madrid y Cataluña. *Rev. Evaluación Programas Políticas Públicas* **2013**, *1*, 72–116. [CrossRef]
25. León Navarro, M.; Tejera Martín, I. Stock de Capital y Creación de Empleo. Un análisis regional para las principales CCAA. In *Centro De Documentación Del Transporte Del Ministerio De Fomento Del Gobierno De España*; Ministerio de Fomento Secretaría General Técnica Centro de Publicaciones: Madrid, Spain, 2015.
26. Jenkins, G.M.; Alavi, A.S. Some aspects of modelling and forecasting multivariate time series. *J. Time Ser. Anal.* **1981**. [CrossRef]
27. Dickey, D.A.; Fuller, W.A. Likelihood ratio statistics for autoregressive time series with a unit Root. *Econom. J. Econom. Soc.* **1981**, *1*, 1057–1072. [CrossRef]
28. Dickey, D.A.; Fuller, W.A. Distribution of the estimators for autoregressive time series with a unit root. *J. Am. Stat. Assoc.* **1979**, *74*, 427–431.
29. Johansen, S. Estimation and hypothesis testing of cointegration vectors in Gaussian vector autoregressive models. *Econom. J. Econom. Soc.* **1991**, 1551–1580. [CrossRef]
30. Johansen, S. Statistical analysis of cointegration vectors. *J. Econ. Dyn. Control* **1988**, *12*, 231–254. [CrossRef]
31. Engle, R.F.; Granger, C.W. Co-integration and error correction: Representation, estimation, and testing. *Econom. J. Econom. Soc.* **1987**, *1*, 251–276. [CrossRef]
32. Phillips, P.C.B.; Ouliaris, S. Asymptotic Properties of Residual Based Tests for Cointegration. *Econometrica* **1990**. [CrossRef]

sustainability

MDPI

Article

Work–Life Balance, Organizations and Social Sustainability: Analyzing Female Telework in Spain

Ana Gálvez [1], Francisco Tirado [2,*] and M. Jesús Martínez [3]

1 Faculty of Psychology and Education Sciences, Universitat Oberta de Catalunya, 08018 Barcelona, Spain; agalvez@uoc.edu
2 Department of Social Psychology, Universitat Autònoma de Barcelona, 08193 Bellaterra, Spain
3 Faculty of Economics and Business, Universitat Oberta de Catalunya, 08035 Barcelona, Spain; mmartinezarg@uoc.edu
* Correspondence: Franciscojavier.tirado@uab.es

Received: 30 January 2020; Accepted: 24 April 2020; Published: 27 April 2020

Abstract: The concept of work–life balance has recently established itself as a key component on route maps drawn up in the pursuit of social sustainability, both on a local scale, represented by individual organizations, and on a more general one, represented by global institutions such as the United Nations. Our article analyzes telework's use as a political tool within organizations that either boost or hinder the development of social sustainability. Additionally, we propose the notion of "life sustainability" to analyze how female teleworkers describe the link between specific work cultures and the possibility of fulfilling social sustainability goals in local work environments through the achievement of a good work–life balance. Our research was performed following a qualitative approach, drawing from a sample of 24 individual interviews and 10 focus groups with a total of 48 participants, all of which are female teleworkers with family responsibilities. Our main findings allow us to summarize the interviewees' social perceptions into two categories, which we have dubbed 'life sustainability ecologies' and 'presence-based ecologies'. We conclude by discussing female teleworkers' claim that work–life balance is directly linked to social sustainability and that the latter goal will remain out of reach as long as the issue of balance goes unresolved.

Keywords: social sustainability; work–life balance; female teleworkers; organizational culture; life sustainability ecologies; qualitative methods

1. Introduction

In 2015, the United Nations established 17 sustainable development goals (SDGs) for the entire planet to work towards and attain by 2030 [1], an initiative supposedly entailing a binding contract for all countries forming part of the organization. Three of the SDGs directly target branches of science with ties to organizational studies (SDG 8: decent work and economic growth; SDG 9: industry, innovation and infrastructure; and SDG 12: responsible consumption and production). It is explicitly stated that these goals will come as an enormous challenge for organizations and will have a significant impact on them in terms of management [2–4]. Likewise, there are at least three other SDGs that prove relevant in this regard (SDG 5: gender equality; SDG 10: reduced inequalities; and SDG 11: sustainable cities and communities). The fact that at least six of the seventeen SDGs established by the United Nations target organizations reflects the crucial role they play in creating a sustainable world and, at the same time, their importance in reducing inequality, with the ultimate goal of ensuring permanent sustainability [5,6].

In this regard, the last decade has seen proposals advocating processes of change in organizations to enhance their commitment to: (a) their surrounding environment; (b) the community in which they carry out their activities; (c) the efficient and clean use of energy; and (d) production and work organization procedures that ensure workers' future well-being and reduce social and economic inequalities [7–10]. Such proposals often overlook the importance of guaranteeing a work–life balance. Oddly enough, this absence is not reflected in the theories posited in academic literature. In fact, there is broad consensus on the fact that work–life balance is of vital importance in industrialized nations and that it is becoming a pressing issue in developing countries as well. In the former case, the massive incorporation of women into the workplace, the rise in the number of single-parent families, and the increase in dependency as a result of ageing populations are some of the factors that explain why the issue of work–life balance has become a key item on the agendas of a number of European Union states [11–18]. In the latter, the sudden creation of companies in areas of Africa and Asia as the result of outsourcing (with the consequent implementation of long working hours), the pace of transformation of local communities and unforeseen changes in age-old family traditions make this balance a new and urgent problem [19,20].

Reflecting the conclusion of academic literature, recent years have witnessed examples of companies, organizations and institutions that have introduced meaningful changes in their development agendas to ensure and promote a proper work–life balance. What is interesting about these examples is that the transformations they propose are regarded as strategic and crucial in guaranteeing the very survival of the companies in question, increasing their ability to attract and retain talent, boosting productivity and, in short, sharpening their competitive edge [21–23]. The majority of these transformations involve promoting flexibility in the organization of working time, maternity leave, the right to special childcare-related vacation time and telework. This last item is especially important, as working from home has appeared in the world of organization as a great solution to the problems hindering a proper work–life balance. In this regard, the resolution adopted by the European Parliament and the Council on measures for achieving a work–life balance recommended flexible working models, including teleworking.

Telework has been analyzed from a wide variety of viewpoints, receiving both great support and harsh criticism. Supporters underline telework's great potential to harmonize the different facets of people's lives, permitting space and time management that proves beneficial to workers [24–27], while also cutting costs for organizations [28–30]. However, other authors reveal its more controversial and negative ramifications [31–34]. Their perspective highlights the pernicious impact of teleworking, portraying teleworkers as being overloaded with work as they directly and intensely experience the conflicts and hurdles that arise when salaried, family, domestic and personal work coexist [11,35]. It also points to how, in the case of women, teleworking can bolster the role they are traditionally saddled with as those chiefly responsible for family-related matters [36–39].

Nevertheless, teleworking has not, to date, been examined as a tool that can be used for political denunciation or for proposing organizational transformations that target the seventeen sustainable development and social sustainability goals set by the United Nations. This, it is that this article will examine this very issue. Leveraging work carried out over the course of a number of years with female teleworkers, we will show that they resort to this form of working to point out two extremely important issues. Firstly, they explain which organizational conditions help make teleworking a success or a failure. Secondly, they indicate that difficulties in successfully teleworking and, therefore, in attaining a proper work–life balance, go far beyond technical issues impeding a fit between the rhythms of everyday life and work. Work–life balance appears as one more goal for helping organizations to become sustainable. In other words, it is an important element that must strongly feature on any social sustainability route map, both on a local scale, represented by individual organizations, and on a more general one, represented by global institutions such as the United Nations, with the role of safeguarding human rights. Therefore, our article contributes to the study of the relationship between organizations and the problem of social sustainability by: (a) showing how telework is employed by users as a political tool for denouncing unfavorable employment situations; (b) indicating telework's association with organizations that boost or hinder the development of social sustainability in the field of work; and (c) proposing the notion of 'life sustainability' to analyze how female teleworker describe the link between specific work cultures and the possibility of fulfilling social sustainability goals in local work environments though the achievement of a work–life balance.

As is often the case in qualitative research, our proposals do not adhere to one single theory or set of works. Rather, they are based on two different kinds of academic contributions. First, we find critical and qualitative research providing a number of insights into the perception and experiences that (male and female) employees have of the relationship between their overall quality of life and their work, family and personal activities [40,41]. Additionally, this tradition has established an active and urgent agenda [14,42] to answer the following questions: (a) What practices, cues and rituals do home-based teleworkers rely on to smooth the transition between their home and work roles [43,44]?; (b) How does technology change workers' concept and use of time and space [45,46]?; (c) What paradoxes and dilemmas are created by the discourse surrounding home-based teleworkers and their flexibility [47–49]?; and (d) What binds the relationship between flexibility, telework and identity [41]? Our research takes up the baton in this line of interest and widens its scope by exploring an entirely new topic: the relationship between female telework and social sustainability.

Second, our work sticks to a conceptual framework called "New Urban Studies" [50–52]. This defends the idea that social sustainability is a term overlapping with others such as solidarity, cohesion, integration, etc. In this vein, an umbrella concept encompassing factors including education, mental and physical health, poverty, social equity or participation is also considered. However, studies like these put forward that research grappling with social sustainability tends to forget that this cannot be analyzed in isolation without considering environmental and economic sustainability. In the bind between social and economic sustainability, New Urban Studies establishes a new theoretical and practical challenge associated with achieving greater social sustainability: the impact teleworking has on it [52]. The Urban Studies framework points out several lines of research to clarify this relationship: (a) establishing how relevant for social sustainability working without commuting between home and work is; (b) analyzing what kind of transformations telework triggers in local and international organizations to align them with the objectives of social sustainability; (c) examining how telework could change our cities and turn them into a more sustainable habitat; (d) understanding how telework producing little transformations in local practices inside organizations can trigger effects on a global scale and contribute to strengthening social sustainability objectives.

As noted above, our research focuses on female Spanish teleworkers and analyzes how this form of work affects, in practice, their work–life balance. The article's second section addresses the vital relationship between work–life balance and social sustainability, completing its analysis with an in-depth look at the importance of teleworking in the knowledge economy, as well as its potential to help redress the issues hindering work –life balance. In the third section, we provide the details of our research methodology. There are two reasons why our sample included only women. The first is that a great deal of literature shows that the issue of work–life balance is gendered [14,19,53–56] and that gender differences remain embedded in the ways in which respondents negotiate their home and work lives [15,57–59]. Therefore, we believe that women experience the greatest number of problems in achieving a proper work–life balance. The second reason is associated with the fact that women with domestic care burdens are those who most commonly take advantage of this form of work and other work flexibility measures [15,60,61]. In the fourth section, we present the results of our research; namely, two types of discourse that summarize the social perception of our interviewees, which we have dubbed 'life sustainability ecologies' and 'presence-based ecologies'. We conclude by discussing how organizations' intention to support work–life balance must be accompanied by their understanding of this balance as a key component of social sustainability, entailing: (a) an improvement in workers' working conditions; (b) greater integration of organizations in the community; (c) a direct commitment to combatting gender differences and promoting equality; and (d) an undertaking to ensure the future of the community and the organization, given that it respects the care and upbringing of dependent persons such as children.

In this vein, our paper contributes to three specific areas of research. Firstly, our own research reflects a line of work that is currently being explored by a number of fields in the organizational world: the analysis of female teleworkers' social perception of their way of working and the relationship it establishes with their work–life balance. Secondly, it shows how telework can become a political tool for denouncing situations of inequality. Lastly, it makes progress in highlighting female teleworkers' claim that work–life balance is directly linked to social sustainability and that the latter goal will remain out of reach as long as the issue of balance goes unresolved.

2. Literature Review and Conceptual Framework

2.1. Wor–Life Balance and Social Sustainability

As pointed out by Rao [23], the drawing up of an agenda for sustainable human development, like that of the United Nations, will not be complete until the issue of work–life balance is approached as a general problem that affects human rights. Work–life balance as an issue firstly relates to personal dignity in the work environment, but it also represents an in-depth approach to gender equality, community development and a future in which children's care and upbringing is not the sole responsibility of their parents. Therefore, work–life balance should be viewed as more than just a way to coordinate work and family time and space. Rather, it should be regarded as an issue that directly impacts on how we organize our societies to make them fairer and more human [62] and as one of the core themes of so-called 'social sustainability'.

This is a notion to which growing importance has been attached in academic literature over the course of the last decade. Its origins are found in the concept of sustainable development [63], the term being coined to emphasize the strong relationship between the sustainable environmental development of human beings and the labor-related and cultural facets involved in their everyday lives. So, while the notion of sustainable development focuses on the relationship between human life and its environmental impact, that of social sustainability reminds us that said lives cannot be analyzed without taking into account cultural dimensions such as those entailed by concepts like 'capitalism', 'work', 'community', etc. [64]. From the standpoint of social sustainability, no real, effective progress can be made in the field of human sustainability without ensuring the involvement of players such as organizations and businesses or without their acceptance of the fact that their agendas for community engagement must include, at the top of the list, the issue of work–life balance.

These are the lines already pointed to by the contributions of other research. For example, Rao [23] suggests that, if we create a culture that truly supports work–life balance, it is also likely to promote sustainable human development though greater role-related engagement of individuals and groupings such as organizations and institutions. Similarly, Di Fabio [9] dares to go a little further and refers to healthy organizations as those whose business structures contemplate work–life balance as a basic component of individual well-being and, therefore, of a more sustainable society. White and Thatcher [65], Mushfiqur et al. [66] and Haar et al. [62] provide good examples of specific research that analyzes work–life balance's direct impact on social sustainability. The first examines the potential role of specific work-related technologies like mobile phones in this balance; the second, a range of work–life balance measures that improved the sustainability of a specific community (Nigerian female medical doctors); and the third, the leading role that work–life balance plays in achieving the SDGs. In a similar way, Kobayashi, Eweye and Tappin [67] have analyzed how managers in a range of Japanese companies tackle and react to the work–life balance phenomenon and its relationship with sustainability.

Another research line [68–70] shows that, while certain governments and international institutions back and promote important work–life balance measures, organizational structures and cultures do not always welcome them with the required engagement. Often times, they may even employ logic that helps to ensure that women continue to bear the brunt of the problems brought on by a work–life balance and, accordingly, prevents men from becoming engaged in them [53,54]. The most commonplace of these are: (a) a workplace organization that rewards staying at one's desk for long working hours; (b) biased perceptions regarding the capacities and responsibilities of each gender with regard to caring for the family; and (c) business environments that value markedly masculine abilities [71–74]. Such logics lead to organizational cultures setting professional careers above caring for the family. They do not, therefore, foster a work–life balance and ultimately become labor, social and economic structures that are to the detriment of social sustainability.

Thus, as a number of authors have shown that an organization's culture can be a hindrance to resolving the work–life balance issue and create a clear gap between the work experience of men and women, exacerbating the reproduction of social inequalities [37,55,56,75–77]. In such cultures, physical presence and a commitment to one's job are key factors in determining the success of one's career. By way of contrast, a concern for work–life balance and family care is seen as an obstacle to workers' professional development and their productivity within an organization. The direct result is a work climate in which women are discriminated against, as they are faced with the dilemma of having to choose between their professional careers and their work–life balance [18,69,78,79]. This is why, for a decade now, some authors have been arguing that organizations need to transform their cultural matrices: in other words, the set of norms that define commitment to one's job, success at work and proper behavior with regard to family commitments [3,80–82]. Nevertheless, as pointed out by a significant part of the literature on the relationship between sustainability and organizational change [83,84], the emphasis placed by organizations in their search for a culture of sustainability focuses on issues associated with the environment, energy efficiency and their direct impact upon the surrounding community, all too often overlooking the importance of the work–life balance dimension.

2.2. The Knowledge Economy, Teleworking and Work–Life Balance

The cultural, economic and labor reality encapsulated in the concept of social sustainability has been characterized as the 'knowledge economy', the 'new economy', the 'digital economy' or the 'network economy'. It represents a significant realignment, in which the consumption of material goods gradually gives way to a prevalence of knowledge and information. As a result, our everyday lives become structured on the basis of intangible resources, knowledge and information technologies. It is thus argued that the opportunities for the development of countries, corporations, organizations and individuals are influenced by techno-scientific advances, knowledge generation and information management [85,86]. Within such a context, telework appears as the star form of working that, among other things, helps solve the seemingly never-ending issue of work–life balance.

Telework first appeared in the 1970s as a new form of labor organization that could provide a solution to many individual, social and organizational problems. It was claimed that it could cut traffic in cities and, therefore, pollution and our dependence on fossil fuels, as well as open up a new arena of employment opportunities for those with difficulties accessing the normal labor market. Similarly, a reduction in employment costs was forecast, as was an increase in productivity and, of course, a social revolution. Its implementation would solve in one stroke the work–life balance problem, increasing job satisfaction and employees' engagement with their organizations' goals [87–91].

Although teleworking is a complex phenomenon that depends upon variables such as contract type, status within an organization, the work's location and the type of task being performed, there is broad consensus in literature when it comes to its definition. It is defined as an employment practice that is decentralized—in other words, undertaken outside of an organization's place of operation—and which depends upon the use of information and communication technologies [92–94].

After a number of decades of implementation and development, a wide range of studies have assessed the real impact teleworking has on our organizations and, particularly, on our everyday lives. For example, there has been a broad examination of how teleworking cuts the cost of investment in infrastructure, equipment, electricity and water [95]. It has also been seen to lead to an increase in productivity and a reduction in absenteeism [92,96]. Nevertheless, other studies point out that telework may also give rise to risks similar to those affecting the self-employed, such as worsening contractual conditions and legal cover for workers [97,98]. Similarly, the implications associated with the social sustainability of telework have been analyzed, and the conclusions do not seem to reach any definitive agreement. While some studies state that it may enhance social sustainability in terms of human resources management and cutting traffic [24,99–101], others reach the exact opposite conclusion [102].

In the last decade, this type of study has undergone an interesting twist. Instead of focusing on telework as a device that fosters certain practices and limits others, researchers have resorted to qualitative methodologies to study the opinions, perceptions, discourses and cultural values of teleworkers with regard to their form of working [103,104]. Our article is framed within this new research perspective. Our qualitative approach allowed us to look at the social perception of female Spanish teleworkers with regard to their form of working. In our research, we encountered two interrelated dimensions that had not yet been subject to much analysis in academic literature. The first is associated with how female teleworkers describe the conditions an organization must implement to help ensure that teleworking is successful in achieving a work–life balance. The second, closely connected to the first, shows that our interviewees refer to telework as something that is much more than a mere work activity tool. They refer to it as a logical framework—one that is directly associated with social sustainability—which allows them to denounce the political climate that dominates in many Spanish organizations. Via telework, interviewees reject the systems preventing them from having a successful professional career and caring for their family at the same time, thereby calling out against organizations which keep the community in which they carry out their activities from functioning properly.

3. Methodology

3.1. Data Collection

Our research was performed following a qualitative approach, drawing from a sample of 24 individual interviews and 10 focus groups, each of which comprised from 4 to 6 participants, totaling 48 in all. Thus, 72 female teleworkers—all with family responsibilities—partook in either an individual interview or a focus group. Broken down by professional category, 8 of the participants were senior-level personnel, 22 were intermediate-level personnel, 7 were university lecturers, 25 were technicians, 6 were administrative secretaries, and 4 were translators. A total of 20% of the women in the study were full-time teleworkers, with the remaining 80% carrying out telework from between one afternoon to three days per week. The sample was drawn up to provide a faithful reflection of the employment situation in Spain. Accordingly, the distribution of the 72 teleworkers based on the type of organization in which they worked was as follows: 22.2% were from private companies, 20.8% from state-owned companies, 36.1% from private universities, 4.2% from state universities, and 16.7% were self-employed and working for several companies at once.

Given their high level of representation, it is important to note that 20 different organizations or companies took part in the study (not including the aforementioned self-employed workers). In all, 60% of these organizations were large companies (with over 500 employees), 20% were medium-sized companies (with between 50 and 500 employees), and the final 20% were small companies (with fewer than 50 employees). In preparing the sample, we sought a variety of organization types and differences in participants' professional category, their weekly time spent teleworking and their family situation. To build the sample based on these criteria, a snowball sampling method was used [105]. To commence this snowball, we contacted individuals in different companies with telework programs and sent emails and different alerts to colleagues who might know others who teleworked. Potential participants were contacted by telephone and reviewed to ascertain whether they fit the selection criteria mentioned above. All interviews and focus groups were recorded after the signing of an informed consent release. The individual interviews lasted from 45 to 60 min, and the focus group sessions, from 2 h to 2 h and 30 min. The interviews were carried out in Spanish, in cities such as Alicante, Barcelona, Bilbao, and Madrid, Spain. The focus group sessions were carried out in closed spaces (meeting rooms, offices, etc.) in the organizations in which participants worked, while individual interviews took place in their homes. The following tables (Tables 1–3) summarize the sample distribution.

Table 1. Telework status, expressed as a percentage.

Percentage	Telework Status
20%	Full-time teleworkers
80%	Part-time teleworkers (carrying out telework from between one afternoon and three days per week)

Table 2. Organizations participating in the sample, distribution by percentage.

Organization	Distribution
Private companies	22.2%
State-owned companies	20.8%
Private universities	36.1%
State universities	4.2%
Self-employed workers	16.7%

Research was performed using two different interview guides. One was prepared especially for individual interviews and covered the following topics: (a) motivations for choosing telework; (b) the pros and cons of teleworking; (c) the relationship between telework and everyday home life; (d) the impact of the job on their domestic organization; (e) opinions on gender differences in the teleworking-work/life balance relationship; (f) telework and professional career; and (g) acceptance of telework in the workplace. The second was aimed at focus groups and was structured around the following issues: (a) the effectiveness of telework in achieving a work–life balance; (b) the relationship between gender and telework; (c) telework and space and time reorganization in the home; (d) the pros and cons of telework for the organizations using it; and (e) gender differences and telework. These guides were designed to offer a flexible framework that could be adapted according to participants' responses by adding new questions and themes on the fly [105].

3.2. Data Analysis

As noted above, consent was given by the participants to record and transcribe the interviews and focus groups. From the transcripts, fragments were extracted, called 'verbatims'. These fragments consisted of opinions or assertions that are particularly relevant in responding to or clarifying one of the issues raised in the interview guide. The verbatims were analyzed for their thematic content, taking place in three phases: pre-analysis, codification, and categorization. In the first stage, our aim was (a) familiarization with the data as a whole; (b) organization of information for analysis; and (c) identification of relevant content in line with the research objectives. In the second stage, we divided up the interviews according to our findings in the first stage. We established a context unit for every relevant piece of content in order to properly understand and interpret it. Then we catalogued the analysis units according to the following criteria: (a) meaning; (b) frequency of appearance; and (c) evaluation by the interviewee. In the final stage, we organized and classified the analysis units into categories. Qualitative content analysis was carried out using the ATLAS.ti program.

4. Results: Life Sustainability Ecologies vs. Presence-Based Ecologies

Our results are opinions, which we show using what are called 'verbatims' in qualitative perspectives. These relevant fragments spoken by our interviewees have been selected due to their value in illustrating an important topic in the research. The set of all verbatims shed light on our interviewees' social perception of the relationship between telework and work–life balance. Their opinions, and the verbatims representing them, have been grouped into three different dimensions. We view the dimensions as types of discourse because they revolve around specific topics, highlight the coherence and logic used, and present a set of issues on which this general logic is built. The three dimensions are:

(a) The assessment of how organizations implement, promote and deploy telework;
(b) The everyday use of this form of working and its integration into one's home life; and
(c) The effects of telework on one's everyday life and professional career.

In presenting the results, the dimensions are given the following names:

Axis 1: the implementation of telework
Axis 2: integration into domestic and family life
Axis 3: the effects of telework

In turn, the opinions expressed in these three axes make up two large-scale categories of social perception, which we have named 'life sustainability ecologies' and 'presence-based ecologies'. In what follows, we will provide a detailed description of these two categories and, for each one, present certain verbatims spoken by our participants to illustrate their opinions with respect to the three axes.

There are two reasons behind our decision to name the two categories as we have done. The first is that our interviewees directly described their organizations as having one of these two viewpoints. They pointed out that some companies lay the groundwork for life sustainability—a philosophy similar to social sustainability—and that in work environments such as these it is easy and simple to find a harmonic work–life balance. Meanwhile, in other companies, priority is given to a more classical presence-based logic, in which finding such a balance proves impossible. The second reason is associated with the word 'ecology', which prevails in our research over other, more commonplace terms, such as 'culture' or 'system'. This is because our participants' explanations of their experiences included references to their organizations as a whole or as an environment in which they were positioned, with this positioning working as either a catalyst for certain actions or a disrupter of or hindrance to others. As some authors [106] point out, the notion of 'ecology' goes beyond that of 'culture', focusing on aspects such as meanings, rituals and signals in referring to a whole that delimits a set of social relationships and the meanings attached to them. Additionally, it goes beyond that of a 'system' in that it stresses ecological perspectives' focus on a subject within a particular context which, in turn, establishes the subject's behavior by means of intrapersonal, interpersonal, institutional, community and public policy-related factors [107,108].

4.1. First Category: Life Sustainability Ecologies

The three discourse axes mentioned above are expressed in this social perception category as follows:

4.1.1. Axis 1: The Implementation of Telework

The first of our axes is associated with the manner in which telework is implemented within an organization. The first issue to clearly appear in our interviews is related to the technological support required for this form of working. Our interviewees stated that their organizations make the technological equipment required to successfully carry out teleworking available to their workers.

> *… the facilities … with ADSL, er … and a VPN, a … secure line, and I'm working at home, or anywhere, a hotel, or even an internet café, with my computer, with a private line and at a reasonable speed, and … it's like I was here at the office. So, there, also, well … well the telephone connection you can make … er … with some numbers in Spain that are toll-free, shall we say, so that you can call anywhere (…) And so I'm connected like I would be here […], in this sense they have it well sorted, because, er, there are measures, well, programs for flexibility and teleworking is one of them, and, well, it suits me and I take advantage of it … (I017_manager_part-time teleworking)*

The second issue detected relates to whether the organization has explicit work–life balance programs or offers flexible working measures, in which telework is a real possibility that staff whose duties so permit can take advantage of.

> *But I ... what I'm referring to, and in this I agree with you, however, there must be a regulatory framework, put it that way, which ... which allows all teleworkers to in some way benefit either from teleworking or from a work–life balance, and that, on this basis, obviously, everyone is responsible for their work, because obviously ... the fact of introducing telework implies the organization trusts people, right? (FG3_005_training manager_part-time teleworking)*

A third issue relates to the support openly expressed by senior management and non-teleworking staff, both of whom regard teleworking measures as positive and show great respect for each worker's family situation.

> *... well, here everyone's got something, in my case I do it for the kids, but I have women coworkers who have really elderly parents and, well, everyone ... has something going on, and in that regard the organization shows respect, they don't ask that of us ... if you have young children ... but it's taken for granted that everyone has their needs. (FG9_060_assistant manager_full-time teleworking)*

Support from senior management is a key factor in ensuring that telework operates properly. The most frequently mentioned aspect associated with this is the peace of mind that they will not be penalized simply for not being physically present in the organization. Directly related to this support are organizations' methods for planning work based on clear, explicit goals.

> *It needs to be assessed. A results-based assessment, with the establishment of carefully calculated goals, on a monthly basis, systems for this assessment in a year ... in a year, goals cannot be assessed, as nobody has a year's long-term memory. Goals need to be ... shorter in timescale for labor relations much more thought out and then, see how telework, well regulated and well done, so, it fits in all of this. In the company's own entire work organization, right? (FG3_005_ training manager_part-time teleworking)*

Sometimes, our interviewees stated that the subject of goal-based planning gives way to a kind of cultural or value-based metaorganization.

> *What we do ... this is a ... this is very important: company XXX, as a company, fosters values-based management, OK? Let's say, I don't know if you've spoken to other companies, but until a few years ago it was results-based ... we go a bit further and do it by values, in other words: "The company has some cultural values that also entail business results", I mean, they're included, that's key, and what really ... what we do, we've ... we have, we set some personal goals, they're called ... personal ... BCs ... personal business commitments ... oof! (laughs), this is a personal commitment, in other words ... I ... yep, from top to bottom ... They are documented and continuously monitored, in other words ... and the same goes for me and my staff. I have my business goal, which everyone is aware of, and the goals, not so much business ones, but of personal development, aligned with the company's values, OK? (I031_business unit manager_part-time teleworking)*

4.1.2. Axis 2: Integration into Domestic and Family Life

For this second axis, we looked at the integration between telework and these women workers' daily lives. Here, telework appears linked to the possibility of self-managing one's time and that this means being able to autonomously arrange the different aspects of one's everyday life. In life sustainability ecologies, such arrangements are presented as fluid and harmonious. The most noted example is the ability to manage and carry out different daily tasks and handle various responsibilities in accordance with one's individual needs, as they appear as pieces of a puzzle that have to be fit together throughout the course of the day.

> *Time is what's most important, it's all, I dunno. From the silliest thing that in another job would be a disaster, like your washing machine breaks down and they come to fix it, it's crucial, you're working and the technician comes and repairs it. In another company you'd have to arrange ... well, it'd be a nightmare. These might seem like small things, but they're really important. (I040_social media specialist_part-time teleworking)*

The feeling of independence and the appearance of a strong sense of controlling one's life in and out of work were key factors for many interviewees, as clearly reflected in the following verbatim:

> *The way I am, the key advantage of teleworking is that it gives me the flexibility to organize my many roles as mother (...), studying, and so on ... if not, it would be impossible. And, for me, perhaps the key advantage is that ... above all, my work–life balance and everything stemming from it. The key advantage I find in it is that it leaves you with quality time for planning, for thinking clearly about the projects you're doing. I take a day, a day and a half where I feel I'm uninterrupted so you're not leading a life where you're always running around like a headless chicken. (I032_managing partner_part-time teleworking)*

The ways and times in which teleworkers do their jobs is usually decided upon by the teleworkers themselves. They organize the relationship between the type of tasks performed and when they are done. It is true that, in many jobs, the work rhythm is not constant and certain times require more dedication than others. Similarly, family demands also vary. In the case of families with children, holiday periods, or when the children are ill, are times when female teleworkers spend less time on their jobs, which they make up for at other times.

4.1.3. Axis 3: The Effects of Telework

In the third axis, an assessment of the effects and consequences of teleworking in the context of these life sustainability ecologies was performed. The first consequence identified by our interviewees is an increase in on-the-job performance. This they attribute, basically, to two things. This first is associated with teleworkers' ability to concentrate on their work better and distance themselves from the interruptions generally created in traditional work environments, while the second is directly related to the goal-based organization of work commented on above. Our interviewees note that these goals allow them to work more intensely and efficiently.

> *I think that those of us who telework, in general, increase our productivity; if they have this debate on the increase in productivity, it's for both the worker and the company. I think it's a very subjective assessment, I think that one of the big problems that we have in knowledge-related jobs is to see what everyone is contributing. I believe that everyone thinks that this goes on a lot and is really productive, but it's difficult to prove and difficult to measure; so, having a good goal-based policy in a company is vital, but it's really not easy. (I032_managing partner_part-time teleworking)*

In addition to the above, the interviewees point to the great importance of a perception of control over their lives. This control is closely linked to the freedom they experience when it comes to organizing their time and space. This self-management and self-organization is described as a fluid and harmonious set of options that offers them new stability and life sustainability:

> *The freedom to choose when to work, and the times that are the deadest, here, or the busiest, you're more productive there, at home, to use it in another ... there are no down times, there are no moments when you say ... "What should I be doing?" Nope. There's always something to do, whether it's for you, for work, for the kids, or for the home. So, [you can] choose how to ensure the best fit between your time and ... work time. The freedom to choose when to work, how to work ... (FG9_060_assistant manager_full-time teleworking)*

This feeling of control leads to other specific effects associated with their relationship with the organization in which they work. We are referring, firstly, to the loyalty that this form of working inspires; these women workers state that they would not change employer even if they were offered a higher salary, as the advantages telework offers them more than offset any others stemming from other forms of compensation or reward. Secondly, there is the resulting engagement. The following quotes make explicit reference to these two effects:

> *I'm aware that I'm lucky, ok? That ... that ... you can't take this for granted, I mean, that ... the fact is that the more advantages you have, the harder it is for you ... to give up, right? In other words, you suddenly find that ... you assume it's normal, and anything short of these expectations seems horrible. (FG6_045_computer technician_part-time teleworking)*

From all of the above, our interviewees can be seen as describing telework as something beyond a mere technical tool which allows them to achieve a better fit between their work and personal lives. It appears as an employment logic or system with a clear political component. Telework is a means of providing life sustainability. Thanks to it, two important facets of their lives can be coordinated, without the need for either one to prevail over the other or to renounce either of them. Additionally, telework is a means of describing the type of organizations in which they work. They are described as wholes (senior management, technological resources, flexible working programs, support, etc.) that foster this sustainability.

Three core factors broadly define what we have dubbed life sustainability ecologies. The first refers to a concern for implementing clear and specific work–life balance-related policies within flexible working programs implemented in a fair and equitable way among all staff. Such programs need to be accompanied by the organization of work based on specific, measurable and quantifiable goals. The second relates to how such policies are greatly appreciated by workers. Furthermore, such measures are seen as a sign of an organization's commitment and the trust it places in its employees. Female teleworkers in organizations of this type view telework as a tool that gives them a boost on the road towards balancing and enjoying the different facets of life (personal, family, professional, etc.). This satisfaction translates to enhanced commitment to the organization to which they belong. Although they are not always physically present there, they are not under the impression that they are renouncing or losing any advantage in their professional careers and believe that they have achieved what they define as a degree of life sustainability that is desirable for all workers. In this regard, these factors show that so-called 'life sustainability' is a key dimension in what we have previously called 'social sustainability'. The third and final factor refers to the fact that sustainability technologies are shaped in organizations in which work and life cultures based on factors such as equality and respect for workers' non-job-related needs are upheld and actively promoted. This factor should be mentioned and borne in mind, as it represents a fundamental difference with what we have named 'presence-based ecologies'.

4.2. *Second Category: Presence-Based Ecologies*

In our research, we found a significant number of women who, although teleworking, did not attest to a life sustainability ecology such as those noted above. Quite the opposite. They stated that their job was carried out in environments in which telework was not appreciated and more importance was attached to a presence-based culture where spending long days at the workplace dominated the work environment. This situation is defined as a 'presence-based ecology', as the logic governing its working hours is based on the value attached to spending many hours at the workplace. The discourse-based axes shaping presence-based ecologies are as follows:

4.2.1. Axis 1: The Implementation of Telework

As in the case of life sustainability ecologies, the first axis in this other type of ecology is associated with the implementation of telework in organizations. In this case, technical support for telework is minimal and, in the majority of interviews, it was indicated that it was the teleworker herself who had to bear the costs of this technology. With regard to teleworking programs, the interviewees stated that, although there were flextime programs in their organizations that included the option of teleworking, this did not mean that everyone could take advantage of them. Telework was granted by senior management on a discretional basis.

> *Let's see, the first thing I'd like to say is that I telework, but it's not, it's not in my contract or anything. I mean, it's a benefit I can ... which I can ... , well, I can make work because ... I've got a manager who ... who thinks it's alright. Basically because he's an online manager and he's not Spanish. XXX gives you ... certain benefits, but those who I know working here at a local level, with local bosses, the fact is that they don't, they don't telework, or if they do it's only very sporadically. Because it's not understood. If you're at home, you're not working, and they have to see you at work, you have to be the last to leave, like at any other company here. (...) What's more, I know people it'd suit right down to the ground, and they don't get it. (I011_project manager_full-time teleworking)*

Telework can thus appear as part of an organization's policies. Nevertheless, its implementation here is discretional and its criteria, with regard to both implementation and usage, are not communicated transparently. In this regard, our interviewees complained about the lack of support in their organizations. This is due to the fact that the organizational culture is based on physical presence; that is, the time spent at one's desk is highly regarded as a means of assessing performance, engagement and commitment to the organization. In these kinds of dynamics, teleworking is often organized to emulate traditional, presence-based working hours.

> *... I mean that there are, for example, people who, even though you're teleworking, impose working hours ... in other words, you have to be connected until six in the evening, while there are others who ... for whom it's enough that you're connected for three hours .... (I037_computer programmer_part-time teleworking)*

Interviewees stated that there were great tensions between presence-based working hours and teleworking ones. Female teleworkers in this environment strongly criticized this system and complained that, even though their organizations provided the possibility of teleworking as a measure for achieving a work–life balance, the clash between the realities of telework and the presence-based culture were huge. Unlike in life sustainability ecologies, there is no goal-based organization of work; instead, a worker's engagement and performance is assessed on the amount of time he or she is present at the workplace. Our interviewees expressed their complete disagreement with such dynamics, the effects of which will be examined in the third axis.

4.2.2. Axis 2: Integration into Domestic and Family Life

In the case of the second axis in presence-based ecologies, which associates telework with domestic and family life, a painful conflict between the two spheres is made clear:

> *I think so, in principle at least, but we pay a price, obviously. But, I mean, in theory, yes, I'd agree. Now, to achieve a balance between your work, family and personal lives, it entails ... I dunno ... working from 11 at night to 3 in the morning, because you're connected, and you achieve a balance, yeah, yeah. Thanks to teleworking you achieve this balance, but ... it's that ... I think ... I, at least, feel we pay a price. (FG3_007_lecturer_part-time teleworking)*

This conflictive relationship basically finds expression in the excessive workload experienced by these female teleworkers. Our interviewees referred to this situation in terms of exploitation and have asserted that, to a great extent, they themselves are responsible for it. As they arrange their time with a certain degree of freedom, they aspire to 'do it all', be it professionally or in terms of family or household activities, etc. This feeling of excessive workload also leads them to sometimes define telework as a sort of exploitation of oneself by oneself:

I don't know ... I don't know what, what characteristics we should have ... as ... I already work on the basis that it's ... it's a sort of self-exploitation you're doing, isn't it? (FG2_073_executive assistant_part-time teleworking)

With this kind of dynamic, it is common to hear teleworking referred to as a trap you can fall into. Flexible working hours means that telework makes more time available for the family and the home but the paid work still has to be done, and so family and work commitments end up taking over all their time and creating, on occasion, situations of tiredness, stress and even depression.

But you've also got to qualify this balance a lot ... in other words, of the cases we've raised here, I've at certain times hinted, but I think that no one's understanding telework, be it part-time or not, as I telework, and I give the baby his bottles and clean and go to the bank. Obviously, this is not achieving a work–life balance, this is like ... obviously, it's being superwoman. [...] I work and do 50 other things at the same time, that's no kind of balance ... (FG5_020_ middle manager_part-time teleworking)

4.2.3. Axis 3: The Effects of Telework

In this third axis, an assessment is made of the effects and consequences of teleworking in presence-based ecologies. The first consequence brought up by our interviewees is directly associated with what we have noted with regard to presence-based cultures. These female teleworkers state that, in such contexts, telework means missing out on career opportunities:

Hmm, well, in a way ... it always depends on the company you're in, but, but, it tends to limit your profess ... your promotion. Well, in the case of teleworking, I dunno, because ... only results matter, they don't know how long you've actually been at it, there's no way of knowing, but when you're in a company, what's important is being there. That you're visible. (I001_translator_full-time teleworking)

There is a clear denouncement of the equating of responsibility and commitment with a high degree of physical presence. They make constant criticisms of promotion criteria and policies, as they entail, among other things, becoming involved in pointless logics associated with complete wastes of time, referring to such situations with expressions like brownnosing, lobbying, desk warming, etc. In this regard, there is agreement in asserting that one indispensable precondition for promotion in today's organizations is simply remaining continually physically present.

Because, the way companies do things, why ... do you promote yourself? Well, so that your bosses see that the work you do is good, and how do they see that? With a report you submit to them every six months? They have to see you, they have to ... picture you, that's what I say, OK? (FG5_021_ commercial manager_part-time teleworking)

It is interesting to note that many women assume the fact that teleworking may put their career at risk. In the words of one of the interviewees, "they put it on the line" even in those companies in which teleworking is portrayed as an employment option one can freely take advantage of. This situation is expressed by means of the assumption that there will be no chance of promotion, as they are not regarded as true professionals.

Compared with the previous perceptions of organizations offering conditions for what we have dubbed life sustainability, here we clearly see the perception of ecologies in which teleworking is unviable and unsustainable, causing people to experience feelings of guilt and suffering, despite the fact that many of these women argue that telework helps them be more productive and efficient. In addition to all of this, many female teleworkers added that their organizations were still convinced that problems may only be solved through physical presence. This belief means that job dynamics are organized on the basis of one's physical presence, and agreed teleworking times are not respected. Small-scale practices such as the times arranged for face-to-face meetings, working group updates, etc., constantly ignore the working hours established for female teleworkers. The following example is highly illustrative of this:

> *I mean that there are, for example, people who, although you're teleworking, impose specific hours … in other words, you have to be connected until six in the evening, while there are others who … for whom it's enough that you're connected for three hours, they may well call you at eight in the evening, and if you're connected, well, you can do something … an incident … anything else, and … well, if you're not connected, well, it doesn't matter. (I037_computer programmer_part-time teleworking)*

Unlike in the previous case, in this type of organizational ecology there is no sense of control over one's work–life balance. Teleworking is carried on in a climate of mistrust and penalization. Efforts to achieve a work–life balance tend to cause conflict and stress. In this regard, the majority of interviewees were very clear in expressing the fact that they felt subject to situations of gender inequality. Given that it is women who tend to opt for teleworking, because they directly shoulder the responsibility to achieve this balance, their career progression is interrupted or they are penalized in comparison with their male colleagues.

> *And, as they don't trust you, I think that often, it's not that … they require you to work more, but … they're more demanding, eh, in what you're doing, right? The fact that handing things in there, because you're there … eh … it could be that you're there and, and … you don't finish that day, but as you're there, at the job you're doing, well, heck, at least you've put the hours in. But … if you don't hand things in perhaps even more quickly … when you're teleworking, they don't … don't trust you, they might be thinking, "Honestly, who knows what she's up to?", the same demands in terms of deadlines, or demands, I dunno … in assignments, right? (FG2_072_journalist_part-time teleworking)*

Lastly, it must be added that women who telework in this kind of ecology find it very difficult to escape from the feeling or attitude of always being available or connected in some way. The environment in which they work forces them to be available like this:

> *It's clear that you're now in a situation in terms of … of … technology that gives you the 24/7, the 24/7 that we foster in company, that you have a company that can be … looking at your products or winning customers or available 24/7, so this means that, nowadays, what you say happens, that you have work 24/7 … in other words, you're working 24 hours a day, 7 days a week, right? (FG7_048_middle manager_part-time teleworking)*

There is one very clear factor that operates intensely and that defines, ultimately, what presence-based ecologies entail. We are referring here to the time physically spent (or not) at the workplace. In organizations with this type of ecology, teleworking does not constitute an acceptable way of carrying out one's job. It is regarded as a privilege, an eccentricity or a quasi-penalizing regime used by those not fully committed to their job. Furthermore, our female teleworkers stated that presence-based cultures reject or shun family or private life, as it is considered completely secondary to work, the only environment in which one can achieve full personal realization. It is precisely in this point that there is a denouncement of organizations with this type of culture as unsustainable undertakings. For our women interviewees, it is obvious that a culture that does not foster life outside of work, a work–life balance or personal satisfaction beyond one's job is a culture that, due to its inhumanity, is neither sustainable nor has any future.

A summary of our results are listed in Table 3 below:

Table 3. Summary of the main results of the analysis.

	1. The Implementation of Telework	2. Integration into Domestic and Family Life	3. The Effects of Telework	General Results
Life Sustainability Ecologies	-Organizations offer adequate technological support for teleworking -Organizations offer explicit work–life balance programs -Senior managers and non-teleworking staff openly express their support	-Time is self-managed -Autonomy -Independence -Strong sense of control over one's life	-Better job performance -Perception of control over one's life -Harmonious self-management -More loyalty and engagement with the organization	-All staff can telework -Physical absence is not penalized -Teleworkers do not feel that their professional career is threatened
Presence-Based Ecologies	-Minimal technical support for teleworking -Teleworking is considered a perkfor senior managers -Tensions exist between presence-based working hours and teleworking ones	-Teleworking is considered a trap as it translates to more working hours	-Teleworking entails missing out on career opportunities -Responsibility and commitment are equated to a high degree of physical presence -No control over one's work–life balance -Teleworkers end up being available to the organization 24/7	-Use of telework is discretional -Teleworking is a perk reserved for senior managers -The issue of work–life balance is not considered relevant -Presence-based working is seen as the rule governing an organization's entire behavior

5. Discussion: Organizations, Work–Life Balance and Social Sustainability

There is an interesting factor that we have not yet mentioned and that appears to influence the shaping and defining of life sustainability or presence-based ecologies. This is the size and the sector of the organization in which our interviewees work. Sustainability ecologies appear in the discourse of those working in large companies, while a presence-based ecology does so in those working for small and medium-sized enterprises. Similarly, the former tends to appear in organizations in the communications sector, while the latter does so in other types of organizations. Lastly, mention should be made of the fact that the former type of ecology is defined by those working in organizations with clear corporate social responsibility policies, while the latter appears in companies in which this issue is not regarded as important.

Given all of the above, we see that the impact that teleworking may have on one's everyday life depends upon the following factors: (a) the support offered by an organization, from both senior managers and non-teleworking staff members; (b) the degree of autonomy permitted when it comes to organizing one's own time and space, as well as the tasks to be performed; and (c) the degree of penalization associated (or not) with this new form of working by the organization. The so-called life sustainability ecologies allow all staff to telework, do not penalize one's physical absence from the workplace, and women workers do not experience any threats to their professional careers. On the other hand, in presence-based ecologies, the use of telework as a form of employment is discretional; it is not based on clear criteria, is considered a perk, is at the mercy of decisions made by senior management and is not associated with achieving a work–life balance. Furthermore, presence-based working is seen as the rule governing organizations' entire behavior.

Compared with such a presence-based mentality, life sustainability ecologies prescribe flexibility as a solution. Work is planned on a goal-based approach, assessments are not made on the basis of time physically spent at the workplace and results are evaluated in terms of quality. This type of ecology tends to set more realistic goals in terms of fulfilment and takes into account workers' personal and family situations. Efforts are made not to organize meetings after school hours, during the school holidays or at weekends. This is not the case in presence-based ecologies, which require workers to be available 24/7. Additionally, we can state that life sustainability ecologies show a greater respect for equality of rights between genders and reject any kind of discrimination. The careers of their women workers are as respected and safeguarded as those of their male colleagues. In this regard, it is no exaggeration to state that organizations with a life sustainability ecology are fully compliant with the goals sought by social sustainability. By way of contrast, presence-based ecologies are associated with organizations that are standing in the way of their fulfilment.

6. Conclusions

The word telework may appear to denote a homogenous reality, usually characterized by two dimensions. On the one hand, it is seen as a technology-based way of working. On the other, it has an organizational connotation that often relates to issues surrounding the way in which work is managed through this form of employment. Nevertheless, as shown in Table 3, this reality is, in fact, heterogeneous, hiding differences and a range of problems brought on by political, cultural, ethical and very much everyday issues. It is clear that teleworking entails an increase in flexibility for its users—something clearly posed by a lot of our interviewees. It can also prove to be a useful tool for achieving a work–life balance. However, this form of work invokes widely varying experiences. Successes, failures and misunderstandings in its usage are intermeshed with cultural issues in organizations that foster or hinder such experiences. This proves evident when comparing the two columns of Table 3. Ultimately, organizations attempting to use telework as a measure for achieving a work–life balance while also retaining a strong presence-based culture are setting themselves up for failure.

The two ecologies detected in our research—life sustainability ecologies and presence-based ecologies—highlight the fact that telework is much more than a new way of working. The opinions of the female teleworkers in our study show us that it is also used as a political tool and as an instrument for denouncing certain organizational practices. Similarly, our study participants commented on how the success of telework as a measure for achieving a work–life balance establishes productive harmony between the individual, the organization and the community. Therefore, telework has proved itself to be a key component of organizational realities that are aligned with social sustainability agendas. Although it can help workers achieve this work–life balance, telework on its own is no guarantee of success in this regard, nor as a tool that per se fosters such sustainability. It needs to be surrounded by a context of support and promotion, which is directly related to organizational cultures. Changing these cultures to foster this form of working and the general sustainability that its employment can entail is undoubtedly one of the great challenges facing the knowledge-based economy.

Author Contributions: Conceptualization: A.G., F.T., M.J.M.; Data curation: A.G., F.T.; Formal Analysis: A.G., F.T.; Methodology: A.G., F.T.; Writing-original draft: A.G., F.T., M.J.M.; Writing-review editing: A.G., F.T. All authors have read and agreed to the published version of the manuscript.

Funding: This research received no external funding.

Conflicts of Interest: The authors declare no conflict of interest.

References

1. United Nations. 17 Goals to Transform Our World. Available online: http://www.un.org/sustainabledevelopment (accessed on 1 April 2019).
2. George, G.; Howard-Grenville, J.; Joshi, A.; Tihanyi, L. Understanding and tackling societal grand challenges through management research. *Acad. Manag. J.* **2016**, *59*, 1880–1895. [CrossRef]
3. Warren, M.; Donaldson, S.; Lee, J.; Donaldson, S. Reinvigorating Research on Gender in the Workplace Using a Positive Work and Organizations Perspective. *Int. J. Manag. Rev.* **2019**, *21*, 498–518. [CrossRef]
4. Savaneviciene, A.; Stankeviciute, Z. Smart Power as a Pathway for Employing Sustainable Human Resource Management. *Eng. Econ.* **2017**, *28*, 198–206. [CrossRef]
5. Delmas, M.A.; Lyon, T.P.; Maxwell, J.W. Understanding the role of the corporation in sustainability transitions. *Organ. Environ.* **2019**, *32*, 87–97. [CrossRef]

6. Vogel, D. Promoting Sustainable Government Regulation: What We Can Learn from California. *Org. Environ.* **2019**, *32*, 145–158. [CrossRef]
7. Crifo, P.; Durand, R.; Gont, J.P. Encouraging Investors to Enable Corporate Sustainability Transitions: The Case of Responsible Investment in France. *Organ. Environ.* **2019**, *32*, 125–144. [CrossRef]
8. De Stefano, F.; Bagdadli, S.; Camuffo, A. The HR role in corporate social responsibility and sustainability: A boundary-shifting literature review. *Hum. Resour. Manag.* **2017**, *57*, 549–566. [CrossRef]
9. Di Fabio, A. The Psychology of Sustainability and Sustainable Development for Well-Being in Organizations. *Front. Psychol.* **2017**, *8*, 1534. [CrossRef]
10. Baumgartner, R.; Rauter, R. Strategic perspectives of corporate sustainability management to develop a sustainable organization. *J. Clean. Prod.* **2016**, *140*, 81–92. [CrossRef]
11. Sorensen, S. The performativity of choice: Postfeminist perspective on work-life balance. *Gen. Work Organ.* **2017**, *24*, 297–313. [CrossRef]
12. Freeney, M.K.; Stritch, J.M. Family-friendly policies, gender, and work-life balance in public sector. *Rev. Public Pers. Adm.* **2019**, *39*, 422–448. [CrossRef]
13. Lewis, S.; Beauregard, T. The meanings of work-life balance: A cultural perspective. In *The Cambridge Handbook of the Global Work-Family Interface*; Johnson, R., Shen, W., Shockley, K.M., Eds.; Cambridge University Press: Cambridge, UK, 2018; pp. 720–732.
14. Emslie, C.; Hunt, K. Live to work or work to live? A qualitative study of gender and work-life balance among men and women in mid-life. *Gen. Work Organ.* **2009**, *16*, 151–172. [CrossRef]
15. Gregory, A.; Milner, S. Work-life balance: A matter of choice? *Gen. Work Organ.* **2009**, *16*, 1–13. [CrossRef]
16. Halrynjo, S. Men's work-life conflict: Career, care and self-realization: Patterns of privileges and dilemmas. *Gen. Work Organ.* **2009**, *16*, 98–125. [CrossRef]
17. Maume, D.; Sebastian, R.; Bardo, A. Gender, work-family responsibilities, and sleep. *Gen. Soc.* **2010**, *24*, 746–768. [CrossRef]
18. Watts, J.H. Allowed into a man's world meanings of work-life balance: Perspectives of women civil engineers as "minority" workers in construction. *Gen. Work Organ.* **2009**, *16*, 37–57. [CrossRef]
19. Adisa, T.; Abdulraheem, I.; Isiaka, S. Patriarchal hegemony: Investigating the impact of patriarchy on women's work-life balance. *Gen. Manag.* **2019**, *34*, 19–33. [CrossRef]
20. De Klerk, M.; Mostert, K. Work-home interference: Examining socio-demographic predictors in the South African context. *J. Hum. Resour. Manag.* **2010**, *8*, 10. [CrossRef]
21. Hsiao–Ping, C.; Chi–Ming, H.; Meei–Ying, L.; Han–Shen, C. Examining the Moderating Effects of Work–Life Balance between Human Resource Practices and Intention to Stay. *Sustainability* **2019**, *11*, 4585.
22. Klindzic, M.; Maric, M. Flexible work arrangements and organizational performance -the difference between employee and employer-driven practices. *J. Gen. Soc. Issues* **2019**, *28*, 89–108.
23. Rao, I. Work-Life Balance for Sustainable Human Development: Cultural Intelligence as Enabler. *J. Hum. Behav. Soc. Environ.* **2017**, *7*, 706–713. [CrossRef]
24. Alina–Mihaela, D.; Tuclea, C.E.; Vrânceanu, D.M.; Tigu, G. Sustainable Social and Individual Implications of Telework: A New Insight into the Romanian Labor Market. *Sustainability* **2019**, *11*, 3506.
25. Malenfant, R. Risk, Control and Gender: Reconciling Production and Reproduction in the Risk Society. *Organ. Stud.* **2009**, *30*, 205–226. [CrossRef]
26. Tietze, S.; Musson, G. Identity, identity work and the experience of working from home. *J. Manag. Dev.* **2010**, *29*, 148–156. [CrossRef]
27. Lister, K.; Harnish, T. Workshifting Benefits: The Bottom Line. 2010. Available online: http://www.workshifting.com/downloads/downloads/Workshifting%20Benefits-The%20Bottom%20Line.pdf (accessed on 1 September 2014).
28. Mirchandani, K. The best of both worlds and Cutting my own throat: Contradictory images of home-based work. *Qual. Sociol.* **2000**, *23*, 159–182. [CrossRef]
29. Gregg, M. *Work's Intimacy*; Polity Press: Cambridge, UK, 2011.
30. Kanellopoulos, D. How Can Teleworking Be Pro-Poor? *J. Enterp. Inf. Manag.* **2011**, *24*, 8–29. [CrossRef]
31. Daniels, K.; Lamond, D.; Standen, P. Teleworking: Frameworks for organizational research. *J. Manag.* **2001**, *38*, 1151–1185. [CrossRef]

32. Pyöriä, P. Managing Telework: Risks, Fears and Rules. *Manag. Res. Rev.* **2011**, *34*, 386–399. [CrossRef]
33. Sarker, S.; Xiao, X.; Sarker, S.; Ahuja, M. Managing employees' use of mobile technologies to minimize work-life balance impacts. *MIS Q. Exec.* **2012**, *11*, 143–157.
34. Vega, R.; Anderson, A.; Kaplan, S. A within-Person Examination of the Effects of Telework. *J. Bus. Psychol.* **2015**, *30*, 313–323. [CrossRef]
35. Wheatley, D. Good to Be Home? Time-Use and Satisfaction Levels among Home-Based Teleworkers'. *New Technol. Work Employ.* **2012**, *27*, 224–241. [CrossRef]
36. Hilbrecht, M.; Shaw, S.; Johnson, L.; Andrey, J. Remixing work, family and leisure: Teleworkers' experiences of everyday life. *New Technol. Work Employ.* **2013**, *28*, 130–144. [CrossRef]
37. Lewis, S. Restructuring workplace cultures: The ultimate work-family challenge? *Women Manag. Rev.* **2001**, *16*, 21–29. [CrossRef]
38. Tremblay, D. *Work-Family Balance: What Are the Sources of Difficulty and What Could Be Done?* Research Note, n°2004-03A of Canada Research Chair on the Socio-Organizational Challenges of the Knowledge Economy; Université du Québec: Quebec, QC, Canada, 2004.
39. Gurstein, P. *Wired to the World, Chained to the Home: Telework in Daily Life*; University of British Columbia Press: Vancouver, BC, Canada, 2001.
40. King, E.B.; Botsford, W.E.; Huffman, A.H. Work, Family, and Organizational Advancement: Does Balance Support the Perceived Advancement of Mothers? *Sex Roles* **2009**, *61*, 879–891. [CrossRef]
41. Wilson, M.; Greenhill, A. Gender and teleworking identities in the risk society: A research agenda. *New Technol. Work Employ.* **2004**, *19*, 207–221. [CrossRef]
42. Brannen, J. Time and the Negotiation of Work–Family Boundaries: Autonomy or illusion? *Time Soc.* **2005**, *14*, 113–131. [CrossRef]
43. Fonner, K.; Stache, L. All in a day's work, at home: Teleworkers' management of micro role transitions and the work–home boundary. *New Technol. Work Employ.* **2012**, *27*, 242–257. [CrossRef]
44. Nätti, J.; Tammelin, M.; Anttila, T.; Ojala, S. Work at home and time use in Finland. *New Technol. Work Employ.* **2011**, *26*, 68–77. [CrossRef]
45. Halford, S. Hybrid workspace: Re-spatialisations of work, organisation and management. *New Technol. Work Employ.* **2005**, *20*, 19–33. [CrossRef]
46. Ibrahim, Y. Temporality, space and technology: Time-space discourses of call centres. *New Technol. Work Employ.* **2012**, *27*, 23–35. [CrossRef]
47. Fogary, H.; Scott, P.; Willians, S. The half-empty office: Dilemmas in managing locational flexibility. *New Technol. Work Employ.* **2011**, *26*, 183–195. [CrossRef]
48. Jaakson, K.; Kallaste, E. Beyond flexibility: Reallocation of responsibilities in the case of telework. *New Technol. Work Employ.* **2010**, *25*, 196–209. [CrossRef]
49. Gold, M.; Mustafa, M. 'Work always wins': Client colonisation, time management and the anxieties of connected freelancers. *New Technol. Work Employ.* **2013**, *28*, 197–211. [CrossRef]
50. Block, A.; Farias, I. *Urban Cosmopolitics: Agencements, Assemblies, Atmospheres (Questioning Cities)*; Routledge: London, UK, 2016.
51. Farias, I.; Benders, T. *Urban Assemblages: How Actor-Network Theory Changes Urban Studies (Questioning Cities)*; Routledge: London, UK, 2010.
52. White, P.; Christodoulou, G.; Mackett, R.; Titheridge, H.; Thoreau, R.; Polak, J. The impacts of Teleworking on Sustainability and Travel. In *Social Sustainaibility in Urban Areas: Communities, Connectivity and Social Fabric*; Manzi, T., Lucas, K., Lloyd-Jones, T., Allen, J., Eds.; Earthscan: London, UK, 2010; pp. 141–160.
53. Burnett, S.B.; Gatrell, C.J.; Cooper, C.L.; Sparrow, P. Well-balanced families? A gendered analysis of work-life balance policies and work family practices. *Gen. Manag.* **2010**, *25*, 534–549.
54. Dilmaghani, M.; Tabvuma, V. The gender gap in work–life balance satisfaction across occupations. *Gen. Manag.* **2019**, *34*, 398–428. [CrossRef]
55. Tang, N.; Cousins, C. Working time, gender and family: An East-West European comparison. *Gen. Work Organ.* **2005**, *12*, 527–550. [CrossRef]
56. Strazdins, L.; Broom, D. Acts of love (and work) gender imbalance in emotional work and women's psychological distress. *J. Fam. Issues* **2004**, *25*, 356–378. [CrossRef]

57. Beham, B.; Präg, P.; Drobnic, S. Who's got the balance? A study of satisfaction with the work–family balance among part-time service sector employees in five Western European countries. *Int. J. Hum. Resour. Man.* **2012**, *23*, 3725–3741. [CrossRef]
58. Coltrane, S. Gender theory and household labor. *Sex Roles* **2010**, *63*, 791–800. [CrossRef]
59. Gerson, K. Dilemmas of involved fatherhood. In *Gender and Work in Today's World*; Sacks, N., Marrone, C., Eds.; Westview Press: Cambridge, UK, 2004; pp. 378–386.
60. Chung, H.; Van der Horst, M. Women's employment patterns after childbirth and the perceived access to and use of flexitime and teleworking. *Hum. Relat.* **2017**, *71*, 47–72. [CrossRef]
61. Sullivan, C.; Lewis, S. Home-based telework, gender and the synchronization of work and family: Perspectives of teleworkers and their co-residents. *Gen. Work Organ.* **2001**, *8*, 123–145. [CrossRef]
62. Haar, J.; Carr, S.; Arrowsmith, J.; Parker, J.; Hodgetts, D.; Alefaio-Tugia, S. Escape from Working Poverty: Steps toward Sustainable Livelihood. *Sustainability* **2018**, *10*, 4144. [CrossRef]
63. World Commission on Environment and Development. *Our Common Future*; University Press: Oxford, UK, 1987.
64. Chandra, V. Work-life balance: Eastern and western perspectives. *Int. J. Hum. Resour. Man.* **2012**, *23*, 100–113. [CrossRef]
65. White, E.; Thatcher, A. How Mobile Phones Affect the Sustainability of the Work/Life Balance of Their Users. In *International Conference on Augmented Cognition*; Springer: Cham, Switzerland, 2015; pp. 393–400.
66. Mushfiqur, R.; Mordi, C.; Oruh, E.; Nwagbara, U.; Mordi, T.; Turner, I. The impacts of work-life-balance (WLB) challenges on social sustainability: The experience of Nigerian female medical doctors. *Empl. Relat.* **2019**, *40*, 868–888. [CrossRef]
67. Kobayashi, K.; Eweje, G.; Tappin, D. Employee wellbeing and human sustainability: Perspectives of managers in large Japanese corporations. *Bus. Strateg. Environ.* **2018**, *27*, 801–810. [CrossRef]
68. Fleetwood, S. Why work-life balance now? *J. Hum. Resour.* **2007**, *18*, 351–375. [CrossRef]
69. Gambles, R.; Lewis, S.; Rapoport, R. *The Myth of Work-Life Balance: The Challenges of Our Time for Men, Women and Societies*; Wiley: Chichester, UK, 2006.
70. Houston, D.M. *Work-Life Balance in the 21st Century*; Palgrave Macmillan: Basingstoke, UK, 2005.
71. Foucreault, A.; Ollier–Malaterre, A.; Julie Ménard, J. Organizational culture and work–life integration: A barrier to employees' respite? *J. Hum. Resour.* **2018**, *29*, 2378–2398. [CrossRef]
72. Crompton, R.; Lyonette, C. Occupational class, country and the domestic division of labour. In *Women, Men, Work and Family in Europe*; Crompton, R., Lewis, S., Lyonette, C., Eds.; Palgrave: London, UK, 2007; pp. 116–132.
73. Duncan, S. Mothers' work-life balance: Individualized preferences or cultural construction? In *Gender Divisions and Working Time in the New Economy: Changing Patterns of Work, Care and Public Policy in Europe and North America*; Perrons, D., Fagan, C., McDowell, L., Ray, K., Ward, K., Eds.; Edward Elgar: Cheltenham, UK, 2007; pp. 127–147.
74. Singley, S.; Hynes, K. Transitions to parenthood: Work-family policies, gender and the couple context. *Gen. Soc.* **2005**, *19*, 376–397. [CrossRef]
75. Adame, C.; Eva–María Caplliure, E.M.; María–José Miquel, M.J. Work–life balance and firms: A matter of women? *J. Bus. Res.* **2016**, *69*, 1379–1383. [CrossRef]
76. Russo, M.; Shteigman, A.; Carmeli, A. Workplace and family support and work–life balance: Implications for individual psychological availability and energy at work. *J. Posit. Psychol.* **2016**, *11*, 173–188. [CrossRef]
77. Thompson, C.A.; Prottas, D. Relationships among organizational family support, job autonomy, perceived control, and employee well-being. *J. Occup. Health Psychol.* **2005**, *10*, 100–118. [CrossRef] [PubMed]
78. Cooper, M. Being the "go-to-guy": Fatherhood, masculinity and the organization of work in Silicon Valley. *Qual. Sociol.* **2000**, *23*, 379–405. [CrossRef]
79. Rapoport, R.; Bailyn, L.; Fletcher, J.K.; Pruitt, B.H. *Beyond Work-Family Balance*; Jossey-Bass: San Francisco, CA, USA, 2002.
80. McDonald, P.; Brown, K.; Bradley, L. Explanations for the provision–utilisation gap in work–life policy. *Women Manag. Rev.* **2005**, *20*, 7–55. [CrossRef]
81. Haar, J.; Russo, M.; Suñe, A.; Ollier–Malaterre, A. Outcomes of work–life balance on job satisfaction, life satisfaction and mental health: A study across seven cultures. *J. Voc. Behav.* **2014**, *85*, 361–373. [CrossRef]

82. Siu, O.; Lu, J.; Brough, P.; Lu, C.; Bakker, A.; Kalliath, T.; O'Driscoll, M.; Phillips, D.; Chen, W.; Lo, D.; et al. Role resources and work–family enrichment: The role of work engagement. *J. Voc. Behav.* **2010**, *77*, 470–480. [CrossRef]
83. Roscoe, S.; Subramanian, N.; Jabbour, C.; Chong, T. Green human resource management and the enablers of green organisational culture: Enhancing a firm's environmental performance for sustainable development. *Bus. Strategy Environ.* **2019**, *28*, 737–749. [CrossRef]
84. Jaramillo, J.; Sossa, J.; Mendoza, G. Barriers to sustainability for small and medium enterprises in the framework of sustainable development—Literature review. *Bus. Strategy Environ.* **2018**, *28*, 512–524.
85. Díaz, A.; Sainz, J.; Torrent, J. The competitiveness of small network-firm: A practical tool. *J. Bus. Res.* **2016**, *69*, 1769–1774. [CrossRef]
86. Díaz, A.; Ficapal, P.; Torrent, J. Did small and medium enterprises maintain better jobs during the early years of the recession? Job quality multidimensional evidence from Spain. *Eur. Manag. J.* **2017**, *35*, 396–413. [CrossRef]
87. Barber, L.K.; Grawitch, M.J.; Maloney, P.W. Work-life balance: Contemporary perspectives. In *The Psychologically Healthy Workplace: Building a Win-Win Environment for Organizations and Employees*; Grawitch, M.J., Ballard, D.W., Eds.; American Psychological Association: Washington, DC, USA, 2016; pp. 111–133.
88. Angell, I. *The New Barbarian Manifesto: How to Survive the Information Age*; Kogan Page: London, UK, 2000.
89. Bailey, D.E.; Kurland, N.B. A review of telework research: Findings, new directions, and lessons for the study of modern work. *J. Organ. Behav.* **2002**, *23*, 383–400. [CrossRef]
90. Handy, C. *The Age of Unreason*; Arrow Books: London, UK, 1990.
91. Kowalski, K.B.; Swanson, J.A. Critical success factors in developing teleworking programs. *Benchmark. Int. J.* **2005**, *12*, 236–249. [CrossRef]
92. Baruch, Y. The status of research on teleworking and an agenda for future research. *Int. J. Manag. Rev.* **2001**, *3*, 113–120. [CrossRef]
93. Loubier, A. Benefits of Telecommuting for the Future of Work. 2017. Available online: https://www.forbes.com/sites/andrealoubier/2017/07/20/benefits-of-telecommuting-for-the-future-of-work/#7e6db2c116c6 (accessed on 20 November 2019).
94. Pinola, M. Differences between Telecommuting and Telework. 2018. Available online: https://www.lifewire.com/difference-between-telecommuting-and-telework-2378090 (accessed on 15 November 2019).
95. Karia, N.; Muhammad, A. Innovation Capability: The Impact of Teleworking on Sustainable Competitive Advantage. *Int. J. Technol. Pol. Manag.* **2016**, *16*, 181–194. [CrossRef]
96. Kazekami, S. Mechanisms to improve labor productivity by performing telework. *Telecom. Policy* **2020**, *44*, 101868. [CrossRef]
97. Moon, C.; Stanworth, C. Ethical issues of teleworking. *Bus. Ethics* **1997**, *6*, 30–34. [CrossRef]
98. Sennett, R. *The Corrosion of Character*; Norton & Company: New York, NY, USA, 1998.
99. Aguilera, A.; Lethiais, V.; Rallet, A.; Proulhac, L. Home-based telework in France: Characteristics, barriers and perspectives. *Transp. Res. Part A Policy Pract.* **2016**, *92*, 1–11. [CrossRef]
100. Lee, S.-H.; Shin, Y.; Baek, S.I. Task Characteristics and Work Engagement: Exploring Effects of Role Ambiguity and ICT Presenteeism. *Sustainability* **2017**, *9*, 1855.
101. Yoo, W.; Oh, I. Effect of Work-Family Balance Policy on Job Selection and Social Sustainability: The Case of South Korea. *Sustainability* **2017**, *9*, 849. [CrossRef]
102. Hynes, M.; Rau, H. Environmental Gains and Social Losses? Critical reflections on the sustainability potential of telework. In Proceedings of the XVIII ISA World Congress of Sociology, Yokohama, Japan, 13–19 July 2014.
103. Felstead, A.; Jewson, N. *In Work at Home. Towards and Understanding of Homeworking*; Routledge: London, UK, 2000.
104. Tietze, S.; Musson, G. When Work Meets Home: Temporal flexibility as lived experience. *Time Soc.* **2002**, *11*, 315–334. [CrossRef]
105. Patton, M. *Qualitative Research and Evaluation Methods*; Sage: Thousand Oaks, CA, USA, 2002.
106. Lawrence, H. *Ecology. Encyclopedia of Science*; Salem Press: New York, NY, USA, 2013.

107. Green, L.; Richard, L.; Potvin, L. Ecological foundations of health promotion. *Am. J. Health Promot.* **1996**, *10*, 270–281. [CrossRef]
108. Lorway, R.; Lazarus, L.; Chevrier, C.; Khan, S.; Musyoki, H.; Mathenge, J.; Mwangi, P.; Macharia, P.; Bhattacharjee, P.; Isac, S.; et al. Ecologies of security: On the everyday security tactics of female sex workers in Nairobi, Kenya. *Glob. Public Health* **2018**, *13*, 1767–1780. [CrossRef] [PubMed]

sustainability

MDPI

Article

Knowledge Economy Indicators and Their Impact on the Sustainable Competitiveness of the EU Countries

Elena Širá [1], Roman Vavrek [2], Ivana Kravčáková Vozárová [1] and Rastislav Kotulič [1,*]

[1] Faculty of Management, University of Prešov in Prešov, Konštantínova 16, 080 01 Prešov, Slovakia; elena.sira@unipo.sk (E.Š.); ivana.kravcakova.vozarova@unipo.sk (I.K.V.)

[2] Faculty of Economics, Technical University of Liberec, Voroněžská 13, 460 01 Liberec 1, Czech Republic; vavrek.roman@gmail.com

* Correspondence: rastislav.kotulic@unipo.sk; Tel.: +421-51-4880-590

Received: 9 April 2020; Accepted: 18 May 2020; Published: 20 May 2020

Abstract: In today's turbulent world influenced by globalization, knowledge is becoming a key factor in the market. Every economy, if it wants to be successful and competitive, must pay more attention to knowledge and its creation, transfer, and preservation. In this respect, it is a key element in ensuring a country's sustainable position in a competitive environment. Based on this, we set out the main idea of the article as follows: increased emphasis on the factors of a knowledge-based economy affects the growth of the country's competitiveness, which contributes to its better sustainability. To verify the idea, we used a multi-criteria evaluation of countries by the TOPSIS method and a subsequent regression model. We examined developments in the EU countries over a period of 11 years in selected indicators typical for the knowledge economies, in the area of competitiveness. Finally, we examined the sustainability of EU countries. Based on the findings of these methods, we identified the leading country—Sweden—in the field of knowledge economy, competitiveness, and sustainability.

Keywords: knowledge economy; economic growth; competitiveness; sustainable development; Europe 2020

---

1. Introduction

Every successful economy must constantly improve and pay increased attention to key areas. These can ensure sustainability and improve the country's position in a competitive environment. Competitiveness, knowledge, and research and development are the priorities of every country today. However, more than the current position of the country, it is necessary to take into account the long-term sustainability of these areas to build a strong and sustainable economy.

In today's world, sustainability issues are becoming increasingly urgent. Among the different approaches to defining this concept, a common attribute is future orientation. The economy of sustainability is usually based on the idea of resource efficiency. As a sustainable economy is about a long-term future, which is largely unknown, questions about the knowledge that can ensure the country's long-term stability and growth need to be answered.

The knowledge economy is not just a new theoretical concept, but a new epoch, which has a fundamental difference from the era of agrarian and industrial economies. Although it appeared only in the early 1990s, it has already had an impact and caused changes in all spheres of economic and social life, and this influence is constantly growing. The trend of development of a knowledge economy is the formation of a knowledge economy, which will mean the onset of a new stage in the development of the global economy [1]. The idea of a knowledge-based economy dates to the 1990s. Its primary objective was for European countries to catch up with America in technological development. Many theories have emerged that determine the direction of European countries [2]. The issues of sustainable development and the knowledge economy are two directions of development to which most countries of the world, including EU Member States, draw attention. Countries face constant changes in scientific and technical development, but there are also new modern trends in the way they do business. Every participant in this global market is forced to adapt its activities to these rapid changes. Countries strive to increase their level of development depending on the available resources. Resources are a means of achieving development, but, as most resources are limited, they should also be used in the context of meeting the needs of future generations. In most countries today, the process of sustainable development is well in line with the process of developing the knowledge economy. To achieve the appropriate changes, the two processes need to be harmonized [3]. The knowledge economy is often explained as a possible way to transform society to achieve sustainable economic growth as well as to solve the various climate challenges arising from the growing scarcity of resources [4]. Based on this, the main idea of the article is to increase the emphasis on factors related to a knowledge-based economy that affect the growth of the country's competitiveness, which contributes to its improved sustainability. The attention is focused on the mutual influences and overall impacts on the country of these main research areas: knowledge-based economy, competitiveness, and sustainability.

2. Literature Review and Conceptual Framework

The concept of sustainable development is rather dynamic. This means that this issue can be described from several perspectives [5]. From the point of view of most theoretical approaches, the issue of sustainable development distinguishes three components: environmental, economic, and social. Of these three aspects, so far, the environmental dimension of sustainability has received the most attention. If people want to live in a prosperous country with a healthy environment, it is necessary to address the major trends of today's world (such as changing demographics, changing consumer patterns, social change, changes in the use of natural resources, and growing pressure on natural resources and ecosystems) that may worsen the situation. However, the importance of the economic dimension of sustainability is also undeniable in today's globalized world; therefore, this document is focused on the economic component of sustainability. In particular, the economic aspect of sustainability addresses the issue of the development of performance as well as the standard of living. Improving sustainability performance can affect a country's competitiveness. It is therefore necessary to ensure not only suitable conditions but also suitable resources for sustainable economic growth. Education, an educated population, and knowledge are likely to lead to the availability of appropriate resources in the future. Many studies show that the transition to a knowledge-based economy through the introduction of innovation significantly increases a country's performance as well as living standards. Innovations are an important determinant of sustainable competitiveness and the growth of the knowledge economy. They are a fundamental factor in progress in the social, environmental, and economic fields [6]. The way in which individual economies respond to these challenges also has a major impact on their sustainable growth and position in the world's economy. In an effort to better understand the relationships among sustainability, competitiveness, and the knowledge economy, a conceptual framework was also defined for our research. EU countries clearly defined their approach to this issue in the Europe 2020 strategy, one of the objectives of which is to achieve a sustainable future and sustainable growth. The question remains as to how successfully individual EU countries are achieving this convergence. From a conceptual point of view, this work seeks to explain and examine the interrelationship of the impact of the knowledge economy on the competitiveness of the economy, which is reflected in the economic dimension of achieving results for sustainability in individual EU countries. However, it should be noted that the achievement of the sustainable development goals of individual countries must be fulfilled in the context of the necessary interconnections among all three dimensions in order to achieve balance.

Sustainable development is a widely defined term without an exact or strict definition. Sinakou [5], Hanushek [7], Širá et al. [8], Valliere and Peterson [9], Busu and Trica [10], and Kiseľáková et al. [11] identified indicators that are suitable for quantifying economic growth (e.g., GDP, inflation, unemployment, productivity, government departments, and circular economies), but the next important indicator to identify the economic growth in today's world is knowledge From this view, we can argue that development would be limited if knowledge support were limited. However, creating new knowledge is not expensive, but, in most cases, it takes effort and time [12]. Other studies devoted to the sustainability of the knowledge economy include those by Ocak and Findik [13], Cantu-Martinez [14], Mikalauskiene and Atkociuniene [15], Li et al. [16], Chang et al. [17], and Melnikas [18].

For a more accurate understanding of the term "knowledge economy", it is necessary to become acquainted with several approaches to it (Durazzi [19]; Saridogan and Kaya [20]; Sagiyeval et al. [21]; Milewska [22]; Ayan and Pabuccu [23]). There is no single approach or clear concept for defining the term "knowledge economy". The OECD defines knowledge-based economies at a very general level as those that are directly based on the production, distribution, and use of knowledge and information [24]. The knowledge economy can be defined, in one respect, as a way of creating a product based on activities dependent on knowledge and expertise that contribute to the creation of scientific and technological progress. The fundamental determinants of the knowledge economy include a more significant ratio for the dependence of the economy on intellectual abilities than on physical inputs or natural resources in the context of the integration of new knowledge at each level of the production process [25]. The knowledge economy is developing on the basis of two driving forces. The first is the increasing knowledge level of economic operations and the second is the globalization of economic events [26]. According to Dudová [27], the prerequisites for the emergence of knowledge economies include the long-term tendency of a gradual increase in the weight of intangible capital on production factors and the emergence and growth of the diffusion of information and communication technologies. Changes in countries towards the transition to the level of knowledge economy are considered a new trend in the global environment. This transformation has become a necessity, especially for emerging economies, which suffer from a low degree of economic competitiveness. It should be noted, however, that these changes require a clear and effective policy-making approach that responds, in particular, to the needs of these countries and their available resources [28].

According to Milewska [22], achievement of a knowledge-based economy requires a transition from a material perception of the economy to one that exploits innovation potential, human capital, knowledge, and new technologies. The intellectual potential, supported by the constant development of people and the appropriate skills of the workforce, as well as the growing competition in the field of innovation, significantly influences the sustainable development of today's economies. Ayan and Pabuccu [23] argued that the knowledge economy is an economy that invests more in quality information than capital inputs, which is an important determinant for economic development and increased competitiveness. The speed of dissemination of new and current knowledge is an important factor in economic development. This is also confirmed by the fact that the most dynamic and competitive countries in the world have economies that make large investments in information factors. Lüthi et al. [29] defined knowledge economy as a type of economy in which there is a strategic combination of highly specialized knowledge and skills at different stages of the value chain in the context of maintaining a competitive advantage. According to Sagiyeval et al. [21], the knowledge economy participates in the creation of new resources and artificial intelligence and their implementation in all sectors of the national economy in order to substitute natural resources and human intellect. The creation of such a knowledge environment is caused by the introduction of new technologies in an effort to save resources but also by the development of extensive knowledge of new technologies and skills. Collison and Parcel [30] showed the three pillars of the knowledge economy (Figure 1). The first pillar contains people who are willing to learn and share knowledge. The second pillar is the information infrastructure that enables the exchange of knowledge. The third pillar contains processes that facilitate sharing, codification, and knowledge discovery.

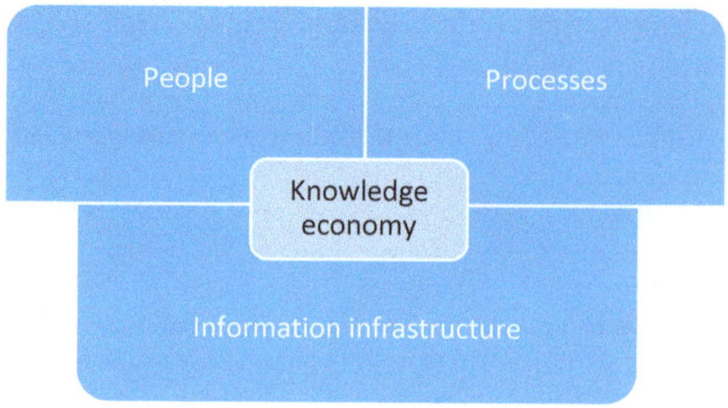

Figure 1. The three pillars of the knowledge economy. Source: own procession according to Collison and Parcel [30].

Sundać and Krmpotić [31] argue that, due to the substance of the term, a successful transition to a knowledge-based economy is often based on the following four basic elements: long-term investment in education, innovative skills, the modernization of information base, and the creation of a favorable business environment. The knowledge-based economy is also a combination of four interconnected items, namely the acquisition of knowledge through scientific research, its subsequent transfer in the process of education, its dissemination through information and communication technologies, and its use in technological innovations [27]. Chen and Dahlman [32] argued that the World Bank also has defined the dimensions of the knowledge economy: economic incentives and the institutional system, educated and skilled human resources, an effective business innovation system, and a modern and appropriate information and communication structure. People, as holders of valuable human capital, represent crucial elements in the knowledge economy [33]. According to Pulic [34], economic growth can no longer come from putting more people to work, i.e., from more resource input, as much of it has in the past. It can come only from a very sharp and continuing increase in the productivity of the resource using knowledge work and knowledge workers.

Therefore, it is necessary to increase the awareness of managers about the constant need for new knowledge [35]. The current situation places new qualitative demands on managers as well as alternative opportunities for their training and education. Effective innovative practices in management education are an increasingly important determinant in shaping the competitiveness of the knowledge economy [36]. Similarly, the empirical results of Barkhordari et al. [37] obtained using the generalized method of moments dynamic panel indicate institutions, human capital and research, infrastructure, and business sophistication are the pillars of a knowledge-based economy that influence significant and positive economic growth.

2.1. Knowledge and Indicators of the Knowledge Economy

In terms of the knowledge economy, the key term is knowledge. Knowledge is a complex term that attracts the attention of both theorists and the practical sphere. Various approaches have been developed [38], but the only thing that seems to be common is the idea that knowledge is more than just data and information itself [39]. Knowledge is sometimes considered as the fifth factor of production in the current economy, and it plays a critical role in economic performance [40]. However, it is indisputable that the knowledge economy is built on knowledge, which is its main capital. The actual functioning of the economy is based on the production of information and knowledge as goods [41]. Knowledge management is important, because knowledge is one of the most strategic means that can lead to sustained increases in profitability [42]. It is important for a knowledge society [43].

According to Rim et al. [44], in today's highly competitive environment, it is necessary to assess the level of actual development in the management of the knowledge economy and to take measures to support and grow accordingly. For this reason, it is essential to identify the key indicators entering into the evaluation in order to subsequently improve the evaluation methodology. To talk about the knowledge economy without being able to measure and evaluate its influence would not be of great utility. Many indicators have been gradually developed to capture these manifestations and impacts. In this section, we introduce some of them and explain their nature and how they are interpreted.

Based on certain similar features, we can divide the indicators of the knowledge economy into two categories. The first category focuses on the basic characteristics of the knowledge economy, and this group of indicators describes the share of the knowledge economy in the whole economy of the country, e.g., the proportion of people working in high-tech industries, or the proportion of people with higher education. In the context of information economy, universities become powerful centers that both consolidate strong intellectual capital and generate new knowledge and technological innovation in their research activities [45]. The second large group consists of the so-called performance or output indicators. These include, among others, the production of high-tech industries, high-tech exports, GDP growth, and labor productivity growth [46].

Let us mention another approach to the classification of indicators. For example, instead of indicators based on the characteristics of the knowledge-based economy, the World Bank talks about the pillars of the knowledge-based economy. It defines four basic pillars:

- a supportive economic and institutional mechanism that provides an incentive scheme to make better use of existing information and generate new knowledge in business;
- an educated and qualified population that generates and uses new knowledge;
- a dynamic information infrastructure for the communication, dissemination, and processing of information; and
- an effective system of innovation for businesses, research centers, and universities to generate new knowledge [32,47].

Roberts [48] divided the knowledge economy indicators into four groups:

- indicators based on innovation and entrepreneurship total R&D expenditure by industry, enterprise R&D expenditure by size of enterprise, and the number of scientific and technical publications per capita;
- indicators based on human capital;
- indicators based on information and communication technologies; and
- indicators based on economic and social impacts.

Human capital is a part of intellectual capital that is not owned by the organization but by the employees themselves. In the environment of the knowledge economy, human capital is defined by the skills of employees, their talent, and their knowledge [49]. The development of a knowledge-based society and a sustainable economy depends considerably on the ability to produce competitive goods and services and to distribute them in the global market. Global economic activity changes fast and heavily impacts the competitive possibilities of developing countries; it is not easy to achieve or to save competitiveness. It is not enough to only be passively open for the free market [50].

2.2. Impact of the Knowledge Economy on the Competitiveness of EU Countries

The current global business environment is shaped by the transition to a knowledge economy, which has moved the competitiveness of business activities to a completely different level. As the issue of the knowledge economy is a fundamental determinant of the economic development of individual economies, its level is considered to be an important indicator in the context of comparing world economies [51]. According to Gorokhova [52], the ability to generate and absorb knowledge and use it effectively helps to create innovations, achieve competitive advantages and economic efficiency, and produce human capital, and in turn determines the effectiveness of economic development. The issue of competitiveness from the perspective of the knowledge economy was analyzed by

Brodowska-Szewczuk [53], Atanassova et al. [54], Lomachynska and Podgorna [55], Dukic et al. [56], and Puškárová and Zajac [57].

The problem of competitiveness in the world economic space is extremely important for any country, especially in the context of globalization of the world economy, where the importance of various forms of external economic relations and the degree of openness of national economies to foreign products, services, and capital are growing sharply [58,59]. Šterbová et al. [60] stated that competitiveness can be understood as a comparative view of the subject and its ability to sell and offer goods and services in a given market. The authors added that attention is paid mainly to the external aspects of the performance of countries or the whole region. The importance of competitiveness has been addressed over the course of history by a number of economists, with a number of independent definitions of competitiveness arising. One of the first is the approach of Scott and Lodge [61], who characterized competitiveness as the ability of the country to produce and distribute products or services in an international environment for profit. According to Štefko [62], competitiveness can be understood as the ability of a company, industry, or country to compete, to lose business interests with leading companies or countries, and to secure at least medium-term prosperity, with the aim of achieving sustainable, long-term prosperity. In this definition, the author placed emphasis mainly on the future, i.e., medium term, and eventually long-term sustainable prosperity as a result of the company's competitive position.

Measurement of competitiveness can be approached from several points of view. The Global Competitiveness Index (GCI) published annually by the World Economic Forum is also used to assess the country's competitiveness. For more than three decades, the World Economic Forum has been an institution concerned with the area of competitiveness and its quantification. Annual reports on global competitiveness compare many factors in the area of national competitiveness. In the case of the Global Competitiveness Index (GCI), several indicators are included in the observation due to the complexity of the outputs in the assessment of this area. The GCI currently comprises 114 indicators divided into 12 pillars. The area of innovation is included in the 12th pillar of the GCI [63].

Maintaining global competitiveness has been one of the main challenges facing countries around the world in recent years. At first, the countries of the European Union sought to achieve this goal through the implementation of the Lisbon Strategy. However, this proved to be very challenging, and, therefore, this goal was subsequently strengthened in the Europe 2020 strategy [6]. The Europe 2020 strategy also aims to improve sustainable growth, environmental protection, and social cohesion [64]. This strategy confirms that the European Union wants to achieve the sustainable development of the EU countries' economies. There are three priorities of Europe 2020:

- smart growth, which is based on the development of the economy using knowledge and innovation;
- sustainable growth, through more efficient use of resources; and
- inclusive growth that supports a high-employment economy with consequent economic, social, and territorial cohesion [65].

3. Materials and Methods

Every economy, if it wants to be successful and competitive, must pay more attention to knowledge and its creation, transfer, and preservation. In this respect, the knowledge is a basic component in ensuring the country's sustainable position in a competitive environment. Competitiveness is in today's world a very important part of every country. It represents the position of the country's rank among other countries. However, in this case, it is very important to gain the appropriate competitive level for a long time, so as to build a sustainable economy. Based on this, we set out the main idea of the article as follows: we increase the emphasis on the factors of a knowledge-based economy affecting the growth of the country's competitiveness, which contributes to its improved sustainability. The attention is focused on these main research areas, their interconnections, and their interactions. The research is based on the evaluation of the relationships between them, as shown in Figure 2.

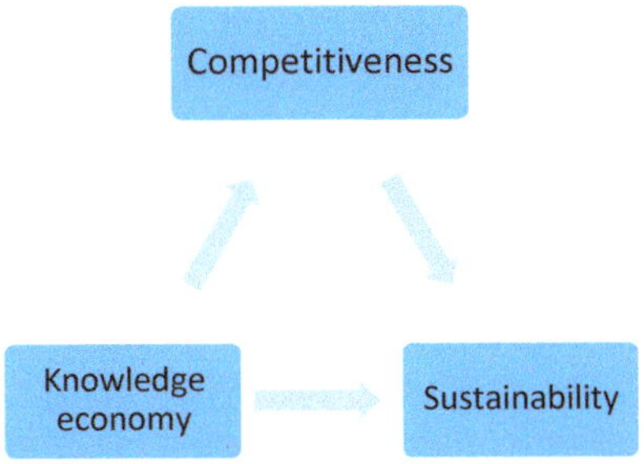

Figure 2. Main research areas. Source: own procession.

The principal goal of this article is to find the EU country with the strongest competitive position. The secondary objectives are to determine how the selected indicators of the knowledge economy affect the country's competitiveness in their interaction and whether competitiveness affects the sustainability of the economy. This was realized by the statistical evaluation of the following hypotheses.

Hypothesis 1. *There are statistically significant differences in the comprehensive assessment of the competitiveness of EU countries using the CV (Coefficient of Variance)–TOPSIS (Technique for Order Preference by Similarity to Ideal Solution) technique.*

The area of competitiveness was quantified according to the overall outputs of the TOPSIS technique. The CV–TOPSIS inputs were as follows:

- tertiary education as a percent of population;
- Research and Development (R&D) expenditure as a percent of gross domestic product;
- total amount of patents per million population; and
- score in the 12th pillar of the GCI.

The second hypothesis was established on the basis of proven differences between individual countries.

Hypothesis 2. *There is a statistically significant positive dependence of competitiveness (12th GCI pillar) on the knowledge economy of individual EU countries.*

The positive dependence is based on the fact that, when better outputs are achieved in indicators of a country's knowledge economy, its position in the 12th GCI pillar also improves. When formulating the hypothesis, we started from already conducted research by several authors. Schiuma et al. [66] demonstrated the impact of knowledge in the company on its performance. Kianto et al. [67] validated the positive effect of knowledge on competitiveness. Krstić and Stanišić [68] also validated the positive effect of knowledge on competitiveness at country level.

We evaluated the level of the knowledge economy according to selected indicators:

- tertiary education as a percent of population;
- R&D expenditure as a percent of gross domestic product; and
- total amount of patents per million population.

The form of reporting these indicators was chosen for a better comparability of countries. When selecting the indicators of the knowledge economy, we were inspired by a team of authors [45], who used these indicators as a basis for the research index. Furthermore, in the works of Batagan [69] and Arundel et al. [46], these indicators are also used as the main indicators assessing the knowledge economy.

It was also necessary to examine the values of competitiveness. This is very specific area with different meanings and interpretations; thus, to make the relevant analysis and conclusions, we needed to quantify it. We chose the World Economic Forum's approach to assess and quantify the country's competitiveness through the GCI. We found the WE Forum approach to be the best for quantification. It was chosen for the reasons given below:

- This institution has been dedicated to competitiveness and its measurement and quantification for over 40 years.
- They publish the ranking regularly (every year).
- This institution compares countries from all over the world.
- The approach has been used by other authors [6,50,54,58,59,68].

This approach has some advantages and some disadvantages. We mention the positive aspects above. A disadvantage of this method is the data and methodology used. GCI materials rely heavily on data collected from surveys and have complex weighted value systems in terms of technology, public agencies, and the macroeconomic environment. One-third of the data are statistical data and two-thirds are obtained on the basis of a questionnaire.

The overall GCI value is influenced by the partial score values obtained in each assessment area. In the GCI, we therefore focused our attention on the 12th pillar, which assessed innovation. Within this pillar, we considered country scores. Based on the above, this hypothesis can be built in various variants and thus as follows:

Hypothesis 2A. *There is a statistically positive dependence of competitiveness (12th GCI pillar) on the level of tertiary education.*

Hypothesis 2B. *There is a statistically positive dependence of competitiveness (12th GCI pillar) on spending on science and research.*

Hypothesis 2C. *There is a statistically positive dependence of competitiveness (12th GCI pillar) on the number of patents.*

Based on the assumed differences at the country level, the third and final research hypothesis was set out as follows.

Hypothesis 3. *There are statistically significant differences between dependence of competitiveness (12th GCI pillar) on knowledge economy at the level of individual EU 28.*

The economic dimension of the sustainability of the overall development of the EU community, as one minor goal of this article, is emphasized by the Europe 2020 strategy. We only analyzed the economic dimension of sustainability, because of the penetration of this area with knowledge economy and competitiveness—our main research areas. This strategy has set priorities and targets that EU countries are scheduled to meet by 2020, which also covers our research period. For this reason, this strategy was chosen as a comparable factor to investigate the sustainability in the period under review and in the conditions valid for EU countries. Moreover, one of the priority objectives of this strategy is that of the aim we are investigating: "The aim of the Europe 2020 in the field of knowledge and innovation is to reach the expenditures on R&D as 3% of gross domestic product for the EU countries" [65].

As a sample of countries, we chose the countries forming the EU. The selection was also conditioned by the commitment of the EU 28 to the Europe 2020 strategy. The current contribution also includes the United Kingdom within the EU, as we evaluated the period of 11 years, i.e., from 2007 to 2017. To verify the idea, we used a multi-criteria evaluation of countries by the TOPSIS method and a subsequent regression model. We evaluated the development of these countries in the given years as well as the structure of the evaluation of overall results in specific countries.

The above objectives and hypotheses were fulfilled and evaluated using several mathematical–statistical methods. The above-mentioned TOPSIS method was chosen as the main tool for assessing "countries' competitiveness" as one value for evaluating the level of each monitored area. The perception of the advantages and disadvantages of this method differs due to their use in different situations and contexts. Following a comparison with other relevant methods (AHP, ELECTRE, etc.), Shih et al. [70] outlined the following advantages of the TOPSIS method: the logic representing the rationality of human choice, the general value which takes into account the best and worst values of the criteria, the use of a simple calculation that can be easily programmed, and the alternative results which can be illustrated by a polyhedron (minimum two dimensions). Bhutia and Phipon [71] also added the advantages of easy use, the ability to work with all types of criteria (subjective and objective), and rationality and understanding. Kandakoglu et al. [72] and Shih et al. [70] considered the absence of the possibility of allocating weights to the criteria and the lack of consistent control by the decision maker as the main disadvantages of the TOPSIS method. For this reason, we chose the Coefficient of Variance as a suitable method for this kind of processing (as applied by Vavrek and Chovancová [73]). Our team of authors has rich experience with this method [74–76].

According to Zavadskas et al. [77], this technique can be considered one of the most frequently used MCDM (Multi Criteria Decision Making) methods (for more details, see [78,79]). The result could be characterized as a solution with the shortest distance to a positive ideal solution (PIS) calculated using the Euclidean distance [80]. The TOPSIS technique offers a solution that is closest to the above-mentioned PIS and also furthest from the negative ideal solution at the same time [81]. Moreover, Carayannis et al. [82] studied this method with respect to the specifics of the knowledge-based economy. He focused on the development and methodological characteristics within the MCDA that are influenced by a given area of interest.

The individual steps of the TOPSIS technique were developed by Vavrek et al. [74], and these characterize the next sequence of this method:

(a) Build the criterion matrix, which represents the ranking of possibilities in accordance with the set characteristics:

$$D = \begin{pmatrix} & X_1 & X_2 \ldots & X_j \ldots & X_n \\ A_1 & x_{11} & x_{12} \ldots & x_{1j} \ldots & x_{1n} \\ A_2 & x_{21} & x_{22} \ldots & x_{2j} \ldots & x_{2n} \\ \vdots & \vdots & \vdots & \vdots & \vdots \\ A_i & x_{i1} & x_{i2} \ldots & x_{ij} \ldots & x_{in} \\ \vdots & \vdots & \vdots & \vdots & \vdots \\ A_m & x_{m1} & x_{m2} \ldots & x_{mj} \ldots & x_{mn} \end{pmatrix} \tag{1}$$

where Ai is the ith alternative and Xij is the value of the jth parameter achieved by the ith alternative.

(b) Build the normalized criterion matrix. To get this matrix, calculate the next formula:

$$r_{ij} = x_{ij} / \sqrt{\sum_{j=1}^{j} x_{ij}^2} \tag{2}$$

where r_{ij} is the normalized value of the jth criterion and x_{ij} is the value of the jth criterion reached by the ith alternative.

(c) Assign weights to each parameter:

$$v_{ij} = w_{ij} \cdot r_{ij}, \tag{3}$$

where vij is the weight of the normalized value and wij is the weight of the parameter.

(d) Find and label PIS and NIS alternatives. These fictitious limits comprise real values, in most cases, and hypothetical alternatives:

$$H_j = \max(w_{ij}), D_j = \min(w_{ij}), \tag{4}$$

where *Hj* is PIS, and *Dj* is NIS.

(e) Compute the distance from these alternatives:

$$d_i^+ = \left[\sum_{j=1}^{k} (w_{ij} - H_j)^2\right]^{1/2}, d_i^- = \left[\sum_{j=1}^{k} (w_{ij} - D_j)^2\right]^{1/2} \tag{5}$$

where *d+* is the distance from the PIS alternative and *d−* is the distance from the NIS alternative.

(f) Calculate the relative distance from the PIS alternative (in terms of alternatives, minimizing the distance from the PIS (d+) and maximizing the distance from the NIS (d−) are desired):

$$c_i = \frac{d_i^-}{d_i^- + d_i^+}, \tag{6}$$

where *ci* is the relative distance from the PIS alternative.

Within each of the MCDM methods, an equally important part of the procedure is to find out how important each of the selected indicators is. Keršuliene et al. [83] divided approaches to weighting into four groups: subjective, expert, objective, and integrated (which are a mix of previous approaches). In the present study, we worked with a group of objective methods that determine the weights of indicators based on a predetermined mathematical model unique to each method, without the decision maker having an influence on this result. Among the objective methods we can include, e.g., CRITIC (CRiteria Importance Through Intercriteria Correlation), MW (Mean Weight), SD (Standard Deviation), and SVP (Statistical Variance Procedure) s. For processing purposes, the CV method was used and calculated according to Singla et al. [84]. This method was described in more detail by Yalcin and Unlu [85] and was also used in research by Vavrek and Chovancová [73].

The results of the CV–TOPSIS technique were then used in a multiple regression model with an additive type of linkages between independent variables:

$$\text{GCI} = \text{a*Patent} + \text{b*R\&D} + \text{c*TeDe}, \tag{7}$$

where Patent is the number of patents per million population; R&D is the research and development expenditure as a percent of gross domestic product; and TeDe is the tertiary education as a percent of population.

The explanatory power was evaluated by the coefficient of determination:

$$R^2 = \frac{\sum_{i=1}^{n} (y_i - \hat{y}_i)^2}{\sum_{i=1}^{n} (y_i - \overline{y}_i)^2} \tag{8}$$

where y_i is the measured value of the dependent variable; $\hat{y}_i$ is the estimated value of the dependent variable; and $\overline{y}_i$ *is the* average value of the dependent variable.

The results obtained in this way were complemented by another apparatus of mathematical–statistical methods (depending on the nature of the data), with which we can include, in addition to the moment characteristics:

- The Shapiro–Wilk test:

$$SW = \frac{(\sum u_i x_i)^2}{\sum u_i^2 \sum (x_i - \overline{x})^2} \tag{9}$$

where u_i is the constant; x_i is the value of the *i*th statistical unit; and $\overline{x}$ is the average value of the variable.

- The Kruskal–Wallis test:

$$Q = \frac{12}{n(n-1)} \sum_{i=1}^{I} \frac{T_i^2}{n_i} - 3(n+1) \quad (10)$$

where n is the number of observations or file size; n_i is the number of observations in the ith group; and T_i^2 is the total number of ranks in the ith group.

- Levene's test:

$$W = \frac{(N-k)}{(k-1)} \frac{\sum_{i=1}^{k} N_i (Z_i - Z_{..})^2}{\sum_{i=1}^{k} \sum_{j=1}^{N_i} \left(Z_{ij} - Z_{i.}\right)^2} \quad (11)$$

where k is the number of values of the observed categorical variable; N is the total number of observations; N_i is the number of observations in the ith group; Y_{ij} is the gained value of the jth unit of the ith group; $\overline{Y_l}$ is the average value of the ith group; $\widetilde{Y}_i$ *is* the median of the ith group; $Z_{..}$ *is the* average of groups Zij; and $Z_{i.}$ is the average Zij for the ith group.

All analysis and data processing were performed in MS Excel, Statistica 13.4, and Statgraphics XVIII.

4. Results

4.1. The Efficiency of EU Countries Measured in the Context of the Knowledge Economy and Competitiveness Indicators

The tertiary education was evaluated as a percentage of the country's population. We chose this form for the sake of improved comparability of the results obtained, which minimized the differences caused by the different size of individual countries. In this comparison, the results in the EU countries were achieved without any significant differences. Over the period under review, the results ranged from 3.72% to 4.03% on average in the EU. There were also values outside this interval during the 11 monitored years. The lowest population with tertiary education measured as a percent of the inhabitants was in 2008 in Malta (2.33%), while the highest in Greece (6.83%) in 2017. Overall, the countries with the most stable development of this indicator were the United Kingdom and Bulgaria. On the contrary, the greatest variance of the achieved values was recorded in Romania, Cyprus, and Lithuania. In 2017, Greece, Denmark, and Finland represented the countries with the best performance in this indicator.

The R&D area as an indicator of the knowledge-based economy was evaluated by expressing the volume of the research and development expenditure as a percentage of gross domestic product. The countries with the lowest average of this indicator were Cyprus (0.46%) and Romania (0.47%). Within these countries, the lowest value was achieved throughout the reference period. In contrast, the best performances of this indicator were in Finland (3.73%) and Sweden (3.49%). The United Kingdom represented in the analyzed period the country with the most stable development.

We evaluated the number of patents as a value per million inhabitants. This was for improved comparability of countries' performances. However, this indicator showed significant differences between countries. The best-performing countries were worth around 300 patents per million inhabitants (Finland and Sweden). At the same time, the weakest countries as Bulgaria, Greece, Romania, and Croatia achieved values ranging from 0.5 to 10 patents per million inhabitants.

The competitiveness of the country was evaluated in relation to the area in question using the GCI. In this index, the 12th pillar is focused on assessing the competitiveness of an area called Innovation. The countries could reach a score of 1–7 in the period 2008–2017. The worst results (2.9) in our sample of countries were achieved by Bulgaria (2009), Slovakia and Romania (both in 2011), and Croatia (2017). The best results were obtained in Sweden in 2011 (5.76) and in Finland in 2013 (5.79). The countries with the most stable development in this pillar included Poland and Denmark.

4.2. Evaluation of Hypothesis Testing

First, we focused our attention on the testing of Hypothesis 1. In a comprehensive assessment, EU countries (with the exception of Luxembourg) were evaluated for the period 2008–2017. The structure of these results is shown in Figure 3.

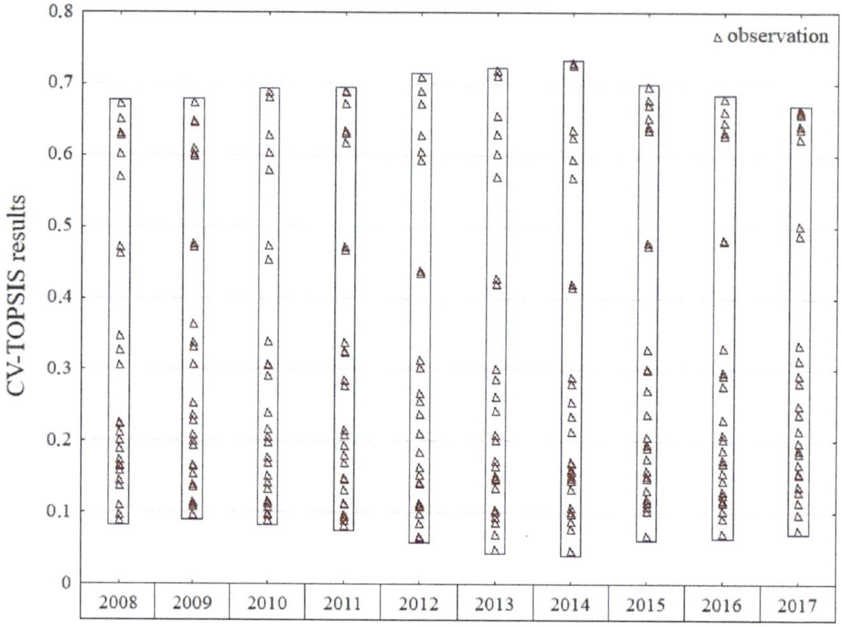

Figure 3. Evaluation of the structure using the CV–TOPSIS method in 2008–2017.

The overall results can be considered stable, which confirmed the variation range of individual annual results in the range of 0.577–0.682 of relative distance to the PIS alternative as well as their confirmed homoskedasticity (LE = 0.066; $p = 0.99$). From the distribution point of view, we observed a slightly positive skewness, i.e., a higher incidence of below-average countries, which is also illustrated in Figure 3. This characteristic persisted across the whole reporting period and did not change the mean value of the results (Q = 2.100; $p = 0.98$).

From the point of view of individual countries, shown in Figure 4, it was possible to observe significant differences, which, due to variability of results, can be described as long term, as opposed to persisting in the period under review. The differences between countries were thus confirmed in the mean value of their results (Q = 238.555; $p < 0.01$) as well as in the variance (LE = 2.976; $p < 0.01$). The countries with the most stable results are Denmark ($v_{DK} = 3.16\%$), Estonia ($v_{EE} = 3.34\%$), and Portugal ($v_{PT} = 3.56\%$). On the contrary, the countries with the highest variability of results include Slovakia ($v_{SK} = 39.19\%$) and Lithuania ($v_{LT} = 29.54\%$).

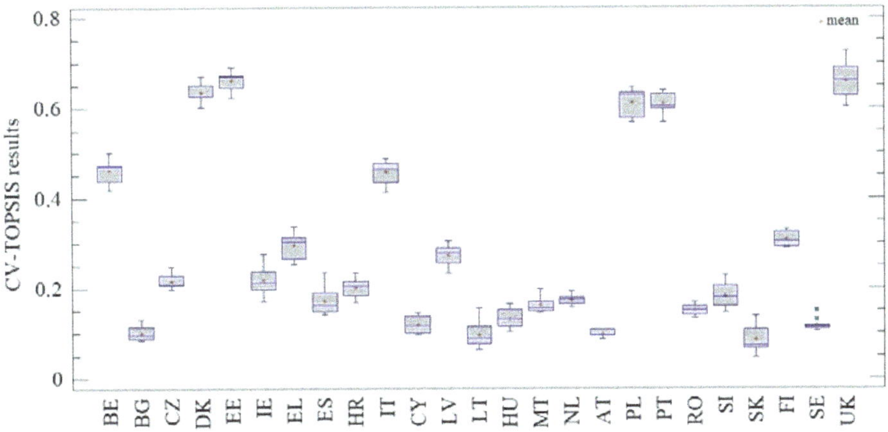

Figure 4. Evaluation of the structure using the CV–TOPSIS method at the country level.

However, the results of individual countries can not only be seen in terms of absolute results, but also in the context of the results of other countries. One option is, for example, to assess countries by placement in each year, as shown in Figure 5. Of course, the differences between the countries in the mean values or variation remained unchanged, but we can observe changes in the variability of such results. Latvia was the only country out of 27 to rank in the same place each year (12th). For countries with stable placement, we can include, e.g., the Netherlands (v_{NL} = 4.21%) or Cyprus (v_{CY} = 4.27). An interesting fact is that Denmark as one of the countries with the lowest variability of the absolute results showed a higher variability of placements in different years (v_{DK} = 14.55%).

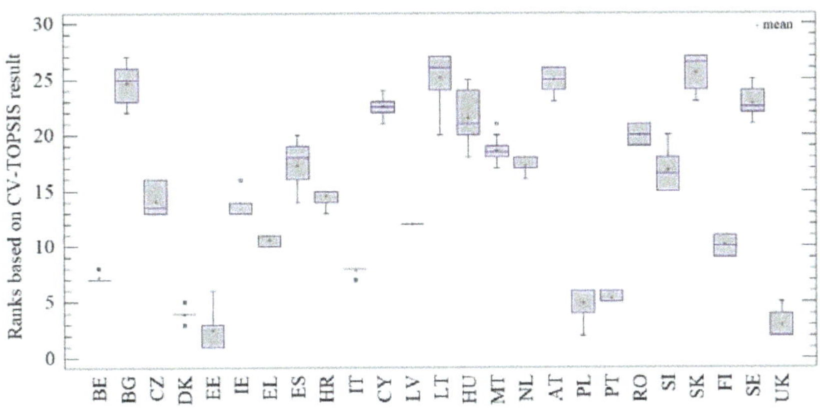

Figure 5. Ranking of countries based on the results of CV–TOPSIS.

Considering both views of the overall results shown in Table 1, Sweden (SE) can be described as the best-ranked country, with a narrow lead over Finland (FI) and Germany (DE). The worst-ranked countries (shown in Figure 6) include Romania (RO) and Cyprus (CY).

Table 1. Mean value (median) of absolute results and placements in individual years 2008–2017.

Country		MED c_i	MED Rank	Country		MED c_i	MED Rank
SE	Sweden	0.684071	1	ES	Spain	0.204981	15
FI	Finland	0.660245	2	PT	Portugal	0.177833	16.5
DE	Germany	0.670887	3	HU	Hungary	0.174564	17
DK	Denmark	0.627575	4	EL	Greece	0.163008	18
AT	Austria	0.603422	5	LT	Lithuania	0.155194	18.5
NL	Netherlands	0.628195	6	PL	Poland	0.150543	20
BE	Belgium	0.471093	7	LV	Latvia	0.131205	21
FR	France	0.464415	8	HR	Croatia	0.116751	22.5
UK	United Kingdom	0.332186	9	SK	Slovakia	0.112336	22.5
SI	Slovenia	0.303795	10	BG	Bulgaria	0.096345	25
IE	Ireland	0.30315	11	MT	Malta	0.095575	25
IT	Italy	0.278197	12	CY	Cyprus	0.087886	26
CZ	Czechia	0.210837	13.5	RO	Romania	0.072488	26.5
EE	Estonia	0.213831	14				

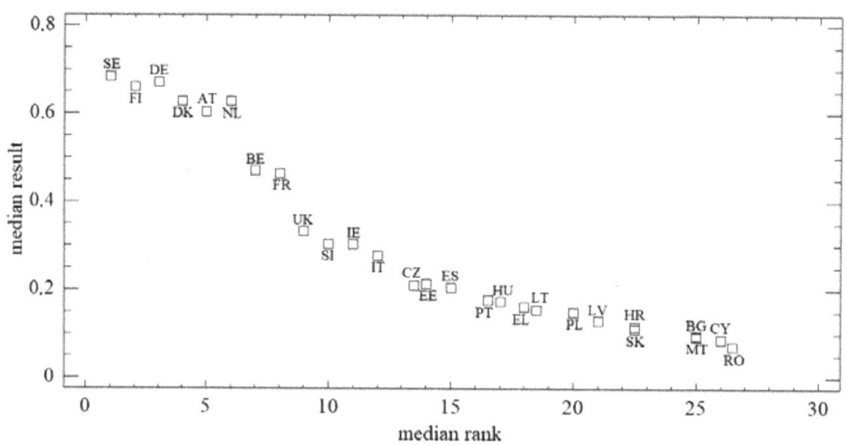

Figure 6. Ranking of countries based on the results CV–TOPSIS method in terms of median.

4.3. *Identification of Causes of Results Using Regression Analysis*

In the above section, we look at the overall results of the multi-criteria assessment, which was assessed by countries simultaneously on the basis of three indicators—Patents, R&D, and TeDE. To evaluate the hypotheses, we tried to set the influence of these indicators on the score of the 12th GCI pillar using multiple regression, which was as follows in Table 2.

Each of the calculated regression models showed a high predicative ability (R2 > 98.5%), and we could divide individual countries into four groups based on the results. The first group includes the countries where each of the three indicators positively influenced the score of the 12th GCI pillar. These countries include Sweden (SE), Croatia (CR), and Estonia (EE). The second group consisted of countries such as the United Kingdom (UK) and Bulgaria (BG), for which we may consider the impact of the Patents indicator as negative. The third group of countries is represented by Finland (FI) and Czech Republic (CZ), where the negative impact of the R&D indicator was recorded. The fourth group is represented by countries with a negative influence from the TeDe indicator, e.g., Italy (IT) and Cyprus (CY).

Table 2. Impact of dependent variables within the applied regression model at the country level.

	Country	Patents	R&D	TeDe		Country	Patents	R&D	TeDe
BE	Belgium	+	-	+	LT	Lithuania	-	+	+
BG	Bulgaria	-	+	+	HU	Hungary	+	+	+
CZ	Czechia	+	-	+	MT	Malta	+	-	+
DK	Denmark	+	+	-	NL	Netherlands	+	+	+
DE	Germany	+	+	-	AT	Austria	+	+	-
EE	Estonia	+	+	+	PL	Poland	+	+	+
IE	Ireland	-	+	+	PT	Portugal	+	-	+
EL	Greece	+	-	+	RO	Romania	+	-	+
ES	Spain	+	+	+	SI	Slovenia	+	+	-
FR	France	+	+	+	SK	Slovakia	+	+	+
HR	Croatia	+	+	+	FI	Finland	+	-	+
IT	Italy	+	+	-	SE	Sweden	+	+	+
CY	Cyprus	+	+	-	UK	United Kingdom	-	+	+
LV	Latvia	+	+	+					

Table 3 gives a comprehensive view of individual groups that were classified based on the results by the impact of selected indicators on the score of the 12th pillar of the GCI.

Table 3. Division of countries into groups according to the impact of indicators on competitiveness.

1st Group	2nd Group	3rd Group	4th Group
Estonia	Bulgaria	Belgium	Denmark
Spain	Ireland	Czechia	Germany
France	Lithuania	Greece	Italy
Croatia	UK	Malta	Cyprus
Latvia		Portugal	Austria
Hungary		Romania	Slovenia
Netherlands		Finland	
Poland			
Slovakia			
Sweden			

As shown in Figure 7, it is not possible to determine the impact of the monitored indicators on individual groups of countries, so it is not possible to predict, with the increase or decrease of a single indicator, the score of the 12th pillar of the GCI of a country.

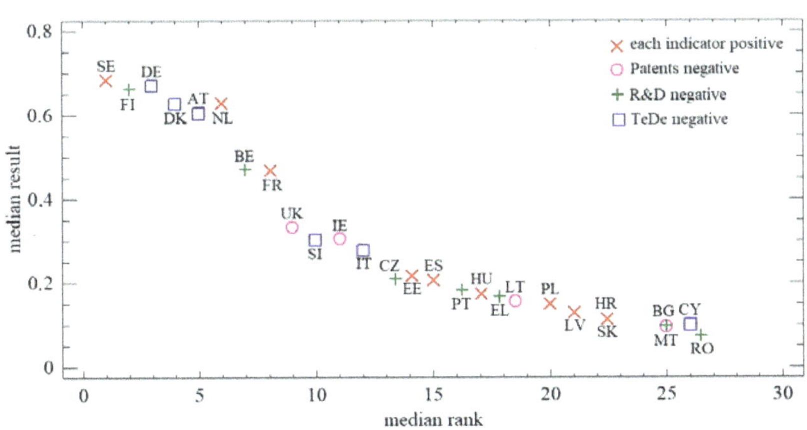

Figure 7. Influence of indicators on the score of the 12th pillar of the GCI in the context of overall placement.

5. Discussion

Nowadays, there is a constant dialogue about the knowledge economy and its importance, both in the field of business environment and in the academic sphere [22]. Krstić and Stanišić [68] argued that a knowledge-based economy is more efficient, which is mainly due to the use of knowledge as a basic source of development. The results of their research confirm the need for the implementation and realization of innovation policies, greater investment in education and training, the development of technological capabilities, and information infrastructure. The authors' analysis confirmed the importance of stimulating economic environments in an effort to use knowledge and expertise effectively in the field of production, services, and exports of EU countries. Jednak and Kragulj [3] confirmed that the EU has achieved quite positive results in R&D investments, which represented 2.02% of the GDP in 2013. Positive results have been achieved in education, too. These authors argued that a knowledge economy focusing on education supports the growth in productivity, innovation potential, and the country's competitiveness. Support for research and development contributes to the creation of innovation, which, in line with the efficient use of natural resources, leads to an increase in the competitiveness of a country on a global scale. Dima et al. [6] divided the assessment approach of the country's competitiveness into two perspectives. The first was an evaluation based on soft dimensions, including R&D expenditure as a percentage of GDP, lifelong learning, and tertiary education. On the other hand, the hard dimensions include the level of GDP, the energy intensity, and the debt-to-equity ratio. Their empirical analysis confirmed that innovation and education are among the most important factors in competitiveness. According to them, it is well known that innovations lead to smart economic growth, and knowledge creation increases a country's chances of economic success in today's competitive and globalized world economy.

Moreover, in their research, Fagerberg et al. [86] identified the variables that are important for economic growth and economic competitiveness. Their results show that, when it comes to competitiveness, there is a clear gap between developed countries with healthy economic growth and the rest of the world. The basic determinant of this development is an optimally set policy in developed countries, which systematically places great emphasis on improving technologies and supporting the knowledge economy.

According to Melnikas [18], the issue of sustainable development, as well as the issue of the transition to a knowledge-based society and economy, is very interdisciplinary. Scientists must reach a consensus on approaches to social and economic development, technological progress, and environmental protection. The regional perspective is an important aspect of research on this issue, as regions differ in terms of different social, economic, technological, and ecological conditions. Thelen [87] argued that differences in the organization of business and work, as well as differences in the approach of institutions that structure mutual relations with each other and with the state, have led these countries along different paths in terms of their level of implementation of the knowledge economy. However, Brodowka-Szewczuk [53] argued that adequate state policy relevantly determines the progress of innovativeness in companies. In this way, it also minimizes the risk of destabilization and deterioration in the economic situation and stimulates high-tech changes in the economy. The internal factors existing within a company define the company's innovative needs and means that can be used for innovations, the human resources in innovative processes, and the importance of innovation for the further development of the company. The basic variable that is a part of expenditure indices is the amount of expenditure on R&D, presented as a percentage of gross domestic product.

6. Conclusions

As shown above, the knowledge-based economy is a very important part of the world today and in many respects affords countries a competitive advantage, which can more or less be reflected in the country's competitiveness. Based on the above analyses, test results, and other conclusions, we can evaluate the established hypotheses and the aim of this study.

From the point of view of individual countries, it was possible to observe significant differences, which, due to variability of results, can be described as long term as opposed to persisting in the period under review. The differences between countries were thus confirmed in the mean value of their results ($Q = 238.555$; $p < 0.01$) as well as in the variance ($LE = 2.976$; $p < 0.01$). The analysis confirmed statistically significant differences in the evaluation of the competitiveness of EU countries and this statement confirmed Hypothesis 1.

In Hypothesis 2, we assumed a positive dependence of competitiveness (12th GCI pillar) on the knowledge economy of individual EU countries. This hypothesis was built in three variants. Based on the results presented in Table 2, we can see that, in some countries (placed in Group 1), positive dependencies are achieved in all three indicators. In other countries (Groups 2–4), only some of the indicators showed positive dependencies. Overall, Hypothesis 2 (based on variants H2A, H2B, and H2C) was not confirmed for all EU countries. The dependence of competitiveness on the knowledge economy was not positive.

In Hypothesis 3, we assumed statistically significant differences in terms of competitiveness on the knowledge economy between individual EU countries. As show in Figure 7, it is not possible to assign the impact of the monitored indicators to individual groups of countries, thus it is not possible to predict, with the increase or decrease of a single indicator, the score of the 12th pillar of the GCI of the country. Since the findings presented in Table 3 show differences in the nature of dependencies across countries, Hypothesis 3 was confirmed.

The main aim of this study was to identify the EU country with the strongest competitive position. Based on the results obtained, considering the broader context and the results of CV–TOPSIS as well as the data in Table 1, it was Sweden. This country, as the only one mentioned here, also took into account the sustainability factor discussed below. Sweden was followed by Finland and Germany. We also wanted to determine the impact that selected indicators of the knowledge economy have on the country's competitiveness in their interaction. We investigated this fact based on the results arising from the testing of Hypotheses 2 and 3. In the case of Sweden, a positive dependence was noted for all examined indicators. Finally, we checked whether competitiveness affects the sustainability of the economy. Taking into account the starting points, Sweden was also a leader in this area. An evaluation of this last area is given below.

The Europe 2020 strategy emphasizes the economic sustainability of the overall development of the EU community. Among other objectives, the strategy aims to achieve R&D spending of 3% of GDP by 2020. This is a target value for all member countries. Because sustainability is a long-term issue, countries must pay attention to factors that provide them with long-term growth. The research and development issue seems to be significant for a country to achieve competitiveness and sustainability. Focusing on prosperous knowledge economies could be the right path to give whole societies a sustainable standard of living and a more meaningful life. During our selected period of time, we can assess how each EU country has contributed to this goal. If a country managed to increase this value every year to a desired level by various measures, we can discuss building a long-standing competitive position of the country, building sustainability in the economy. Increased R&D spending improves the level of the knowledge-based economy, thereby building the country's sustainability in a competitive environment in the long run.

In this case, sustainability was assessed by comparing EU countries' achievements with the set Europe 2020 target of 3% of GDP. In 2017, only four countries (Denmark, Germany, Austria, and Sweden) achieved or exceeded R&D spending of 3% of GDP. Only in the case of Sweden was the value of this indicator higher than 3% over the entire monitored period. In Austria, the target value has been reached and exceeded since 2014. In the case of Denmark, in 2009, the value of this indicator was above 3%; subsequently its level fell and again exceeded 3% in 2015. In Germany, the value was higher than 3% only in 2017. It is worth mentioning Finland, where from 2007 to 2014 the values of this indicator were higher than 3%, but decreased slightly in 2015 and fell to 2.73% in 2017.

Based on this comparison, we can claim that sustainability was only identified in countries that have long sought to achieve the required indicator values. These countries were Denmark, Germany, Austria, and Sweden. We would also include Belgium, which has not yet reached the required value of 3%, but the values of this indicator are increasing annually and at the same time they are closest to the required threshold in comparison to other EU countries.

The study has some limitations. From the viewpoint of the future orientation of scientific tasks, it is essential to focus on other knowledge economy indicators that may affect the competitiveness and the sustainability of the country. Research should consider such indicators not only with respect to the knowledge economy but also their impact on competitiveness. It would be interesting to determine the indicators that affect or do not affect competitiveness. It might be useful to begin new research on the indicators considered here on a wider group of countries. By expanding the research with new countries and enlarging the sample size, new conclusions and interactions between the research areas may emerge. Another suggestion for future studies is to replace the GCI in the quantification of competitiveness. Instead of using the GCI, another approach or an index that represents the competitive position of the country in numerical terms could be used.

The scientific community can apply this conceptual view to understand how the sustainability and competitiveness of countries integrate with each other and are supported by the transition to a knowledge-based economy. The methods used in the analytical part of this study could be used to assess a sample of countries from other regions. The study also provides useful references for policy makers to understand the importance of transition to a knowledge-based economy in order to ensure the country's sustainable competitiveness.

Author Contributions: Investigation, supervision, and resources, E.Š.; Funding acquisition and project administration, R.K.; Conceptualization, E.Š., I.K.V., R.V., and R.K.; Formal analysis and software, R.V.; methodology, E.Š. and R.V.; Validation, R.V.; Data curation and visualization, E.Š. and R.V.; and Writing—original draft, review and editing, E.Š., I.K.V., and R.V. All authors have read and agreed to the published version of the manuscript.

Funding: This research was funded by the Scientific Grant Agency of the Ministry of Education, Science, Research, and Sport of the Slovak Republic and the Slovak Academy of Sciences, grant numbers VEGA 1/0578/18 and VEGA 1/0082/19; by the Cultural and Educational Grant Agency of the Ministry of Education, Science, Research and Sport of the Slovak Republic, grant numbers KEGA 011PU-4/2019 and KEGA 024PU-4/2020; and by the OP VVV—International Mobilities of Researchers of the TUL [CZ.02.2.69/0.0/0.0/16_027/ 0008493].

Acknowledgments: The authors also thank the journal editor and anonymous reviewers for their guidance and constructive suggestions.

Conflicts of Interest: The authors declare no conflict of interest.

References

1. Zhuparova, A.; Sagiyeva, R.; Kalmakova, D. The Development Knowledge-Based Economy: A Literature Review. In *Strategica: Challenging the Status Quo in Management and Economics: Proceedings of the 6th International Academic Conference on Strategica-Challenging the Status Quo in Management and Economics, Bucharest, Romania, 11–12 October 2018*; Bratianu, C., Zbuchea, A., Vitelar, A., Eds.; Tritonic Publishing House: Bucharest, Romania, 2018; pp. 555–572.
2. Metaxiotis, K. *Knowledge-Based Development for Cities and Societies: Integrated Multi-Level Approaches: Integrated Multi-Level Approaches*; IGI Global: Hershey, PA, USA, 2010.
3. Jednak, S.; Kragulj, D. Achieving Sustainable Development and Knowledge-Based Economy in Serbia. *Manag. J. Sustain. Bus. Manag. Solut. Emerg. Econ.* **2015**, *20*, 1–12. [CrossRef]
4. Režný, L.; Buchanan White, J.; Marešová, P. The knowledge economy: Key to sustainable development? *Struct. Chang. Econ. Dyn.* **2019**, *51*, 291–300. [CrossRef]
5. Sinakou, E.; Boeve-de Pauw, J.; Van Petegem, P. Exploring the concept of sustainable development within education for sustainable development: Implications for ESD research and practice. *Environ. Dev. Sustain.* **2019**, *21*, 1–10. [CrossRef]
6. Dima, A.M.; Begu, L.; Vasilescu, M.D.; Maasen, M.A. The Relationship between the Knowledge Economy and Global Competitiveness in the European Union. *Sustainability* **2018**, *10*, 1706. [CrossRef]

7. Hanushek, E.A. Economic growth in developing countries: The role of human capital. *Econ. Educ. Rev.* **2013**, *37*, 204–212. [CrossRef]
8. Širá, E.; Radvanská, K.; Kravčáková Vozárová, I. Government gross debt and unemployment in selected European countries. In *CER Comparative European research 2014: Proceedings of the 2nd Biannual CER Comparative European Research Conference*; Sciemcee Publishing: London, UK, 2014; pp. 25–28.
9. Vallerie, D.; Peterson, R. Entrepreneurship and economic growth: Evidence from emerging and developed countries. *Entrep. Reg. Dev.* **2009**, *21*, 459–480. [CrossRef]
10. Busu, M.; Trica, C.L. Sustainability of Circular Economy Indicators and Their Impact on Economic Growth of the European Union. *Sustainability* **2019**, *11*, 5481. [CrossRef]
11. Kiseľáková, D.; Širá, E.; Šofranková, B. The ease of doing business index in selected countries. *J. Manag. Bus. Res. Pract.* **2019**, *11*, 8–14.
12. Smulders, S. Environmental policy and sustainable economic growth. *De Econ.* **1995**, *143*, 163–195. [CrossRef]
13. Ocak, M.; Findik, D. The Impact of Intangible Assets and Sub-Components of Intangible Assets on Sustainable Growth and Firm Value: Evidence from Turkish Listed Firms. *Sustainability* **2019**, *11*, 5359. [CrossRef]
14. Cantu-Martinez, P.C. Economy of Knowledge for Sustainability. *Rev. Econ. Soc.* **2017**, *22*, 71–83. [CrossRef]
15. Mikalauskiene, A.; Atkociuniene, Z. Knowledge Management Impact on Sustainable Development. *Monten. J. Econ.* **2019**, *15*, 149–160. [CrossRef]
16. Li, Y.; Song, Y.; Wang, J.; Li, C. Intellectual Capital, Knowledge Sharing, and Innovation Performance: Evidence from the Chinese Construction Industry. *Sustainability* **2019**, *11*, 2713. [CrossRef]
17. Chang, D.L.; Sabatini-Marques, J.; Moreira da Costa, E.; Selig, P.M.; Yigitcanlar, T. Knowledge-based, smart and sustainable cities: A provocation for a conceptual framework. *J. Open Innov. Technol. Mark. Complex.* **2018**, *4*, 1–17. [CrossRef]
18. Melnikas, B. Sustainable development and creation of the knowledge economy: The new theoretical approach. *Technol. Econ. Dev. Econ.* **2010**, *16*, 516–540. [CrossRef]
19. Durazzi, N. The political economy of high skills: Higher education in knowledge-based labour markets. *J. Eur. Public Policy* **2019**, *26*, 1799–1817. [CrossRef]
20. Saridogan, H.O.; Kaya, M.V. Knowledge Economy and Economic Performance: Comparison of Turkey and the European Union. *J. Mehmet Akif Ersoy Univ. Econ. Adm. Sci. Fac.* **2019**, *6*, 916–935. [CrossRef]
21. Sagiyeval, R.; Zhuparova, A.; Ruzanov, R.; Doszhan, R.; Askerov, A. Intellectual Input of Development by Knowledge-Based Economy: Problems of Measuring in Countries with Developing Markets. *Enterp. Sustain. Issues* **2018**, *6*, 711–728. [CrossRef]
22. Milewska, A. Knowledge Based Economy: Opportunities and Challenges. In *International Scientific Conference on Economic Sciences for Agribusiness and Rural Economy. Proceedings of the 2018 International Scientific Conference–Economic Sciences for Agribusiness and Rural Economy, Warsaw, Poland, 7–8 June 2018*; Golebiewski, J., Ed.; University of Warsaw: Warsaw, Poland, 2018; pp. 313–318. [CrossRef]
23. Ayan, T.Y.; Pabuccu, H. The assessment of knowledge economy efficiency: Comparing Turkey with the European Union countries. *Zb. Rad. Ekon. Fak. Rijeci Proc. Rij. Fac. Econ.* **2018**, *36*, 443–464. [CrossRef]
24. Godin, B. The knowledge-based economy: Conceptual framework or buzzword? *J. Technol. Transf.* **2006**, *31*, 17–30. [CrossRef]
25. Powell, W.W.; Snellman, K. The knowledge economy. *Annu. Rev. Sociol.* **2004**, *30*, 199–220. [CrossRef]
26. Houghton, J.; Sheehan, P. *A Primer on the Knowledge Economy (Working Paper No. 18)*; Victoria University of Technology: Melbourne, Australia, 2000.
27. Dudová, I. *Ekonómia Vzdelávania*; EKONÓM: Bratislava, Slovakia, 2011.
28. Alnafrah, I.; Mouselli, S. The Knowledge Society Vis-a-vis the Knowledge Economy and Their Potential Development Impacts in Russia. *J. Knowl. Econ.* **2019**, *10*, 205–220. [CrossRef]
29. Lüthi, S.; Thierstein, A.; Bentlage, M. Interlocking firm networks in the German knowledge economy: On local networks and global connectivity. *Raumforsch. Raumordn.* **2011**, *69*, 161–174. [CrossRef]
30. Collison, C.; Parcel, G. *Knowledge Management*; CP Press: Brno, Czech Republic, 2005.
31. Sundac, D.; Krmpotic, I.F. Knowledge Economy Factors and the Development of Knowledge-Based Economy. *Croat. Econ. Surv.* **2011**, *13*, 105–141, WOS:000435261900003. Available online: http://hrcak.srce.hr/67344 (accessed on 10 January 2020).

32. Chen, D.; Dahlman, C. The Knowledge Economy, the KAM Methodology and World Bank Operations. 2005. Available online: http://siteresources.worldbank.org/KFDLP/Resources/KAM_Paper_WP.pdf (accessed on 15 January 2020).
33. Jergová, N.; Bednárová, L. Human Capital Investigation and Identification Its Key Criteria of the Article. *Hum. Soc. Sci.* **2016**, *23*, 161–166. [CrossRef]
34. Pulic, A. Measuring the performance of intellectual potential in knowledge economy. In Proceedings of the 2nd McMaster Word Congress on Measuring and Managing Intellectual Capital by the Austrian Team for Intellectual Potential, Hamilton, ON, Canada, 21–23 January 1998; pp. 1–20.
35. Hudáková, M.; Masár, M. The Assessment of Key Business Risks for SMEs in Slovakia and Their Comparison with other EU Countries. *Entrep. Bus. Econ. Rev.* **2018**, *6*, 145–160. [CrossRef]
36. Mushynska, N.; Kniazian, M. Social Innovations in the Professional Training of Managers under the Conditions of Knowledge Economy Development. *Balt. J. Econ. Stud.* **2019**, *5*, 137–143. [CrossRef]
37. Barkhordari, S.; Fattahi, M.; Azimi, N.A. The Impact of Knowledge-Based Economy on Growth Performance: Evidence from MENA Countries. *J. Knowl. Econ.* **2019**, *10*, 1168–1182. [CrossRef]
38. Alavi, M.; Leidner, D.E. Review: Knowledge management and knowledge management systems: Conceptual foundations and research issues. *MIS Q.* **2001**, *25*, 107–136. [CrossRef]
39. Greiner, M.E.; Böhmann, T.; Krcmar, H. A strategy for knowledge management. *J. Knowl. Manag.* **2007**, *11*, 3–15. [CrossRef]
40. Rajnoha, R.; Štefko, R.; Merková, M.; Dobrovič, J. Business intelligence as a key information and knowledge tool for strategic business performance management. *Econ. Manag.* **2016**, *19*, 183–203. [CrossRef]
41. Bencsik, A.; Juhász, T.; Mura, L.; Csanádi, Á. Formal and Informal Knowledge Sharing in Organisations from Slovakia and Hungary. *Entrep. Bus. Econ. Rev.* **2019**, *7*, 25–42. [CrossRef]
42. Choi, B.; Lee, H. Knowledge management strategy and its link to knowledge creation process. *Expert Syst. Appl.* **2002**, *23*, 173–187. [CrossRef]
43. Tomčíková, M.; Bednářová, L.; Naščáková, J. The knowledge society and offer of qualified workers. In Proceedings of the 13th International Conference on Emerging eLearning Technologies and Applications (ICETA), Stary Smokovec, Slovakia, 26–27 November 2015; pp. 1–6. [CrossRef]
44. Rim, G.N.; Kim, G.S.; Hwang, S.H.; Ko, U.D. Some Problems in Statistically Assessing the Level of Knowledge Economy. *J. Knowl. Econ.* **2019**, *10*, 974–996. [CrossRef]
45. Shkarlet, S.; Kholiavko, N.; Dubyna, M. Information Economy: Management of Educational, Innovation, and Research Determinants. Marketing and management of innovations. *Inf. Econ.* **2019**, *10*, 126–141. [CrossRef]
46. Arundel, A.; Hansen, W.; Kemp, R. *Knowledge Economy Indicators: State of the Art on the Knowledge-Based Economy*; European Commission: Brussel, Belgium, 2008.
47. Smith, K. *Innovation Indicators and the Knowledge Economy: Concepts, Results and Policy Challenges*; STEP Group: Oslo, Norway, 2000.
48. Roberts, S. *Measuring the Knowledge-Based Economy: A Statistical Framework for Measuring Knowledge in the Australian Economy and Society*; Economic and Social Commision for Asia and the Pacific, Working group of Statistical Experts: Bangkok, Thailand, 2001.
49. Sharabati, A.; Jawad, S.; Bontis, N. Intellectual capital and business performance in the pharmaceutical sector of Jordan. *Manag. Decis.* **2010**, *48*, 105–131. [CrossRef]
50. Aleksejeva, L. Country's Competitiveness and Sustainability: Higher Education Impact. *J. Secur. Sustain. Issues* **2016**, *5*, 355–364. [CrossRef]
51. Hadad, S. The geographic distribution of Knowledge Economy (KE) within the European Union (EU). *Manag. Mark. Chall. Knowl. Soc.* **2018**, *13*, 1089–1107. [CrossRef]
52. Gorokhova, M. Resource Potential of the Knowledge Economy. *Upr. Manag.* **2018**, *9*, 20–25. [CrossRef]
53. Brodowska-Szewczuk, J. Determinants of the Development of Enterprises' Innovativeness in the Aspect of Competitiveness of the Economy. *Enterp. Sustain. Issues* **2019**, *7*, 1279–1295. [CrossRef]
54. Atanassova, V.; Doukovska, L.; Kacprzyk, A.; Sotirova, E.; Radeva, I.; Vassilev, P. InterCriteria Analysis of the Global Competitiveness Reports: From Efficiency- to Innovation-driven Economies. *J. Mult. Valued Log. Soft Comput.* **2018**, *31*, 469–494.
55. Lomachynska, I.; Podgorna, I. Innovation Potential: Impact on the National Economy's Competitiveness of the EU Developed Countries. *Balt. J. Econ. Stud.* **2018**, *4*, 262–270. [CrossRef]

56. Dukic, B.; Dukic, S.; Dugandzic, S. Knowledge Management in the Function of Ensuring Competitiveness of Slavonian Economy. In Proceedings of the 7th International Scientific Symposium Economy of the Eastern Croatia–Vision and Growth, Osijek, Croatia, 24–26 May 2018; Tonkovic, A.M., Crnkovic, B., Eds.; 2018; pp. 94–102.
57. Puškárová, P.; Zajac, Š. Innovation and Competitiveness of the Slovak Economy: New Evidence of International Impacts in the Knowledge Accumulation Process. *Int. J. Manag. Econ.* **2014**, *42*, 81–97. [CrossRef]
58. Bondareva, I.; Tomčík, R. Vplyv inovácií na konkurencieschopnosť Slovenskej republiky. *J. Knowl. Soc.* **2013**, *2*, 1–6.
59. Chapčáková, A.; Hečková, J.; Gira, D.; Valentíny, T.; Zbihlejová, L. Quantification of the selected macroeconomic impacts on the EEA countries competitiveness assessment. *Monten. J. Econ.* **2019**, *15*, 155–171. [CrossRef]
60. Šterbová, L.; Černá, I.; Čajka, R.; Bolotov, I. *Mezinárodní Obchod ve Světové Krizi*; Grada: Praha, Czech Republic, 2013; p. 364.
61. Scott, B.R.; Lodge, G.C. *US Competitiveness in the World Economy*; Harvard Business School Press: Boston, MA, USA, 1985.
62. Štefko, R. *Personálna Práca v Hyperkonkurenčnom Prostredí a Personálny Marketing*; R. S. Royal Service: Bratislava, Slovakia, 2001; p. 235.
63. Schwab, K.; World Economic Forum. The Global Competitiveness Report 2017–2018. Available online: http://reports.weforum.org/global-competitiveness-index-2017-2018/ (accessed on 7 December 2019).
64. Martens, W. Europe 2020 and beyond. *Eur. View* **2010**, *9*. [CrossRef]
65. Barroso, J.M. Europe 2020—A Strategy for Smart, Sustainable and Inclusive Growth. 2010. Available online: https://ec.europa.eu/eu2020/pdf/COMPLET%20EN%20BARROSO%20%20%20007%20-%20Europe%202020%20-%20EN%20version.pdf (accessed on 17 January 2020).
66. Schiuma, G.; Andreeva, T.; Kianto, A. Does knowledge management really matter? Linking knowledge management practices, competitiveness and economic performance. *J. Knowl. Manag.* **2012**, *16*, 617–636. [CrossRef]
67. Kianto, A.; Andreeva, T.; Pavlov, Y. The impact of intellectual capital management on company competitiveness and financial performance. *Knowl. Manag. Res. Pract.* **2013**, *11*, 112–122. [CrossRef]
68. Krstić, B.; Stanišić, T. The influence of knowledge economy development on competitiveness of southeastern Europe countries. *Industrija* **2013**, *41*, 151–167. [CrossRef]
69. Batagan, L. Indicators for Knowledge Economy. *Inform. Econ.* **2007**, *11*, 60–63.
70. Shih, H.; Shyur, H.; Lee, E.S. An extension of TOPSIS for group decision making. *Math. Comput. Model.* **2007**, *45*, 801–813. [CrossRef]
71. Bhutia, P.W.; Phipon, R. Application of AHP and TOPSIS Method for Supplier Selection Problem. *J. Engine* **2012**, *2*, 43–50. [CrossRef]
72. Kandakoglu, A.; Celik, M.; Akgun, I. A multi-methodological approach for shipping registry selection in maritime transportation industry. *Math. Comput. Model.* **2009**, *49*, 586–597. [CrossRef]
73. Vavrek, R.; Chovancová, J. Assessment of economic and environmental energy performance of EU countries using CV-TOPSIS technique. *Ecol. Indic.* **2019**, *106*, 105519. [CrossRef]
74. Vavrek, R.; Kotulič, R.; Adamišin, P. Evaluation of municipalities management with the topsis technique emphasising on the impact of weights of established criteria. *Lex Localis J. Local Self Gov.* **2015**, *13*, 249–264. [CrossRef]
75. Vavrek, R.; Adamišin, A.; Kotulič, R. Multi-Criteria Evaluation of Municipalities in Slovakia–Case Study in Selected Districts. *Pol. J. Manag. Stud.* **2017**, *16*, 290–301. [CrossRef]
76. Kravčáková Vozárová, I.; Kotulič, R.; Vavrek, R. Assessing Impacts of CAP Subsidies on Financial Performance of Enterprises in Slovak Republic. *Sustainability* **2020**, *12*, 948. [CrossRef]
77. Zavadskas, E.K.; Turskis, Z.; Kildiene, S. State of art surveys of overviews on MCDM/MADM methods. *Technol. Econ. Dev. Econ.* **2014**, *20*, 165–179. [CrossRef]
78. Hwang, C.L.; Yoon, K. *Multiple Attributes Decision Making Methods and Applications*; Springer: Berlin, Germany, 1981.
79. Yoon, K. *Systems Selection by Multiple Attribute Decision Making*; Kansas State University: Manhattan, KS, USA, 1980.
80. Streimikiene, D.; Balezentis, T.; Krisciukaitiene, I.; Balezentis, A. Prioritizing sustainable electricity production technologies: MCDM approach. *Renew. Sustain. Energy Rev.* **2012**, *16*, 3302–3311. [CrossRef]

81. Zavadskas, E.K.; Mardani, A.; Turskis, Z.; Jusoh, A.; Nor, K.M. Development of TOPSIS Method to Solve Complicated Decision-Making Problems: An Overview on Developments. From 2000 to 2015. *Int. J. Inf. Technol. Decis. Mak.* **2016**, *15*, 1–38. [CrossRef]
82. Carayannis, E.G.; Ferreira, J.J.M.; Jalali, M.S.; Ferreira, F.A.F. MCDA in knowledge-based economies: Methodological developments and real world applications. *Technol. Forecast. Soc. Chang.* **2018**, *131*, 1–3. [CrossRef]
83. Keršuliene, V.; Zavadskas, E.K.; Turskis, Z. Selection of rational dispute resolution method by applying new step-wise weight assessment ratio analysis (Swara). *J. Bus. Econ. Manag.* **2010**, *11*, 1611–1699. [CrossRef]
84. Singla, I.; Ahuja, I.S.; Sing Sethi, A. Comparative Analysis of Technology Push Strategies Influencing Sustainable Development in Manufacturing Industries Using Topsis and Vikor Technique. *Int. J. Qual. Res.* **2017**, *12*, 129–146. [CrossRef]
85. Yalcin, E.; Unlu, U. A Multi-Criteria Performance Analysis of Initial Public Offering (IPO) Firms Using Critic and Vikor Methods. *Technol. Econ. Dev. Econ.* **2018**, *24*, 534–560. [CrossRef]
86. Fagerberg, J.; Srholec, M.; Knell, M. The competitiveness of nations: Why some countries prosper while others fall behind. *World Dev.* **2007**, *35*, 1595–1620. [CrossRef]
87. Thelen, K. Transitions to the Knowledge Economy in Germany, Sweden, and the Netherlands. *Comp. Political* **2019**, *51*, 295–315. [CrossRef]

MDPI
St. Alban-Anlage 66
4052 Basel
Switzerland
Tel. +41 61 683 77 34
Fax +41 61 302 89 18
www.mdpi.com

Sustainability Editorial Office
E-mail: sustainability@mdpi.com
www.mdpi.com/journal/sustainability

CPSIA information can be obtained
at www.ICGtesting.com
Printed in the USA
LVHW071818040322
712645LV00012B/1003

9 783039 368228